# Revisiting the Critical Legacy of Shah Ismail

# Studies in Critical Social Sciences Book Series

Haymarket Books is proud to be working with Brill Academic Publishers (www.brill.nl) to republish the *Studies in Critical Social Sciences* book series in paperback editions. This peer-reviewed book series offers insights into our current reality by exploring the content and consequences of power relationships under capitalism, and by considering the spaces of opposition and resistance to these changes that have been defining our new age. Our full catalog of *SCSS* volumes can be viewed at https://www.haymarketbooks .org/series_collections/4-studies-in-critical-social-sciences.

# REVISITING THE CRITICAL LEGACY OF SHAH ISMAIL

## An Inquiry into the Lost Gnostic Tradition of Khatai

### SEYED JAVAD MIRI

Haymarket Books
Chicago, IL

First published in 2025 by Brill Academic Publishers, The Netherlands
© 2025 Koninklijke Brill NV, Leiden, The Netherlands

Published in paperback in 2026 by
Haymarket Books
P.O. Box 180165
Chicago, IL 60618
773-583-7884
www.haymarketbooks.org

ISBN: 979-8-88890-796-2

Distributed to the trade in the US through Consortium Book Sales and
Distribution (www.cbsd.com) and internationally through Ingram Publisher
Services International (www.ingramcontent.com).

This book was published with the generous support of Lannan Foundation,
Wallace Action Fund, and the Marguerite Casey Foundation.

Special discounts are available for bulk purchases by organizations and
institutions. Please call 773-583-7884 or email info@haymarketbooks.org for more
information.

Cover design by Jamie Kerry and Ragina Johnson.

Printed in the United States.

Library of Congress Cataloging-in-Publication data is available.

# Contents

# The Gnostic Legacy of Shah Ismail

The discussion of Shah Ismail initially appears straightforward, as he is widely recognized as the founder of the Safavid dynasty, a pivotal figure in Iranian history. Extensive historical scholarship has elucidated his origins, detailing his upbringing in Gilan, Iran, during what is often referred to as the "hidden period," prior to his emergence alongside the Qizilbash[1] onto the historical stage. Together, they orchestrated significant transformations not only in Ardabil, Azerbaijan, and Iran but also exerted profound influence beyond the country's borders. However, Shah Ismail's significance transcends mere historical documentation. Despite his undeniable impact on Iran's trajectory and global geopolitical dynamics, his persona remains enigmatic, particularly within the contexts of Ardabil, Azerbaijan, and the broader Islamic world. This dual nature of recognition and obscurity surrounding Shah Ismail necessitates a rigorous reassessment of his multifaceted character. How do we reconcile the paradox of his simultaneous familiarity and unfamiliarity? Why does this phenomenon persist despite limited engagement from scholars in Iran's humanities? These inquiries underscore the urgent necessity for a deeper exploration of Shah Ismail's enduring legacy and its profound implications for our collective historical consciousness.

Drawing upon the language of sociology and social theories, researchers embark on a journey to defamiliarize Shah Ismail. Despite initial impressions, Shah Ismail, particularly in his multifaceted role as a Khatai—poet, sage, mystic, and librarian king—remains shrouded in obscurity. A thorough reevaluation of Shah Ismail is now imperative. This endeavor necessitates transcending personal biases of affection or aversion. While Shah Ismail holds personal significance for many, the scholarly aim transcends the individual. Rather than emoting about a historical figure from centuries past, the focus is on delving into a tradition and opening a new chapter of inquiry. The goal is to chart uncharted territories, shedding light on a neglected facet of history. The intent is to explore Shah Ismail beyond the confines of individual sentiment, investigating his broader impact and legacy. Through this approach, new insights and perspectives can be unlocked, enriching our understanding of Shah Ismail and his enduring significance.

---

1  The Qizilbash hailed from Azerbaijan, a region in the northwest Caucasus near Iran, and were comprised of ethnic Persians and Turks. Their appellation, "Qizilbash," derives from their distinctive red headgear, symbolizing their identity.

I have symbolically christened this tradition "the Gnostic Tradition of Shah Ismail" and propose a research project tailored for aspiring young scholars to illuminate the future. I fervently hope this proposition transcends mere rhetoric, fostering an environment where "Dar Al-Ershad of Ardabil" or The Sufi Center for Spiritual Wisdom becomes a prominent hub for the Gnostic Tradition of Shah Ismail. I envision Ardabil University as more than a physical institution; it should epitomize an ethos of academic rigor and intellectual vibrancy. Researchers worldwide should converge upon Ardabil, drawn by its scholarly atmosphere and intellectual dynamism, to explore the nuances of this tradition, infused with the essence of Shah Ismail and Khatai, and carrying the cadence of Turkish. Thus, I aspire for Ardabil University to serve as the epicenter of this intellectual revival, paving the way for future generations to explore and enrich our understanding of the Gnostic Tradition of Shah Ismail on a global scale.

This research endeavor serves as a potential catalyst, igniting the spark for others to become custodians of this emerging trend. However, every movement and research initiative require a foundational problem or set of questions to incite debate and discourse. In the realm of the philosophy of science, conflict doesn't solely denote discord; rather, it signifies the presence of an objective and substantive problem that prompts individuals to approach it from diverse perspectives, fostering reflection and culminating in varied conclusions. It is through this divergence of opinions and viewpoints that a diverse fabric of intellectual controversies emerges, fortifying the tradition. These disputes serve to strengthen and refine the trajectory of research, enriching our understanding and propelling the tradition forward.

Today, Shah Ismail exists not as a living person but as a textual representation. The Diwan[2] Shah Ismail has been meticulously corrected and published by professor Rasool Ismailzadeh (Ismailzadeh, 2010). But what does it mean for Shah Ismail to be manifested as a text? How and why has this textual representation faded from the annals of Iranian cultural and intellectual developments? Many historians and philosophers, both Iranian and non-Iranian, posit that following the collapse of the Sassanids, Shah Ismail spearheaded the first all-encompassing state in the name of Iran across the region. While debatable, my focus transcends historical debates; rather, I seek to scrutinize the strategies that led to Shah Ismail's relegation to obscurity as a Khatai. My inquiry delves into what transpired to cause such a significant and influential figure to vanish

---

2   In the Islamic cultures spanning the Middle East, North Africa, Sicily, and South Asia, a Diwan (Persian: دیوان, divân, Arabic: دیوان, diwan) typically refers to a compilation of poems by a single author, typically excluding their longer works, such as mathnawī.

from the realms of Iranian and Islamic thought and culture. In essence, I question how the Diwan Shah Ismail Khatai slipped beyond our grasp and faded into obscurity.

Three crucial points warrant discussion here. Firstly, within historiography, two prominent currents emerge: cultural historiography and nationalist historiography. Nationalist historiography, entrenched in the concept of the modern nation-state, constructs a narrative of civilization or land evolution within the confines of contemporary national boundaries. This approach often formulates the past in terms of the present, projecting current cultural, religious, and intellectual frameworks onto historical contexts. For instance, in the 1700s, the entity known as Germany did not exist in its modern form, and writers in German did not necessarily espouse the same cultural identity as contemporary Germans. However, when chronicling the formation of the German nation-state, historians tend to retroactively interpret historical events through a nationalist lens, potentially overshadowing the diversity and plurality of cultural, religious, and intellectual expressions that characterized the past. In contrast, cultural historiography transcends national boundaries, offering a broader understanding of cultural evolution that extends beyond contemporary geopolitical borders. This approach acknowledges the rich tapestry of languages, traditions, and influences that have shaped cultural heritage, fostering a more inclusive and nuanced interpretation of history.

In today's context, nations largely adhere to the cultural-political framework of the nation-state, shaping their social and collective affairs accordingly. Under this paradigm, each country typically designates a standard language around which its history and cultural identity are constructed. Presently, Persian serves as the official language of Iran. However, Iran's cultural landscape is far more diverse, with a multitude of languages contributing to its rich heritage over centuries of historical, cultural, and civilizational evolution. Among these languages, Turkish holds particular significance. Texts and works in Turkish have played a pivotal role in shaping Iran's cultural history. By adopting a cultural historiography approach, divorced from nationalist biases, scholars can revisit and engage with these texts, thereby reevaluating and discussing the Gnostic Tradition embodied by the poets and sages who once inhabited this region. Through this lens, a more comprehensive understanding of Iran's cultural tapestry can emerge, transcending narrow nationalist narratives.

To illustrate our discussion, consider the case of Seyyed Hossein Nasr, a preeminent philosopher and author renowned for his extensive writings on Sufism, theoretical Irfan, Hekmat, and philosophy within the Islamic world, with a particular emphasis on Iran. While much of Nasr's oeuvre is in English, many of his works have been translated into Persian. In 2013, he penned an article in English for the magazine *Hekmat and Sufism*, edited by Seyed Salman Safavi. Titled "History of Sufism and Theoretical Irfan in Iran from Ancient Times to Present" (Nasr, 2013, 1–35), the article delves into the historical trajectory of Sufism in Iran. Notably, while Nasr acknowledges figures like Sheikh Safiuddin Ardabili, he conspicuously overlooks any mention of Shah Ismail, also known as Khatai, and neglects to explore Shah Ismail's Diwan or broader contributions. This omission is particularly striking given Nasr's esteemed reputation as a leading authority in Hekmat, philosophy, Irfan, and Sufism, as well as his esteemed role within the "Maryamiyya Tariqat".[3] The absence of any reference to Shah Ismail in Nasr's examination of Sufism's evolution prompts critical reflection on the factors underlying this oversight.

Let us explore another example in the realm of philosophy and Hekmat or Gnosis studies in Iran, focusing on Mohammad Ali Foroughi, a pivotal figure in both Iranian culture and politics during the early 20th century. Foroughi authored a significant work at the beginning of the last century, around the early 1300s in the Persian calendar (Foroughi, 2020l). Titled *The Journey of Hekmat or Gnosis in Europe*, the book ostensibly discusses the development of Hellenic rationality and Greek philosophy, tracing its evolution from antiquity through figures like Descartes and Kant to the modern era. While the title suggests a focus on "Hekmat or Gnosis," the content primarily centers on Western philosophical thought.

However, even if I generously interpret the term "Hekmat or Gnosis" in the context of Foroughi's work, a glaring omission remains: the absence of any mention of Shah Ismail. Despite a temporal distance of roughly four centuries between Foroughi and Shah Ismail, the intellectual and social chasm between them seems vast. It is perplexing that a figure as influential as Foroughi, deeply engaged in shaping Iran's modernity, would overlook Shah Ismail's contributions, especially considering Shah Ismail's reputation as a sage who expressed his thoughts and beliefs through poetry.

Moreover, the oversight becomes more pronounced when considering that questions about the nature of Hekmat or Gnosis have been central to philosophical, theological, mystical, and jurisprudential inquiries across various civilizations for at least the past 2500 years. This inquiry extends beyond Iranian

---

3   The Maryamiyya Order, established by Sheikh Isa Nur ad-Din–Frithjof Schuon (1907–1998), is a Sufi order, or tariqa, belonging to the lineage of the Shadhiliyya-Darqawiyya-Alawiyya order. With followers in Europe, the Americas, and the Islamic world, it adheres to a doctrine rooted in what it perceives as universal truths of pure esotericism. Its approach aligns with the fundamental principles of the Sufi path.

and Islamic cultures, resonating with philosophical dialogues in civilizations such as India, China, ancient Greece, and modern Western societies.

The relationship between "Hekmat or Gnosis" and governance lies in their potential to create a society rooted in wisdom, knowledge, and thoughtful planning. To forge a dialectic between these realms, I can integrate philosophical and spiritual principles into practical governance through educational reforms that emphasize critical thinking and ethics, foster inclusive dialogue among philosophers, spiritual leaders, and policymakers, and cultivate ethical leadership focused on the common good. Many philosophers, including Plato, grappled with structuring a society that harmonizes with reason, wisdom, and Hekmat or Gnosis. Plato famously attempted to implement his intellectual system on an island in Italy, but his efforts fell short, leading him to retreat to theory, believing the true world merely mirrored an "ideal" realm. Nonetheless, his efforts inspire modern attempts to align governance with higher principles, striving for an enlightened social order.

In contrast, a sage and mystic like Shah Ismail achieved what Plato could not: establishing a government grounded in his insights and theoretical Irfan. Shah Ismail's rule was informed by his mystical understanding and governing principles, offering a tangible example of how Hekmat or Gnosis could be applied to governance. For contemporary thinkers, philosophers, and sages like Hakim Lahiji, author of influential works such as "Gawhar-e morād" (Capital of Faith), "Showarq Al-Ilam," and "Kamela Al-Taiba," the challenge lies in envisioning a government built upon the foundational principles of their wisdom.

In the case of Shah Ismail, it is no longer a matter of speculation; his governance stands as a concrete reality. To truly gauge the significance of Shah Ismail's accomplishments, one must contextualize them within the historical backdrop of his era. Shah Ismail emerged onto the world stage during a period marked by the rise of vast empires like Spain and Portugal, alongside significant developments within Iran's borders, juxtaposed against the formation of the expansive Ottoman Empire. Internally, Iran grappled with deep divisions, yet Shah Ismail managed to establish a system rooted in his intellectual framework and Hekmat or Gnosis, stemming from the Gnostic Tradition of Ahl al-Bayt.

The puzzling aspect arises when considering how such a profound phenomenon, with its foundations deeply rooted in wisdom, could remain largely overlooked, with its principal architect sidelined throughout history. Despite Shah Ismail's pivotal role, his intellectual legacy seems to have been omitted from mainstream narratives, including the annals of literature in Iran. While figures like Ferdowsi, Saadi, and Hafez are celebrated in Iranian literary history, Shah Ismail Khatai's poetry is notably absent. This omission begs the question:

how can such a significant figure and his contributions to wisdom and governance be so conspicuously disregarded? This collective forgetfulness poses a profound enigma that warrants further exploration and explanation.

The influence of nationalist historiographical notions has effectively obscured Shah Ismail and his Gnostic Tradition from mainstream discourse, a phenomenon evident in the works of prominent intellectuals like Mohammad Ali Foroughi and Sayyed Hossein Nasr. Within this framework, which emphasizes Persian as the sole language of Iranian culture and thought, Shah Ismail's contributions are often sidelined. Notably, Seyyed Javad Tabatabai, in discussing the Iranian identity, cites Mohammad Ali Foroughi's assertion that the Shahnameh Ferdowsi serves as the nation's identity document. While Ferdowsi's legacy is undeniable, the substantial temporal gap of nearly seven hundred years between the Shahnameh's creation and the establishment of Iran as a distinct civilization-political entity, and nearly a thousand years between its creation and Foroughi's era, prompts reflection. Why have figures like Foroughi, steeped in nationalist thought, overlooked the profound impact of figures like Shah Ismail?

Shah Ismail's legacy extends far beyond conventional military valor; he was a figure deeply engaged in both Hekmat or Gnosis and governance. While some critics may regard Shah Ismail as a remarkable yet isolated individual who authored a book, such a view overlooks the gradual evolution of concepts within the sociological framework of knowledge. According to the sociology of knowledge, concepts don't emerge suddenly; rather, they develop over time within a broader cultural and intellectual milieu. Just as Hafez's poetic brilliance was nurtured within the rich tapestry of Persian literature and linguistic advancements, Shah Ismail's Diwan poems and philosophical ideas in Azerbaijani Turkish were deeply rooted in a continuum of thought and tradition. These concepts and ideas attributed to Shah Ismail were part of an ongoing intellectual discourse, with predecessors like Seyed Imadaddin Nasimi contributing to a lineage deeply intertwined with Iranian and Islamic civilizations.

The emergence of Shah Ismail's Diwan poems and philosophical contributions underscores the multifaceted nature of his intellectual legacy. Contrary to the notion of sudden creative genius, Shah Ismail's writings were shaped by a historical and cultural context rich in philosophical inquiry and spiritual tradition. His ideas didn't materialize in isolation; rather, they were part of a broader continuum of thought within Iranian and Islamic civilizations. Understanding Shah Ismail's intellectual contributions requires contextualizing them within this broader tradition, acknowledging the influences of predecessors like Seyed Imadaddin Nasimi and recognizing the dynamic inter-play between language, culture, and philosophical development.

The Gnostic Tradition attributed to Ahl al-Bayt stands as a significant aspect of Iranian cultural heritage. Yet, today, this tradition is often perceived as mar-ginal, raising questions about the perception of Iranian identity. Iran, as a pivotal nation in the region and globally, possesses a rich linguistic diversity, akin to the multifaceted knowledge of esteemed scholars known as "sheikhs of many books." Shah Nimatullah Wali reference to such a sage underscores the importance of broad knowledge in guiding communities. Iranians have his-torically embraced various languages, including Arabic, Turkish, and Persian, each contributing to their cultural tapestry. Some of these languages directly fostered the gnostic legacy and the intellectual tradition of Ahl al-Bayt, reflect-ing the depth of Iranian identity across linguistic boundaries. Revisiting this multilingual heritage offers insights into the nuanced layers of Iranian culture and identity.

In reflecting on Shah Ismail's legacy, it behooves us to approach the subject with reason and evidence, free from unnecessary controversy or exaggeration. Who was Shah Ismail, and what did he achieve? This question warrants consid-eration not only from writers and philosophers but also from those immersed in the realms of Irfan and Nazari. Rereading the text of Diwan Shah Ismail can offer valuable insights into his message and its relevance for the 21st century. In today's world, marked by a pervasive sense of nihilism and existential emp-tiness, Shah Ismail's Gnostic Tradition holds particular significance. Central to this tradition is the notion of invitation rather than imposition. Hekmat or Gnosis extends an invitation to humanity, offering answers to existential anxi-eties and addressing profound questions without coercion. Embracing this invitation can provide solace amidst the absurdity of modern life, offering a path towards meaning and fulfillment.

Shah Ismail emerges as one of the most marginalized figures in history, lacking even a thorough biography dedicated to him. Many accounts of Shah Ismail have been marred by satire and personal attacks. Embracing the sur-name "Khatai" and acknowledging himself as the servant of full guilt, he does not claim innocence. Yet, the absence of even a basic biography is glaring. It is my fervent hope that this research marks the commencement of earnest studies on Shah Ismail. He stands as one of the most pivotal yet egregiously overlooked figures in modern Iranian history, wielding significant influence in the evolution of the gnostic tradition, Irfan, and Sufism globally.

My discussion unfolds in two primary threads. Firstly, I delve into why Shah Ismail's pivotal role in the development of Hekmat or Gnosis in Iran and the broader Islamic world has been overlooked and neglected. Secondly, my aim is to reestablish Shah Ismail's stature as a sage and mystic who possessed both a practical ruling apparatus and a profound theoretical framework. I seek to revive the dimensions of the Khatai tradition, encapsulated within his writings, which have been obscured in the annals of Iranian and Islamic history. Interestingly, by delving into "the Gnostic Tradition of Shah Ismail," I anticipate a paradigm shift in my understanding of the historiography of Hekmat or Gnosis in Iran and the Islamic world. This reevaluation promises to unveil broader dimensions, transcending linguistic confines to encompass the rich tapestry of the Iranian and Islamic legacy, thereby enriching my theoretical discourse.

# CHAPTER 1

# Shah Ismail and the Importance of the Gnostic Legacy in the Islamic World

## 1 Introduction

The focus of this chapter revolves around the fascinating figure of Shah Ismail and the profound significance of the gnostic legacy within the Islamic world. However, before delving deeply into this intricate discussion, it becomes essential to address a series of foundational questions that frame the discourse. Why does this topic demand our attention, and what makes it a subject of both historical and intellectual importance? What is the intricate connection between Shah Ismail—a charismatic leader, poet, and the founder of the Safavid dynasty—and the enduring gnostic traditions that have shaped significant aspects of Islamic thought and spirituality? Furthermore, how do sociological and intellectual thinkers, both past and present, perceive the interplay between Shah Ismail's legacy as a political and spiritual leader and the broader currents of gnostic tradition within Islamic culture? By addressing these questions, we set the stage for a nuanced exploration of how Shah Ismail's life and influence serve as a pivotal lens through which to understand the synthesis of political power, spiritual mysticism, and esoteric knowledge in the broader context of Islamic history. This chapter thus seeks to bridge historical analysis and sociological insight, offering a comprehensive understanding of the intersection between Shah Ismail's legacy and the enduring gnostic currents within the Islamic world.

## 2 The Importance of Sciology of Poetry

In Iran, scholars in the field of sociology often draw upon classical sources like Karl Marx, Durkheim, Weber, Pareto, Giddens, and Habermas for teaching sociology courses, considering their works as foundational texts. However, in Europe and America, a shift occurred in the 1970s and 1980s, with the inclusion of courses such as "Sociology of Literature" or "Relationship between Literature and Sociology" within sociology curricula. Over the past few decades, similar courses have been integrated into doctoral and master's programs in sociology in Iran, prompting discussions about the interplay between sociology and literature. While this development is noteworthy, it underscores the unique significance of "literature and novels" within the intellectual landscape of America and Europe, particularly in Western Europe.

In the last two centuries, significant literary figures have emerged world-wide, contributing remarkable works to the fields of novels and short stories. However, when considering the intellectual landscape of Iran, one may question whether the "novel and story" hold the same importance as they do in Europe and America. The answer to this inquiry reveals a notable distinction. Within Iran's intellectual milieu, the art form that occupies both a special place and boasts a longer historical legacy is not the "novel and story," but rather "poetry."

Despite this cultural emphasis, many Iranian sociologists and textbook compilers, perhaps overlooking this fact, tend to translate and teach European and American textbooks on literary sociology without addressing the significance of poetry. Remarkably, there is no dedicated course unit titled "Sociology of Poetry" in Iran, despite the profound cultural heritage and historical depth of poetry within Iranian civilization. The tradition of poetry in Iranian culture spans millennia, dating back at least a thousand years, and even further when considering ancient texts like the "Gathas." Nevertheless, the absence of a "sociology of poetry" raises questions about the reasons behind this oversight and underscores a potential area of weakness in Iranian sociology within this domain.

One of the primary factors contributing to this phenomenon is that Iranian academics and intellectuals often develop their theories within the framework of Europeanism, neglecting to situate themselves within their own temporal and historical context. As a result, concepts of "time" in the geographical sense and "position" in the historical sense remain obscure. Iranian thinkers fail to critically engage with the relationship and dialectic between their own cultural position and the era in which they reside, both within Iranian civilization and the broader Islamic world. Consequently, Iranian researchers and intellectuals overlook their unique issues and fail to pose new, non-European questions. In light of this premise, the question arises: What relevance does this issue have to Shah Ismail?

## 3    Eurocentric Historiography and Ignoring Shah Ismail

In this chapter, Shah Ismail is not merely regarded as one of the prominent founders in modern Iranian history, but rather as a pivotal figure in the "Iranian stage" with significant ties to the Safavid Tariqat. The focal point of the Safavid Tariqat is Dar al-Irshad Ardabil, which, in a way, catalyzes a profound and influential civilizational movement across the Iranian plateau. Consequently, this movement extends its influence to encompass a vast region spanning from Central Asia to Anatolia, Turkey, Albania, the southern Mediterranean, and even as far as Italy's Venice and the Indian subcontinent. Indeed, the emergence of the Gurkans in the Indian subcontinent, including figures like Babur, was profoundly influenced by the Safavid Tariqat, underscoring the pivotal role of the Safavids in these areas.

A crucial question arises: Should cultural history be confined and shaped solely by the framework of the nation-state system, or does the cultural history of a society transcend the boundaries of the nation-state? This question remains largely unexplored within the Eurocentric paradigm. Currently, when historians attempt to chronicle the histories of nation-states such as Iran, Turkey, or Russia, they often adopt a perspective that prioritizes the contemporary "present" over the distant "past," interpreting historical developments through the lens of present societal structures. However, culture is a far-reaching and multifaceted phenomenon that cannot be confined within the narrow confines of the present moment or geographical boundaries. While nation-state historiography may serve to bolster the political and national consciousness of a nation, it fails to fully encapsulate the breadth and depth of cultural history, which extends well beyond the limits of modern national borders.

If it holds true that culture transcends the confines of the nation-state system, then we must ponder how figures like Shah Ismail managed to establish governments. Shah Ismail, the leader of the Safavid Tariqat, embodied this question. The Safavid Tariqat was not solely an ascetic or reclusive order, where adherents withdrew from society to engage solely in spiritual practices. Rather, it was deeply engaged in societal transformation and upheavals, leaving a lasting impact that reverberates through history to the present day. The collective identity forged by the Safavids persists in various forms, shaping our contemporary reality. Despite Shah Ismail's emergence on the world stage in 1501, the legacy of the Safavids endures, profoundly influencing the political boundaries and societal frameworks of our country.

Expanding on our previous discussion, it is worth noting the contributions of prominent figures in Iran's contemporary history, such as Mohammad Ali Foroughi and Seyyed Hossein Nasr. Foroughi, a significant figure of the early 20th century, left indelible marks on some of Iran's most crucial contemporary developments. Similarly, Nasr stands as a towering figure in Iranian thought, spanning the 20th and 21st centuries. Notably, Foroughi authored a seminal work titled *An Introduction to Wisdom in Europe*, which has emerged as a classic source for comprehending the trajectory of Hekmat or Gnosis in Europe (Foroughi, 2022).

In his work, *An Introduction to Wisdom in Europe*, Mohammad Ali Foroughi examines the evolution of philosophy, placing particular emphasis on Hellenic philosophy and rationality, rather than directly addressing the concepts of Hekmat or Gnosis in Europe. This deviation raises questions regarding the rationale behind Foroughi's choice of title for his exploration of philosophical evolution in Europe. However, aside from this inquiry, another significant issue emerges: the lack of attention to "Hekmat or Gnosis in Iran" within Foroughi's discourse. Despite being a pivotal figure in contemporary Iranian culture, Foroughi's work does not engage substantially with the status of Hekmat or Gnosis in Iran or its relationship with European philosophical thought.

The overlooking of "Hekmat or Gnosis in Iran" by contemporary Iranian intellectuals may be attributed to their adoption of a Eurocentric rationality or perspective, wherein Iran's history is perceived through the lens of Eurocentric ideologies. Consequently, they tend to consider the beginning of the Pahlavi era as the zero point of Iran's history, disregarding the complex and multi-faceted historical trajectory of Iran. This oversight has posed numerous challenges, as Iran's rich intellectual tradition, including thought, philosophy, Irfan, and Sufism, flourished during Mohammad Ali Foroughi's time. Thus, while there was significant intellectual activity within Iran, the focus on the course of Hellenic philosophy and rationality in Europe failed to establish a connection with Hekmat or Gnosis and its relationship with governance in Iran.

When Foroughi delves into the topic of Hekmat or Gnosis, notably absent is any mention of Iran's own intellectual tradition, particularly the path of wisdom led by figures like Shah Ismail, also known as Khatai. Interestingly, Seyyed Javad Tabatabai highlights Foroughi's assertion that the epitome of Iranian nationality lies in Hakim Abolqasem Ferdowsi's *Shahnameh*. This stance overlooks the significant temporal gap of nearly a thousand years between Ferdowsi's era and Foroughi's. Conversely, the period between Foroughi and Shah Ismail spans a mere four hundred years, yet Foroughi fails to acknowledge Shah Ismail's pivotal role in Iranian intellectual and cultural history.

The historical trajectory of what we now identify as Iran owes much more to Shah Ismail's governance, philosophy, and spiritual legacy than to Ferdowsi's poetry and *Shahnameh*. Shah Ismail's impact on Iran's political, institutional, social, and cultural landscape is undeniable, yet his name remains conspicuously absent from contemporary discourse. Unlike many other Shahs of Iran, Shah Ismail was not merely a ruler; he was a scholar, philosopher, and thinker in his own right. However, despite his profound influence, discussions on intellectual and theoretical developments, particularly in Hekmat or Gnosis, Sufism, and Irfan, often overlook Shah Ismail and his contributions. This systemic oversight warrants rigorous academic inquiry to understand how such a critical figure was marginalized from historical narratives.

Seyyed Hossein Nasr, born in 1933, nine years before the passing of Mohammad Ali Foroughi, has authored numerous works on Hekmat or Gnosis, Irfan, Sufism, and philosophy. Notably, despite his extensive scholarship in these fields, Nasr remains conspicuously silent about Shah Ismail. His influential book *Teachings of the Sufis from Yesterday to Today* (Nasr, 2003), originally penned in English as *Living Sufism*, stands as a cornerstone of his contributions to Sufi studies. However, the absence of any reference to Shah Ismail and his Turkish Diwan in this seminal work raises questions about Nasr's engagement with this significant figure in Islamic history.

The book is structured into three parts, each delving into different aspects of Sufism. The first section explores fundamental teachings, such as the role of reason and revelation, authority, and guardianship. In the second part, Nasr examines historical contexts, including the relationship between Sufism and Shiism, characteristics of 7th-century Sufism, and the influence of Ibn Arabi's school. The third segment focuses on how Sufism addresses contemporary global issues, including its role in environmental crises, modernization, and the evolution of civilization. Despite its comprehensive scope, Nasr's work notably excludes any mention of Diwan Shah Ismail, a significant figure in Sufi history. This omission raises questions about the reasons behind this apparent oversight and prompts inquiry into the mechanisms that led to the erasure of Shah Ismail's memory from such a pivotal work on Sufism.

It is possible that Nasr addressed this shortcoming in later works and filled in the gaps. Back in 2012, he penned an article titled "Irfan and the Theoretical Developments of Sufism in Iran from the Beginning to Now," shedding light on the evolution of Sufism and mystics. This piece was published in *Transcendent Philosophy: International Journal for Comparative Philosophy and Mysticism*, under the stewardship of Dr. Seyed Salman Safavi in England (Nasr, 2013, 1–35). In it, Seyyed Hossein Nasr delineated the trajectory of Irfan, Hekmat, or theoretical gnosis, and Sufism, tracing their historical journey from inception up until 2013. While the article touched upon Sheikh Safiuddin Ardabili, it notably omitted any mention of Shah Ismail, also known as Khatai, and his Hekami Diwan, along with the framework of Hekmat or Gnosis and Shah Ismail's theoretical Irfan.

It appears that this oversight arises from the predominance of nation-state historiography, which often overshadows cultural historiography. Within the framework of nation-state historiography, which constructs a somewhat artificial entity, "Iranian identity" is predominantly linked to the Persian language. As a result, the multifaceted expressions of Iranian culture conveyed through other languages spoken within the country's borders have been largely neglected, leading to a systematic erasure of memory. Scholars studying Iranian identity frequently view it solely through the lens of the Persian language, overlooking the rich diversity of linguistic expressions present within Iran.

However, the cultural history of Iran transcends its political boundaries. Iranians have historically spoken various languages and produced significant works across diverse linguistic landscapes. For instance, the regions of Aq Qoyunlu and Qara Qoyunlu, located in Tabriz, were integral parts of Iran's cultural landscape despite not aligning with its modern political borders. Yet, when examining the historical development of Hekmat or Gnosis, theoretical Irfan, and Sufism, there is a tendency to restrict the discussion to works written solely in Persian, thereby neglecting figures like Shah Ismail. Shah Ismail, as the founder of a government rooted in Hekmat or Gnosis and Sufism, and the author of significant works, deserves acknowledgment within this broader cultural narrative.

The relationship between governance and theoretical Hekmat or Gnosis has been a longstanding debate, resonating across various philosophical, theological, and mystical traditions. This dialectic, exploring the interplay between wisdom and government, has captivated thinkers throughout history, including Plato and many others. In contemporary Iranian philosophy, Dr. Sheikh Mehdi Haeri, a disciple of Ayatollah Boroujerdi and Imam Khomeini, stands out for his profound inquiry into this nexus. Shah Ismail, too, contributed to this discourse through his poetry, writings, and Diwan, where he engaged with pivotal theoretical Irfan concepts, drawing inspiration from the deep wellsprings of Irfan Ahl al-Bayt. Within this dialogue, the relationship between rulership and Hekmat or Gnosis remains a central and enduring inquiry.

Shah Ismail stands out not only for theorizing about governance but also for establishing a functioning government grounded in his principles of theoretical Irfan. While other thinkers, philosophers, and sages often contemplate how their governing philosophies might fare in practice, Shah Ismail's case is distinctive: his government is not a hypothetical construct but a tangible reality. Unlike Plato, who encountered obstacles in implementing his republican ideals, Shah Ismail's theoretical insights were manifested not only in his poetry and writings but also in the concrete establishment of a governing system. This unique combination of theoretical contemplation and practical action distinguishes him as a notable figure. Despite this significant achievement, scholars such as Foroughi and Nasr, among others investigating the evolution of Hekmat or Gnosis and theoretical Irfan, often overlook Shah Ismail's pivotal role in bridging theory and action.

The omission of Shah Ismail from the discourse on the evolution of Hekmat or Gnosis and theoretical Irfan, as discussed by figures like Foroughi and Nasr, raises pertinent questions about why his significant contributions are frequently overlooked. Similarly, his absence from discussions regarding Iran's intellectual developments and his role in shaping Iranian identity—particularly through his reverence for Ahl al-Bayt—reflects a broader oversight in recognizing his influence. Furthermore, the neglect of Shah Ismail in conversations concerning the sociology of literature or the intersection between sociology and political traditions in Iran is perplexing. Examining these omissions illuminates various aspects of contemporary Iranian history that warrant further exploration and acknowledgment.

Shah Ismail's characterization often falls prey to the confines of Orientalist historiography, which imposes Eurocentric interpretations onto the histories of non-Western societies. This approach, prevalent among European and American scholars, frames the Safavid dynasty's narrative from Shah Ismail's ascension to Shah Sultan Hussain Safavid's rule, effectively boxing it into a predetermined period in history. However, breaking free from this Eurocentric perspective allows for alternative readings that reject European-centric ideas and seek to understand Iranian cultural history on its own terms. By transcending the limitations of orientalist narratives, we can offer fresh insights into Shah Ismail's legacy and his role in shaping Iranian civilization.

By stepping outside the confines of nation-state historiography and Orientalist readings, there is an opportunity to reinterpret Shah Ismail's legacy in a more nuanced light. This involves rejecting European-oriented frameworks and embracing indigenous perspectives to understand Iranian cultural history authentically. Rather than perpetuating the cycle of Eurocentric interpretations, the aim is to offer alternative readings that shed new light on Shah Ismail's contributions and his significance within the broader narrative of Iranian civilization.

## 4      Shah Ismail as Part of a Tradition

It could be argued that viewing Shah Ismail's Diwan of poetry as a singular exception, born from a stroke of genius, is fundamentally flawed. According to the sociology of knowledge, concepts do not emerge instantaneously; rather, they evolve over time through a complex network of influences. Thus, it is improbable that the Diwan was produced all at once; rather, it likely encountered various obstacles during its formation. This raises a crucial question: what were the contributing factors to these obstacles? Surprisingly, this question has not been adequately addressed within the field of Iranian humanities. Instead of merely pondering why such an event did not occur, there is a pressing need to delve deeper into understanding the components of the challenges faced during the creation of Shah Ismail's Diwan.

In essence, Shah Ismail's intellectual tradition, as manifested in his Diwan, finds its roots in the theoretical Hekmat or Gnosis and the theoretical Irfan of Ahl al-Bayt (a). This historical landmark has left its mark not only in Arabic, Turkish, and Persian but also in various languages across the Islamic world. It is conceivable that traces of this theoretical legacy even extend to languages like Siamese in Thailand, a connection forged during the Safavid era. This enduring link persists today, fueled by the presence of Shiite communities whose lineage can be traced back to figures like Sheikh Ahmad Qomi (Julispong Chularatana, 2008).

The influence of the Gnostic Tradition and the theoretical insights of Ahl al-Bayt (The Family of The Prophet) can also be discerned in languages like Hindi and Urdu. Sufism and Irfan boast diverse theoretical schools, with many tracing their origins back to the spiritual authority of Wilayat Ali (a). Notably, Shah Ismail represents a significant tradition within this framework. Viewing this phenomenon through the lens of the sociology of knowledge reveals that such a tradition, with its multifaceted dimensions, couldn't have emerged instantaneously. Shah Ismail's unique contribution lies in his ability to shape knowledge within the Azerbaijani Turkish language, impacting both Iran and the wider Islamic world within a specific historical context. This knowledge shared a common context and temporal framework with preceding traditions.

Before Shah Ismail Khatai, a lineage of poets, mystics, and wise poets in Iran had already composed works in Azerbaijani Turkish, suggesting that the creation of Diwan Shah Ismail Khatai was within the realm of possibility. This Azerbaijani Turkish language and tradition extended not only across Anatolia, Mesopotamia, Syria, the southern Mediterranean, the North and South Caucasus, Central Asia, but also reached regions as far as Bosnia and Albania in Europe today. Within this linguistic and cultural landscape, a significant portion of our Gnostic Legacy finds crystallization in Azerbaijani Turkish, with Shah Ismail standing as a prominent representative (Savoy, 1980, p. 27). However, despite the richness of this tradition and its widespread influence, it has been largely marginalized in contemporary discourse.

The role of the sociologist of knowledge extends beyond defining issues and concepts solely within European-oriented paradigms. It entails examining matters from perspectives outside of this framework, which often leads to the emergence of new questions and considerations. Ardabil, as a significant center of the Gnostic Legacy and Islamic civilization, holds immense potential that transcends its status as just another city. It symbolizes a crucial movement in civilization, with Shah Ismail and Sheikh Safiuddin Ardabili representing pivotal figures within this context. Unfortunately, this capacity remains largely neglected. Revitalizing this focal point requires an epistemological concern, one that can be directed towards exploring the *Diwan Khatai* and its implications.

# CHAPTER 2

# Overcoming Cognitive Biases in Understanding the Gnostic Legacy of Shah Ismail

## 1    Introduction

Restoring the Gnostic Legacy of Shah Ismail, also known as Khatai, involves more than just exploring the life of an individual; it entails rediscovering and revitalizing an entire tradition. This tradition, rooted in the views of Hekmat or Gnosis and Irfan, draws its inspiration from the Ahl al-Bayt and has flourished in at least three major languages in Iran: Arabic, Persian, and Turkish. The pressing question at hand is not merely the relevance of Shah Ismail to our present context, but rather, how this rich Gnostic Legacy, embodied in texts like the Diwan Shah Ismail and other works, as well as the tradition conveyed in the Turkish language and the Hekmat or Gnosis of Ahl al-Bayt Safavid, has slipped out of our grasp.

Essentially, the focus should not be solely on emphasizing the significance of Diwan Shah Ismail, but rather on acknowledging the deliberate efforts to erase or sideline this text from our shared intellectual heritage. These efforts have been ingrained and institutionalized within Iranian intellectual and cultural spheres. It is remarkable that within the university, which should ideally foster critical thinking and reflection, not only has criticism been discouraged but also the opportunity for reevaluation of Inaccessibility Strategies has been withheld from humanities scholars.

Therefore, what demands attention is not just the historical text itself, but the broader socio-cultural context that has marginalized it. This includes examining the motivations behind such marginalization, the mechanisms through which it has been perpetuated, and the implications for our understanding of Iranian intellectual history. By acknowledging and challenging these strategies of inaccessibility, I can create a more inclusive and nuanced discourse that enriches my understanding of our intellectual heritage.

When examining the trajectory of poetry and literature in Iran, it is evident that Turkish poems are glaringly absent from the historiography of Iranian poetry. Similarly, within discussions of philosophy in Iran, including Hekmat, Gnosis, Sufism, theoretical Irfan, and the history of ideas, works written in Turkish, particularly Azerbaijani Turkish, are routinely disregarded. This systemic neglect, both in institutional frameworks and organizational practices, has effectively rendered a rich linguistic and cultural heritage inaccessible—a repository of knowledge and insight remains untapped.

Thus, to embark on the journey of revitalizing the text of Shah Ismail and others like it, it is imperative to first address the fundamental question: Why are these texts beyond our grasp? Before delving into the content of these texts, I must confront the mechanisms that have marginalized them, recognizing that their exclusion is not merely an oversight but a deeply political act. Texts, in their essence, represent complex and multifaceted entities, and to truly revive them, I must comprehend the intricate strategies employed to suppress them. This understanding forms the foundation upon which I can reclaim and reevaluate these invaluable contributions to our intellectual and cultural heritage.

## 2      Mohammad Ali Foroughi and Inaccessibility Strategies of Texts

One of the prevailing challenges in the contemporary era is the marginalization of texts through the lens of orientalist frameworks, often rooted in Eurocentric perspectives. This approach restricts access to the diverse texts within the gnostic legacy. Central to this discussion is the pivotal work of Mohammad Ali Foroughi. Viewing Foroughi not merely as an individual but as a significant project in the modern history of Iran sheds light on his profound impact on the civilizational landscape of the Shiite world. Foroughi's notable contribution lies in his seminal book titled *An Introduction to Wisdom in Europe* which warrants serious consideration.

This book stands as a cornerstone in Iran's modern intellectual landscape, emerging from the vibrant public and intellectual sphere of the country. Its significance in the ongoing discourse cannot be overstated, particularly when considering its title. Mohammad Ali Foroughi, far beyond being a chronicler of the Pahlavi dynasty, hails from a lineage of considerable influence. Notably, his family encompasses figures like his father, Mohammad Hossein Foroughi, and his brother, Abulhasan Foroughi. Each member contributed distinctively: Mohammad Hossein in the realm of economics, Abulhasan in intellectual pursuits, and Mohammad Ali in politics, philosophy, and enlightenment.

Abulhasan Foroughi's impact on the intellectual landscape of Iran, particularly in influencing figures such as Shariati, is undeniably significant. However, there exists a relative paucity of comprehensive exploration into his works and ideas within Iran's intellectual milieu. For instance, the compelling narrative surrounding Agha Mehdi Arbab's activities in the British colonies of Bombay, where he promoted a Shahnameh-based nationalism among modernist leaders, underscores the family's rich historical legacy. While scholars like Mojtaba Minavi and Jalal Homayi have briefly addressed these aspects, there remains considerable opportunity for a deeper examination and appreciation of the Foroughi family's contributions to Iran's modern history. The relationship between the *Shahnameh* and the process of de-memorizing the heritage of *Diwan Khatai* represents a neglected area in contemporary Iranian historiography that warrants a thorough reevaluation.

As it has been noted earlier, Mohammad Ali Foroughi's book titled *The Path of Hekmat or Gnosis in Europe* may initially suggest a focus on "Hekmat or Gnosis," but upon closer examination, it becomes evident that the book diverges from this theme. In Christian Europe, Henry Corbin asserts that the term "Theosophy" often substitutes for "Hekmat or Gnosis," while in contemporary discourse, some prefer the term "Wisdom Philosophy." However, if we refrain from categorizing "Hekmat or Gnosis" as exclusively an "Eastern" concept, we can recognize its profound roots in Islamic thought. Indeed, this concept finds its genesis within the Islamic world, and one might argue that it bears a distinctly "Quranic" character.

Hekmat or Gnosis, as articulated in the Quran and nurtured within the theoretical tradition inspired by Ahl al-Bayt, embodies a form of illumination (Eshrāq) and intuitive, sagacious thought. It encompasses a depth of knowledge that transcends mere intellectual understanding, encompassing profound insights into existence and spirituality. Therefore, it would be more accurate to view Hekmat or Gnosis as inherently intertwined with Islamic philosophy and spirituality, rather than as a concept exclusively tied to Eastern or Western traditions.

Hekmat or Gnosis is knowledge by presence and is not knowledge by acquaintance; it is endowed upon human being from the Ultimate Source of Being. *The Path of Hekmat or Gnosis in Europe* by Mohammad Ali Foroughi presents a narrative that extends beyond the confines of its title. While the book ostensibly revolves around the themes of "Hekmat or Gnosis," a deeper examination reveals a broader exploration of philosophy within European intellectual history. Notably absent are mentions of significant figures like Jacob Boehme and Immanuel Swedenborg, indicating a departure from a narrow focus on esoteric wisdom. Instead, Foroughi's discourse encompasses a diverse array of philosophical currents and thinkers, offering insights into the multifaceted landscape of European thought across various epochs and intellectual traditions.

Mohammad Ali Foroughi's book, written in Iran at the turn of the 13th to 14th century (around 1921 to 1941), extends the concept of "Hekmat or Gnosis" to encompass Western philosophical movements such as continental philosophy, analytical philosophy, and positivistic philosophy from the French tradition. However, it is worth noting that these philosophical traditions do not inherently align with the principles of "Hekmat or Gnosis," which emphasize the science of knowledge, presence, intuition, and theoretical Irfan. In doing so, Foroughi broadens the scope of "Hekmat or Gnosis" beyond its traditional Eastern understanding. This raises questions about why Foroughi applies this concept to philosophical traditions that are not typically associated with it in Europe and the West.

This question offers two possible explanations for Mohammad Ali Foroughi's choice of substituting "Hekmat or Gnosis" for Western philosophy. The first suggests a deliberate act of terminological innovation on Foroughi's part. However, a deeper exploration reveals a second, more profound interpretation: the coining of "Hekmat or Gnosis" marks an "epistemological break" within Iranian intellectual discourse. Comparable to a stroke-induced disruption in memory and language, Iran experienced a momentary pause in its historical memory and intellectual continuity, particularly evident since the middle of the Naseri period. Foroughi's role becomes emblematic of this civilizational rupture, encapsulating both the challenge of redefining intellectual traditions and the potential for renewal within Iranian society.

Mohammad Ali Foroughi's discourse, while addressing Iranian culture and civilization, as well as the deeper layers of thought significant to the Islamic and Shiite traditions, often employs terminology and concepts divergent from these traditions. Notably absent from his discussions is any mention of the rich philosophical, Gnostic, and theoretical Irfan traditions indigenous to Iran. These traditions, spanning thousands of years and encompassing diverse developments, were vibrant during Foroughi's lifetime, with luminaries existing in Tehran throughout the Qajar and Pahlavi eras. However, Foroughi's work fails to acknowledge this extensive Iranian heritage, with no reference to figures like Shah Ismail or the Iranian Gnostic Tradition. Moreover, the absence of any exploration into the relationship between analytical or continental philosophy and Iran's Gnostic Tradition further underscores the disconnect between Foroughi's discourse and the indigenous philosophical currents of Iran.

Mohammad Ali Foroughi's narrative on Hekmat in Europe reflects a conscious and unconscious adoption of strategies that distance one from tradition. These strategies, ingrained in the educational system of Iran and perpetuated through intellectual currents in contemporary Iranian discourse, contribute to a pseudo-modernity that alienates us from our intellectual and spiritual heritage. Foroughi's work becomes emblematic not of understanding modernity, but of grasping pseudo-modernity—an approach that obscures direct engagement with our Gnostic Tradition. It appears we are compelled to rely on figures such as Louis Massignon or Henry Corbin to reinvigorate our texts through orientalist paradigms, thereby perpetuating a historiographical trajectory reminiscent of Edward Browne's formulations. Although these scholars are esteemed, their revival of our texts frequently adheres to pre-established orientalist frameworks, which may further distance us from our authentic intellectual heritage. Mohammad Ali Foroughi's narrative inadvertently contributes to a framework that sidelines the diverse intellectual contributions of Iran by predominantly focusing on Persian language texts. This narrow lens disregards the richness of Arabic, Turkish, and other texts produced within Iran, which form an integral part of the intellectual tapestry of the Islamic world. By equating Persian language with Iranian identity and even Islamic tradition, Foroughi's approach reinforces the notion that Persian language encapsulates the entirety of Iranian cultural and intellectual heritage. Consequently, both our educational and higher education systems become ensnared within the confines of "Persian language," neglecting the plurality and richness inherent in the broader Iranian intellectual tradition.

Shafiei Kadkani assertion that Persian language serves as the primary language of Irfan and theoretical Hekmat or Gnosis in the Islamic world raises pertinent questions. Despite his deep understanding of Islamic texts, particularly in Arabic, due to his seminary background, Kadkani's claim may overlook the historical reality that many foundational texts in Irfan and Gnosis were indeed written in Arabic. While acknowledging the importance of Persian language, this assertion implies a monopolization of Irfan and Gnosis within a linguistic framework shaped by historical, nationalist perspectives. Such a stance risks marginalizing valuable texts and the broader Gnostic Tradition, limiting accessibility and understanding. It underscores the ongoing challenge of navigating between linguistic, historical, and nationalistic influences that shape our interpretation and access to intellectual traditions.

When delving into the Gnostic Legacy within a specific language, one inevitably encounters Hekmat or Gnosis; for Hekmat or Gnosis transcends borders and is inherently human. Aristotle is often credited as the earliest proponent of Greek Hekmat or Gnosis, followed by Farabi as its second teacher, and even Plotinus, despite being of Jewish origin, contributes to this body of knowledge. Thus, Greek Hekmat or Gnosis is not confined by nationality. Consequently, the exploration of Diwan Shah Ismail's Turkish text serves as a revitalization of Hekmat or Gnosis, and narrow nationalistic perspectives should not overshadow other texts, mystics, and scholars.

In the current intellectual landscape of Iran, Turkey, Arab countries, and various parts of the Islamic world, there is a concerning trend where the rich tapestry of the Gnostic Tradition and the broader cultural heritage of the Islamic world is being fragmented into numerous small, often newly formed national-istic traditions. These traditions, often less than a century old, risk alienating various ethnicities and groups, fostering cultural alienation that breeds differ-ent forms of ethnocentrism. This fragmentation gives rise to ideologies like Pan-Arabism, Pan-Persianism, Pan-Turkism, Pan-Kurdism, and so forth. These ethnocentric ideologies highlight our failure to embrace the entirety of our cultural identity, reducing it to singular components. Consequently, I struggle to formulate a comprehensive collective identity.

Mohammad Ali Foroughi's ambitious project aimed to disrupt our access to the rich tapestry of the Gnostic Tradition across various languages of the Islamic world, including Turkish, Arabic, Persian, and others. Through diverse epistemological strategies, this endeavor achieved some success in limiting our engagement with these traditions.[1]

## 3      Seyyed Hossein Nasr and Inaccessibility Strategies of Texts

Before the revolution, Seyyed Hossein Nasr stood as a prominent figure straddling the realms of thought and politics in Iran. His subsequent move to America following the revolution expanded his sphere of influence significantly, par-ticularly among students from Islamic nations like Iran, Turkey, Malaysia, Syria, Iraq, as well as among those from Western countries who either were born Muslim or embraced Islam later in life. Notably, Ibrahim Kalin, an impor-tant student of Nasr, mastered English, Persian, and Arabic alongside his native Istanbul Turkish, delving deeply into Sadra's Hekmat or Gnosis under Nasr's guidance. Upon returning to Turkey, Kalin assumed key policymaking roles, serving as a senior advisor to Recep Tayyip Erdogan and presently directing Turkey's National Intelligence Center. Nasr himself, with his profound under-standing of Islam, knowledge, the Gnostic Tradition, and theoretical heritage, wields considerable influence globally. However, his contributions to the Gnostic Legacy often go unrecognized. Discussions on the Gnostic Tradition and the legacy of Shah Ismail inherently necessitate engagement with thinkers such as Nasr, which may lead to a potential conflict of perspectives.

In Seyyed Hossein Nasr's seminal work, *Three Muslim Sages* (Nasr, 2022), he meticulously charts the evolution and diverse streams of theoretical Hekmat or Gnosis in the Islamic world, particularly focusing on Iran. Nasr's narra-tive seamlessly transitions from the Arabic origins of Hekmat or Gnosis to

---

1   The topic is briefly explored in Seyed Javad Miri's book *General Theory of Religious Reform* (2022, Tehran: Criticism of Culture).

its Persian counterpart, tracing a direct line of continuity to contemporary thought. This trajectory forms a crucial triangle, encompassing Edward Brown, Mohammad Ali Foroughi, and Seyyed Hossein Nasr, each contributing a distinct theoretical perspective. Brown laid the groundwork for understanding Iranianness and the Iranian tradition, followed by Foroughi's categorization efforts, and finally, Nasr's profound insights, conveyed through the language of Hekmat or Gnosis. Despite their differing angles, all three scholars operate within the orientalist framework and the European paradigm, shedding light on a tradition that transcends linguistic boundaries, encompassing Arabic, Persian, Azerbaijani Turkish, and beyond.

In *Three Muslim Sages*, Nasr unveils the philosophical musings of these eminent figures, delving into their perspectives on humanity, metaphysics, knowledge, and the intricate relationship between humanity and existence. Their discourse spans a wide range of fields and languages, showcasing proficiency in Arabic, Persian, Azerbaijani Turkish, and more. Nasr's exploration underscores the universality and adaptability of this tradition, which continues to resonate across cultures and linguistic spheres, enriching our understanding of the human condition and the mysteries of existence.

The issue at hand pertains to the exclusive association of the Gnostic Tradition in Iran with the Persian language, which neglects the significance of Azerbaijani Turkish. This oversight is considerable, as notable poets and sages such as Seyedamad al-Din Nasimi, Fazuli, Shah Ismail, Hakim Hidji, and Shahryar have all produced works in Turkish, thereby contributing to the development of the Gnostic Tradition within this linguistic framework. However, this trajectory has abruptly diminished in contemporary discourse. While Persian poetry by figures like Shahriar is widely recognized, their Turkish works remain marginalized, if acknowledged at all. Understanding this phenomenon illuminates the strategies employed to render these texts inaccessible.

The crystallization and zenith of the Gnostic Tradition in Turkish can be traced back to Shah Ismail. Yet, attention to this aspect of the tradition lacks a cohesive policy. Scholars like Seyyed Hossein Nasr have not actively advocated for such a policy, often operating within the confines of an orientalist discourse. One consequence of this discourse is the deliberate obfuscation of the diverse texts comprising the Gnostic Legacy. Consequently, the use of Turkish within the Iranian context may be construed as a challenge to or deviation from Iranianness, further perpetuating the marginalization of Turkish-language contributions.

Central to the cultural and theoretical foundations of Iranianness and its influence on the Islamic world is the paradigm of Ahl al-Bayt. However, orientalist policies have effectively silenced discussions of this component in the

Turkish language. As a result, Turkish, including Azerbaijani Turkish, is not synonymous with the Gnostic Legacy in Iran. Figures like Shah Ismail, pivotal in the revival of the Gnostic Legacy and theoretical Irfan, remain largely unknown and systematically erased from collective memory.

## 4     Abbas Eqbal Ashtiani and Orientalist Discourse Design

When we refer to the "designer" of the orientalist discourse, we do not imply a singular individual orchestrating a conspiracy to dominate intellectual discourse in Iran and the Islamic world. While some may indeed participate in such endeavors, they are not the focus of our discussion here. Rather, we are addressing the development of a mental framework that evolves over time in response to shifts in societal contexts. The question then becomes: Who influenced Seyyed Hossein Nasr's thinking, leading him to adopt Mohammad Ali Foroughi's worldview, which seemingly disregards the diversity within the Gnostic Legacy in Iran?[2]

Abbas Eqbal Ashtiani emerges as a significant architect in shaping language policy, particularly concerning Turkish and Arabic languages. Despite receiving relatively little attention from intellectuals and researchers, his ideas continue to permeate language policies in Iran, influencing philosophers, sages, and historians of various disciplines such as philosophy, Hekmat or Gnosis, Sufism, and Irfan theory. Though his name may be seldom mentioned, and his language policies overlooked, the impact of Abbas Eqbal Ashtiani's doctrine persists.

According to Eqbal Ashtiani, certain languages are inherently linked to notions of security. Thus, as a means to safeguard our cultural identity and ensure security, he advocated for the erasure of these languages from our collective consciousness and historical memory. Abbas Eqbal Ashtiani says:

> If our nation is to survive and at least defend itself in the political arena of language, it must necessarily have a language policy and, for this purpose, design a reasonable plan and implement it with determination and prudence so as not to be defeated in this field. For if, God forbid, we fail at this stage and another language prevails over Persian in Iran, the death knell of Iran and Iranians will have been sounded.
>
> EQBAL ASHTIANI, 1945: 3

---

2   In the book *Re-reading the Idea of the Language of National Unity: Re-reading the Discourse of Archaic Nationalism* written by Seyed Javad Miri (2018, Tehran: Naqd Farhang), five cases of the designers of this thinking are mentioned.

Abbas Eqbal Ashtiani identifies several languages, including Turkish and Arabic, as possessing a security attachment that poses a threat to Iranianness, according to his perspective. In his view, languages like Kurdish, Mazandarani, and Gilaki are deemed less dangerous. Despite elements of our tradition and the Gnostic Legacy being embedded in Turkish and Arabic, Eqbal Ashtiani perceives these languages as inherently risky. He contends that approaching or exploring the Iranian spirit through non-Persian languages, particularly Turkish and Arabic, is tantamount to an attack on Iranianness. Consequently, the significance of Shah Ismail's Gnostic Legacy is diminished in Eqbal Ashtiani's framework. Moreover, its revival may even be construed as a threat to Iranian identity, as per his formulated perspective.

From the mid-Naseri era onward, debates surrounding nationalism have proliferated, laying the groundwork for the emergence of approaches akin to that of Abbas Eqbal Ashtiani. This perspective was not merely theoretical but was actualized as a strategic plan at the highest echelons of Iran's cultural policies. Similar projects were undertaken in other countries, notably Turkey and Iraq, with devastating consequences for the intellectual traditions of the Islamic world. Today, both countries grapple with confusion stemming from the attempt of one identity to overshadow others, asserting itself as the sole representative of Mesopotamian or Anatolian nationality and culture.

## 5    Avoiding Cognitive Biases

This book can only provide initial insights into the Gnostic Legacy of Shah Ismail. Currently, we lack the capacity for a phenomenological exploration of Shah Ismail's Gnostic Legacy and Iran's intellectual tradition in the Turkish language due to cognitive biases. These biases are not solely psychological; they manifest as prejudices. Let us briefly define prejudice before delving into its dimensions within the Iranian context.

Prejudice can be defined as a negative or hostile attitude towards a subject or person. This attitude stems from three factors: cognitive, emotional, and behavioral. The cognitive factor involves our thoughts and opinions, while the emotional factor pertains to our feelings. The behavioral factor can lead to discriminatory actions. In the context under discussion, it appears that prejudices encompass both cognitive and emotional dimensions, leading to specific behavioral actions. Notably, there has been limited research on how these prejudices manifest in the actions of academics.

For instance, it could be insightful to examine the preconceptions of academics regarding the significance of Shah Ismail Khatai's Gnostic Legacy in

Turkish. Consider individuals like Hamid Ahmadi or Seyyed Javad Tabatabai, who depict the Turkish language as an external element that infiltrates and dominates the Iranian essence. While this perspective might initially seem psychological, it is crucial to delve into its underlying foundations and origins.

Cognitive prejudices have structured the educational and higher education systems, as well as academies and cultural organizations, in a manner that impedes a phenomenological engagement with texts. Our discussion in this chapter does not constitute a research project; rather, it presents a mental framework. Unlike a research plan requiring access to sources shaping our current situation, our access to such sources, spanning various languages over the past five centuries, remains fragmented. Despite these challenges, we propose a mental schema centered on Shah Ismail's Gnostic Legacy. However, while we may have a relatively good understanding of the obstacles, establishing meaningful connections with others sharing our journey remains difficult. Iranian researchers, sages, theologians, and thinkers encounter difficulty in phenomenologically engaging with Shah Ismail's Gnostic Legacy due to entrenched cognitive prejudices, which hinder such encounters.

# CHAPTER 3

# Linguistic Classifications and Deletion of the Gnostic Legacy of Shah Ismail

## 1 Introduction

This chapter explores the multifaceted concept of language by addressing three critical questions. First, language is defined as a sophisticated system of communication encompassing sounds, words, and grammar that uniquely enables human interaction and the transmission of ideas. Second, the chapter examines the conceptualization of "local language" within the realm of social literature, investigating how this notion is expressed and the core principles underlying its formation. A pivotal point of reference in this analysis is the fifteenth article of the Constitution of the Islamic Republic of Iran, which provides a legal framework for understanding linguistic categorization. Scholars have highlighted the article's emphasis on distinguishing between the "official language of the country" and "local languages." Persian is recognized as the official language, serving as the nation's *lingua franca* and script, while other languages, including Turkish, Armenian, and Georgian, are acknowledged as local languages, with their use permitted in literature and media. This legal formulation demonstrates the complex interaction between linguistic identity and political considerations within a constitutional framework (Mansour, 2023: Article 15).

From a philosophical perspective, defining language entails addressing its intrinsic and extrinsic dimensions. Language is often considered a uniquely human attribute that differentiates our species from other forms of life, embodying the ability to convey complex ideas, abstract concepts, and emotions through structured systems of symbols and sounds. When language is viewed as a fundamental phenomenon, the classification of languages into categories—such as local, national, official, or common—emerges not as an inherent property of language but as a construct shaped by sociopolitical, historical, and cultural contexts. In the Iranian context, for instance, Persian has been designated as the national, official, and common language, while languages like Turkish, Armenian, and Georgian are regarded as local. This classification underscores the influence of extralinguistic factors, such as historical legacies, geographic boundaries, and sociopolitical considerations, in shaping language policies and practices.

However, these classifications do not derive from the intrinsic nature of language but rather from human conventions and societal constructs. Language itself is a dynamic and evolving phenomenon, reflecting the diverse needs of its speakers over time. The categorization of languages into official or local, national or regional, is shaped by sociocultural and political dynamics, illustrating the intersection of power, identity, and culture in the linguistic landscape. Thus, while language serves as an essential and universal aspect of human life, its classification into various categories is an extralinguistic construct that reflects the broader structures of society and history.

## 2    What Is Language?

According to continental philosophers, language transcends its conventional understanding as a tool for communication or a human construct. It is not merely an imposition or a complication imposed on existence but rather constitutes the very dwelling place of Being itself. Heidegger, for instance, refers to language as the "house of Being," emphasizing its ontological significance in shaping the human experience of reality. Far from being a constraint, language is a source of power and potential, enabling humanity to navigate and expand its understanding of the world. Through language, individuals and societies move from stasis to dynamism, allowing for the articulation of identity, the unfolding of history, and the deepening of self-awareness. In this view, language does not simply reflect reality but actively participates in its construction, serving as the medium through which existence is shaped and given meaning.

Linguistic barriers, within this philosophical framework, are not conceived as mere obstacles to communication but are instead manifestations of language's profound role in structuring and differentiating existence. The multiplicity of languages and the challenges they present signify the richness of human experience, rather than its fragmentation. Each language provides a unique lens through which reality is interpreted and understood, thereby enriching the collective understanding of existence. Language, in this sense, is not a neutral or static medium but the very substrate upon which the complexities of Being unfold. Continental philosophers highlight this perspective by describing language as the "abode of Being," underscoring its centrality to the creation, preservation, and transformation of meaning. This ontological framing challenges utilitarian conceptions of language and positions it as fundamental to the human condition.

Approaching linguistic pluralism through this philosophical lens radically shifts the discourse from conventional pragmatic discussions to an exploration of language as an essential dimension of existence. Instead of viewing linguistic diversity as a challenge to communication, it is celebrated as a manifestation of the dynamic interplay between culture, identity, and reality. The plurality of languages reflects the multiplicity of ways in which existence is articulated, experienced, and understood. Each linguistic tradition contributes to the tapestry of human experience, offering distinct frameworks for interpreting the world and enriching the collective understanding of what it means to be. Thus, linguistic diversity is not a barrier to overcome but a profound expression of humanity's capacity to engage with and shape its own existence.

Noam Chomsky's linguistic theory posits the existence of a universal grammar inherent to human beings, predating the formation of specific language systems like English, Turkish, or Arabic. According to Chomsky, humans are born with this innate linguistic framework, setting them apart from other species like parrots. This universal grammar serves as the foundation for language acquisition and development, guiding the evolution of language within society. In essence, human linguistic determination occurs within the parameters of this pre-existing structure, highlighting the fundamental role of innate grammar in shaping human language.

The classification of languages into categories such as local, national, and official does not seem to be inherent within the structure of language itself, which is predicated on a universal grammar. Instead, this classification appears to be a product of external factors such as politics, culture, and societal norms. Concepts like "locality" and "formality" do not seem to be encoded within the grammar of language; rather, they are constructs imposed on language from outside sources. This implies that linguistic classifications are not solely determined by factors within the language itself but are also shaped by external influences. Before delving deeper into this topic, it is crucial to address another aspect.

## 3     Language Classification in Iran

In the intellectual landscape of Iran, certain assumptions have spurred the Gnostic tradition and philosophy in the Islamic world, prompting profound reflections on language. Among the pioneers of the philosophy of language in the Islamic world stands Farabi, recognized as a foundational figure in this field. Contemporary Iranian philosopher Qasim Pourhassan, in his work

*Al-Farabi and Al-Haruf,* eloquently highlights Farabi's contributions to linguistic studies, particularly in the second chapter of *Al-Haruf,* beginning from the 20th chapter onward (Pourhassan, 2019, p. 406).

In the past century and a half, as intellectuals have increasingly engaged in public discourse in Iran and across the Islamic world, the issue of language has often been overlooked or relegated to a secondary concern. Instead of delving deeply into the phenomenon of language itself, discussions have tended to revolve around linguistic examples, leading to simplistic categorizations such as labeling Persian as the "national language." Critics who raise objections to such classifications are often dismissed, as their critiques are perceived as lacking political acumen or sensitivity to linguistic nuances. However, this approach fails to provide a meaningful solution to the complexities inherent in the language question.

To truly address this issue, we must return to the intellectual tradition of rigorous questioning and criticism espoused by thinkers such as Farabi, Ibn Sina, Ibn Rushd, Abu Rihan al-Biruni, Mulla Sadra, and other great minds of the past. Rather than resorting to superficial categorizations, we should engage in a deeper examination of language and its role in Iranian society. A fundamental question arises: How should language be formulated in Iran? This question necessitates a comprehensive exploration of linguistic theory, cultural dynamics, historical context, and philosophical insights. Only by adopting a nuanced and multidimensional approach can we hope to formulate a language policy that is both equitable and reflective of Iran's rich intellectual heritage.

In Iran, discussions about language span four primary domains: 1) as a mother tongue, 2) as a national language, 3) as an official language, and 4) as a common or mediating language. These aspects are intricately woven into Iran's historical and sociopolitical context. Each facet reflects the evolving dynamics of identity, governance, and cultural diversity within the nation. Understanding these discussions requires a nuanced examination of how language functions both as a personal identifier and as a tool of state policy, navigating the complexities of Iran's linguistic landscape over time.

Before the constitutional era, the term "national" predominantly referred to "nationhood." It was during the constitutional movement that this term began to denote "nation" in the Iranian context. It is imperative to acknowledge that Persian has not universally served as the mother tongue for all Iranians throughout history. In contemporary analysis of language in Iran through phenomenological, ethnographic, philosophical, and sociological lenses, a diverse linguistic landscape unfolds. Beyond Persian, numerous Iranians speak languages such as Turkish, Armenian, Arabic, Georgian, Kurdish, and Balochi as their mother tongues. The categorization of languages, dialects, and accents varies by scholarly criteria, leading to estimates that Iran accommodates any-where between 400 to 80 distinct languages. This multifaceted linguistic diver-sity underscores the complex interplay of cultural, historical, and social factors shaping Iran's linguistic tapestry today.

Linguistic pluralism in Iran is indeed evident. Prior to the constitutional era, the concept of "milla" denoted religion, and religious languages varied widely. For example, Zoroastrians used Pahlavi, Assyrian Catholics spoke Assyrian, and Armenians utilized Armenian. Even Buddhists employed Pali for their texts. Post-constitution, the concept of "nation" shifted to denote a collec-tive social contract, encompassing various ethnicities and cultures coexisting within Iran. Consequently, the diverse languages and cultures present in Iran contribute to its national identity. Thus, Persian alone does not solely consti-tute the national language; rather, it is one component of Iranian nationality. Other languages, such as Georgian, Armenian, Turkish, and Arabic, also con-tribute to the Iranian national identity. It is incorrect to assert that an Iranian citizen born in Iran lacks Iranian cultural or linguistic affiliations. Their iden-tity inherently embodies Iranian heritage, shaped by a diverse array of cultural and linguistic influences.

Conflicts arise within archaeological and neoclassical discourses when claims assert that Turkic and Arabic languages were introduced to Iran solely through the Mongol invasion and Arab conquests, respectively. Such assertions challenge the principles inherent in social contract theory and modern nationality dis-course. Within contemporary discourse, the attribution of language exclusively to an essential "Iranianness" poses significant issues, as it implies a perceived necessity to safeguard the purity of this essence. This essentialist perspective conflicts with the foundational principles of a nation rooted in collective social contract and historical realities. It suggests a stance where any perceived influ-ence deemed to compromise this essence must be eliminated to preserve lin-guistic integrity. However, these viewpoints contradict the dynamic historical evolution of Iran and the evolving concept of nationhood, which encompasses a mosaic of linguistic and cultural influences across its history.

In the Iranian constitution, Persian is designated as the official language of the country, serving as the common and mediating language. However, the choice of the language of mediation can vary depending on the context and cultural dynamics of the setting. For instance, in the bustling markets of Tehran, Turkish may serve as the common language among carpet sellers. Similarly, in provinces like West Azerbaijan, Turkish could be used as a shared language among diverse ethnic groups.

The question of whether a language's identity can be confined to being "local" probes into the origins of linguistic localization: Does it arise internally from the language itself, or is it imposed externally by non-linguistic factors? This inquiry intersects with strategies of de-memorization surrounding Diwan Shah Ismail Khatai, prompting a fundamental exploration into the essence of linguistic evolution and cultural identity. By dissecting this debate, we may unlock pathways to revive forgotten linguistic traditions within Iran and the wider Islamic world, nurturing a deeper appreciation for linguistic diversity and cultural heritage.

4      The Term "Local Language" and the Elimination of
       Language Possibilities

In the sixth part of the sixth chapter of his book *On the Service and Treachery of Intellectuals*, Jalal Al Ahmad presents a theory without providing extensive elaboration (Al-Ahmad, 1400: 138). Subsequent discussions regarding the concept of language in Iran have either overlooked Jalal's theory entirely or actively sought to suppress it. To elucidate this phenomenon, we can turn to a concept from the philosophy of science: undertheorization. This term refers to situations where theories are introduced but not sufficiently developed or explored. To illustrate this concept, let us consider two examples.

When Alaei introduces his "Theory of Consensus" and endeavors to apply it across different domains like culture and cinema, others fail to engage in dialogue with his ideas. Consequently, the theory of consensus remains isolated and over time, it gradually recedes to the periphery, lacking opportunities for further development and expansion. In the language of the philosophy of science, when a theory is presented but lacks thorough conceptualization, it is deemed weak or undertheorized.

Karl Marx's theory on capital, as presented in *Das Kapital*, alongside his insights into historical evolution (Marx, 2006), serves as a foundational framework upon which subsequent researchers, theorists, and thinkers build. Over time, through their interactions and contributions, Marx's original theory expands and proliferates, branching out like a sturdy and sprawling tree. This process of continuous elaboration and refinement eventually leads to the phenomenon known as overtheorization, where the theory becomes dense with additional layers of analysis and interpretation.

Jalal Al-Ahmed's theory asserts that languages, particularly Turkish, have been forcibly removed from the public sphere in Iran, stifling their ability to flourish and develop independently. If we accept this theory, it suggests that the concept of "local language" is an external construct, shaped by political agendas rather than emerging naturally from linguistic dynamics. This viewpoint represents a subject-object relationship within the language field, influenced by political considerations that exclude certain languages from public discourse.

Language encompasses more than a mere collection of words; it embodies culture, perspective, and identity, serving as a crystallization of historical diversity and plurality. Removing a language from public discourse not only erases linguistic elements but also disrupts a significant historical and traditional flow that has shaped identity over time. In essence, the concept of a "local language" is not intrinsic to linguistic matter. Regarding languages like Georgian and Arabic, their designation as "local" or "native" within a particular context, such as Iran, is often a product of external political impositions rather than inherent linguistic realities.

Arabic stands as one of the most prominent languages globally, renowned for its historical significance and continued relevance in contemporary times. However, within the context of Iran, the classification of Arabic as a "local language" is not a natural consequence of linguistic evolution. Instead, it reflects a political imposition onto a cultural phenomenon. This external designation creates a linguistic classification or hierarchy that does not originate from within the language itself but rather results from political dynamics shaping cultural narratives.

The phenomenon of linguistic hegemony, where one language asserts dominance over others within a nation-state system, is not unique to Iran but is pervasive across many countries. In Iraq, for instance, Arabic held sway as the official language until the fall of Saddam Hussein, marginalizing languages like Persian, Kurdish, Azerbaijani Turkish, and Assyrian. Linguistic hegemony is a modern construct closely tied to the nation-state system, which hierarchically structures languages based on political will. This imposition often leads to the suppression or even eradication of minority languages, as seen historically in countries like England, where Scottish, Welsh, and Irish languages faced severe repression. However, with the emergence of discourse promoting cultural diversity in Europe, there are efforts to revive these languages.

The notion that certain languages are inherently superior while others are merely "local" or even considered dialects is erroneous. Every language has the capacity to fully express human thoughts, emotions, and reflections. Viewing the majority of languages as "local" while elevating one as the national or official language perpetuates a false hierarchy. In Iran, for example, the Persian language is designated as an "official language" rather than a "national language" in the country's constitution, challenging the notion of linguistic superiority.

5       The Importance of Paying Attention to the Philosophy of Language

The significance of delving into the philosophy of language cannot be overstated. Unfortunately, many misconstrue discussions regarding language as adversarial toward the Persian language, viewing them as attempts to undermine its hegemony in Iran. Nevertheless, it is crucial to emphasize that such discussions are not motivated by animosity towards Persian. Rather, they aim to explore language dynamics from a metaphysical and philosophical standpoint, questioning whether any language inherently holds superiority over others based on its components. This inquiry is not about diminishing the importance of Persian but rather about understanding language dynamics within their broader philosophical context, free from misconceptions and preconceived notions.

Those who espouse ideologies like Pan-Turkism, Pan-Slavism, Pan-Persianism, Pan-Kurdism, and others often propagate flawed reasoning. One such fallacy is the claim that the Persian language lacks the capacity to convey human emotions. However, anyone familiar with the works of Saadi, Hafez, Ferdowsi, Rudaki, and others understands the immense depth and expressive capability of the Persian language. For instance, poets like Bidel Dehlavi masterfully articulate delicate human emotions in the Indian style, showcasing the profound emotional range inherent in Persian literature. To assert that Persian is deficient in expressing emotions is to disregard the rich literary tradition and expressive prowess of the language. Bidel Dehlavi speaks beautifully about the complexities of meaning:

> Not every bewildered gaze grasps the meaning,
> A sound disposition is virtue, not inherited.
> We have reached the sky, yet not seen the inner secret,
> This circle is suspect, if there's no door outside.
>     BIDEL, 2001: 1187

Likewise, it would be unfounded to assert that the Turkish language lacks the capacity to articulate intricate and philosophical concepts. Across nations like Turkey, Azerbaijan, Uighuristan (Xinjiang, China), Uzbekistan, and others, Turkish (including Istanbul Turkish, Azeri Turkish, Uighur, and Joghtai) serves as a vehicle for rich cultural expressions in music, literature, and history. In Iran, the legacy of Azerbaijani Turkish finds resonance through figures like Seyyed Mohammad Hossein Behjat Tabrizi, known as Shahryar, celebrated both nationally and internationally. Shahryar's poem *Haydar Babaye Salam* stands as a testament to the profound depth of expression achievable in Turkish. Through his work, Shahryar adeptly navigates the intersection of tradition and modernity, capturing the complexities of societal change and personal encounters with unparalleled nuance—all conveyed in the Turkish language.

The focal point of inquiry revolves around investigating the cognitive and creative capabilities of language through a philosophical lens. Before examining specific instances that demonstrate the potency and scope of human language, it is essential to establish a foundational comprehension of its fundamental nature. In Iran, disciplines such as Persian literature, linguistics, and, to a certain extent, the sociology of language address this inquiry with varying degrees of emphasis. Additionally, archaeologists may contemplate the role of language in their research endeavors. However, the domain known as "philosophy of language" does not command substantial attention within Iranian scholarly discourse.

Before delving into specific examples of language, such as the Persian language, it is essential to first explore the fundamental nature of language itself. This entails theoretically formulating linguistic concepts and understanding the relationship between language and existence on a broader philosophical level. When we prioritize examples over general theoretical considerations, we risk substituting the particular for the general. For instance, if we exclusively use the term "melon" instead of the more general concept of "fruit," we encounter difficulties when describing other fruits. This tendency to prioritize specific examples over broader theoretical frameworks can lead to conceptual confusion, particularly within disciplines such as Persian literature, linguistics, language sociology, and language archaeology. Without grounding our analyses in theoretical rationality, philosophical insight, and conceptual imagination, we inadvertently elevate specific languages, like Persian, to a privileged position, thereby measuring other languages against it. This approach perpetuates conceptual confusion and inhibits our ability to develop a comprehensive understanding of language as a universal phenomenon.

In addressing these debates within the Iranian academic milieu, it is essential to recognize the prevalence of political considerations, which often result in overly simplistic classifications of languages. Some arguments, for instance, propose that Turkish is merely a derivative of Persian, tracing its roots to Azeri. However, such assertions disregard the intricate historical trajectories of individual languages and oversimplify the process of classification. Without employing a philosophical approach characterized by abstract reasoning and analytical rigor, there is a risk of becoming entangled in linguistic ambiguities. Rather than delving into specific instances, it is crucial to contemplate language in a more conceptual manner and examine the linguistic landscape within Iran from a broader perspective.

From this vantage point, it becomes evident that the Turkish language cannot be relegated to a non-Iranian status. The historical narrative suggesting that

the Mongols introduced Turkish to Iran is fraught with complexities and inac-
curacies. In reality, languages like Turkish and Arabic are integral components
of Iranian nationality. Attempts to reduce language classification to genealogi-
cal or racial formulations fall short, as they fail to capture the nuanced interplay between language and identity. Overcoming these stereotypes is essential
for engaging with issues like the heritage of Diwan Shah Ismail and Khatai in
a meaningful manner.

## 6      Conclusion

Our exploration of linguistic issues has often neglected the rich insights provided
by ethnographic, anthropological, and sociological perspectives. Overlooking
the social nature of language formation and its role in identity construction
has hindered our understanding. Languages are not static entities but dynamic
social constructs that interact, evolve, and profoundly influence individual
and collective identities. Ethnographically, delving into communities' lived
experiences unveils how language intricately intertwines with cultural practices, norms, and rituals. Anthropologically, language serves as a lens through
which we analyze societal structures, power dynamics, and knowledge systems. Sociologically, language functions as a marker of social belonging and
differentiation, shaping patterns of inclusion and exclusion. Embracing these
interdisciplinary approaches reveals the intricate interplay between language,
society, and identity, enriching our understanding of linguistic phenomena.

The absence of a philosophical approach in the realm of language is con-
spicuous. By philosophical approach, we do not confine ourselves to the discipline of philosophy alone, but rather to the power of conceptualization
inherent in philosophical thinking. The dialectical interplay between national
and local concepts, often subjected to an artificial hierarchy where national is
deemed superior and local inferior, prompts us to question the origins of this
prioritization. Is it an intrinsic aspect of language itself, or have we internal-
ized it as an unquestionable principle, even deeming it taboo to contemplate?
Our inability to grasp and articulate this issue stems from a deficiency in conceptual perspective. Without a theoretical framework for classification and
articulation, as elucidated by contemporary Iranian philosopher Mohammad
Ali Moradi, meaningful discourse becomes elusive. Instead of engaging in genuine dialogue, we find ourselves embroiled in political strife, devoid of conceptual depth. True understanding and theoretical formulation do not arise
from political contention; rather, they necessitate a conceptual approach that
transcends political rhetoric.

# Rereading the Gnostic Legacy of Shah Ismail

The assertion that the Diwan of Shah Ismail is beyond reach does not imply the inaccessibility of its physical existence. Original copies of this significant text are preserved in various prominent institutions, including the Paris Museum, the Saint Petersburg Museum, and historical sites such as the tomb of Shah Ismail or Sheikh Safi-ad-Din Ardabili. Thus, the materiality of the text remains intact and available. However, the notion of inaccessibility arises from a lack of meaningful engagement with its content, rather than the absence or destruction of the text itself. This raises a critical question: why has such an important work, despite its preservation, remained largely unread and underexplored? Addressing this issue requires an examination of the cultural, historical, and intellectual dynamics that have contributed to the neglect of this pivotal literary and historical artifact.

As it has been noted earlier, the philosophy of science includes the concept of undertheorization. This concept elucidates instances where a theoretical framework with significant potential is proposed but fails to gain traction or popularity within the scientific community, resulting in its marginalization and lack of widespread discussion. Consequently, the theoretical framework remains thin and feeble due to its limited application across various fields and issues. Conversely, theories like Karl Marx's, particularly his theory on capitalism and human alienation, have spawned a robust tradition of discourse. Marx's conceptual framework has been extensively deliberated, reinterpreted, and expanded upon within the Marxist tradition, leading to its Overtheorization. When we remark that the text of Diwan Shah Ismail is inaccessible, we imply that it has largely remained unread in Iran. While various reasons for this phenomenon have been discussed earlier, another factor contributing to the unavailability of Diwan Shah Ismail and the Gnostic Legacy Khatai is their inaccessibility.

## 1    Marginalization of the Texts of the Khatai Tradition

The tradition associated with Shah Ismail has not vanished among groups such as "The Followers of The Right Path," "Ghulat," "Ali Elahi," and "Qizilbash," residing outside and on the periphery of Iran. Instead, it has endured and remained accessible to them. Beyond Iran's borders, in regions like Turkey, Syria, Lebanon, Iraq, the South Caucasus, as well as certain areas of present-day Armenia, Bulgaria, and the Balkans, this tradition persists.

Scholars such as Abdülbaki Gölpınarlı, Irene Markov, and Sadettin Nüzhet Ergun have delved into the field of the Khatai tradition, specifically the tradition attributed to Shah Ismail, and the Qizilbash or Alevi Bektashi tradition across various regions worldwide. However, both in the works of these scholars and within the text of Diwan Shah Ismail itself, poems, narratives, and anecdotes have been ascribed to Shah Ismail, the historical accuracy of which remains dubious. The marginalization of the Khatai tradition has led to these texts, known as the texts of the Khatai tradition, being approached with a marginal perspective.

In Iran, the Gnostic Tradition associated with Shah Ismail and Diwan Shah Ismail himself have been largely overlooked, with no discernible discussions on this topic within Iranian scholarly circles. However, beyond Iran's borders, particularly in regions like the Balkans, Bulgaria, and Turkey, this tradition finds resonance among communities marginalized within mainstream society, often regarded as minorities. For instance, adherents to the Khatai tradition in Bulgaria, Turkey, and various Balkan regions, stretching as far as Albania and Iraq, occupy the fringes of their respective communities. Sociologically, texts available to marginalized groups often exhibit a sense of minority mentality and constraint.

When a mindset is characteristic of a minority social group, constantly relegated to society's periphery by the majority, texts within their possession may lose their inclusivity. While minority groups may hold these texts in high regard, considering them sacred, they often lack recognition from the broader society. This dynamic engenders a marginal or abandoned mentality within the minority group, not unique to the Khatai tradition. In contemporary Iran, for instance, a group residing near Taleghan and Qazvin, in a village known as "Ista," are descendants of the Mujtahid of Tabrizi, maintaining a belief in seclusion since the constitutional period to the present day.

This group abstains from involvement in political affairs and societal developments, choosing to remain detached from manifestations of civilization. Departure from the village is permitted, but returning is discouraged. While such minority groups may attain intuitive and esoteric insights, their lack of exposure to societal changes and human civilization's transformations results in texts characterized by a minority viewpoint, distant from global events and societal progressions. These texts, though significant, often lack universal relevance and capacities.

## 2    Rereading the Texts of the Khatai Tradition

The revival and reevaluation of the Gnostic Tradition attributed to Shah Ismail necessitates a comprehensive reassessment, including the identification and preservation of texts associated with this tradition. However, this endeavor must transcend the biases and preconceptions of various groups such as The Followers of The Right Path, Ali-Illahism, Qizilbash, Alawites, and Bektashis. Instead, it requires a fresh perspective untethered to sectarian affiliations, enabling an unbiased reinterpretation. While the goal may appear straightforward, the project faces significant challenges and complexities.

In Bulgaria, communities associated with the Qizilbash are known as the Alian Qezelbash Community, denoting their attribution to Ali, much like the "Ali Elahi" designation in Iran. Predominantly residing in rural or mountainous regions across provinces like Ceylon, Razgrad, Silistra, and Tergovishte, each province boasts its own Qizilbash villages. For instance, in Tergovishte, settlements like Mogilets and Baicheva are inhabited by Qizilbash, while in Silistra, villages such as Preslavci, Chenovik, and Bradvari host Qizilbash communities. Similarly, in Razgrad province, larger populations of Qizilbash are found in vil-. lages like Sevar, Ostrova, Madrevo, Lavino, Bisertsi, Sveshtari, Malko Selo, and Yablanovo in Selivne province.

Despite their geographical proximity and shared Anatolian cultural heritage, Bektashis and Qizilbash exhibit distinct identities influenced by factors like the Balkan climate. Irene Markoff notes that most Qizilbash adopt an eclectic or syncretic approach, drawing elements from Catholicism, Orthodoxy, and pre-Christian religions prevalent in Bulgaria. This syncretism mirrors similar practices among Yarasanis in Iran, who incorporate beliefs from pre-Zoroastrian religions like Mithraism. The dispersal of Qizilbash communities into remote villages and mountainous terrains reflects a history of persecution and marginalization.

Many of these regions were under Ottoman rule for centuries, during which Qizilbash communities faced persecution from adherents of the dominant religion. Unable to comprehend Qizilbash beliefs and practices, Ottoman rulers sought to isolate them from urban centers, resettling them in rural areas. This geographical and social isolation has profoundly influenced the mindset, language, and intellectual framework of Qizilbash communities. As Shariati observes, the perspectives and religious rulings issued by rural authorities differ significantly from those of urban counterparts, reflecting distinct cognitive and socio-cultural contexts shaped by village life.

Essentially, the Khatai tradition is largely rooted in rural contexts, which has adversely impacted the comprehension and articulation of its principles.

Texts attributed to this tradition are often relegated to rural settings, where they are entrusted to elders and mentors whose audience primarily comprises rural dwellers. These figures, while lacking extensive literacy or formal education, rely heavily on oral transmission of beliefs and teachings. Consequently, their understanding of the tradition tends to be simplistic and limited.

The texts associated with the Khatai tradition, preserved within these rural communities, reflect this simplistic framework. If approached with the same rural perspective prevalent during their inception, these texts may appear incompatible with the sophisticated frameworks and assumptions of the modern era. Consequently, our interpretation of the Gnostic Tradition, based on these oral formulations and interpretations of the Khatai tradition, may yield perceptions steeped in superficiality and simplicity.

A fundamental aspect of the Gnostic Tradition lies in the interplay between esoteric and exoteric messengers, fostering a profound relationship that transcends temporal and cultural boundaries, allowing its essence to resonate across generations. However, the current state of texts attributed to the Khatai tradition fails to fully embody this dynamic interaction. Many of these texts lack the depth and coherence required to represent the intricate fusion of esoteric wisdom and exoteric expression central to the tradition. To address this disparity, it becomes imperative to undertake a meticulous process of identification and categorization. This involves distinguishing authentic texts genuinely linked to Shah Ismail and the Khatai tradition from those that erroneously claim affiliation or stem from unrelated sources. Such a scholarly endeavor not only safeguards the intellectual and spiritual legacy of Shah Ismail but also ensures that the profound insights of the Gnostic Tradition are accurately preserved and interpreted for future generations.

Critically revising the texts of the Khatai tradition necessitates moving beyond the worldviews, beliefs, and interpretative frameworks of groups such as the Tajiklars, the Qizilbash communities in Bulgaria and the Balkans, and rural populations. These interpretations, often rooted in the perspectives of minority or lay communities, tend to reflect localized or subjective understandings that diverge from the theoretical and philosophical foundations of the Gnostic Tradition. To ensure a more rigorous and comprehensive analysis, a scholarly approach is essential—one that prioritizes historical authenticity, intellectual coherence, and fidelity to Shah Ismail's original teachings. By disentangling the Khatai tradition texts from the constraints of localized or non-scholarly interpretations, it becomes possible to uncover a more nuanced and accurate representation of the Gnostic Tradition, thereby enriching the understanding of its profound spiritual and intellectual legacy.

In Iran, the Safavid texts of Shah Ismail and the Khatai tradition, including his own Diwan, have not been the focus of significant scholarly investigation. While Shah Ismail's historical authenticity as a king is universally recognized and uncontested—firmly situating him as a historical figure rather than a mythical or legendary one—the scholarly engagement with his literary and intellectual contributions remains limited. Interestingly, outside of Iran, numerous texts attributed to him continue to enrich his legacy, providing a broader perspective on his influence. Within Iran, however, Shah Ismail's primary identity diverges from that of a historical monarch. He is predominantly revered as one of the perfect Murshids (spiritual guides) within the Alavi dynasty, emphasizing his spiritual authority and esoteric significance over his political and administrative roles. This dual perception highlights the complexity of his legacy, which intertwines spiritual leadership with political sovereignty.

According to Alevis, attaining the level of perfection embodied by Shah Ismail within the Gnostic Tradition and the Safavid Tariqat is exceedingly rare. They believe that, aside from prophets and imams, only a handful of individuals over the past 1500 years have reached such a degree of completeness. While the Bektashi, Alavi, Qizilbash, and Safavid dynasties intersected at certain points before diverging, communities outside Iran, like those in Bulgaria and the Balkans, have seen followers of these Tariqats coming together. It could be argued that the Qizilbash, Bektashi, Alavi, and similar Tariqats have, to some extent, converged in these communities.

In critical studies concerning the texts of the Khatai tradition, the preservation of Diwan Shah Ismail, housed in the museums of Paris and Saint Petersburg, remains intact. Scholars like Abdülbaki Gölpınarlı, Nikolai Markov, and Saaduddin Nezhat Ergon have posed inquiries into whether there exist additional texts attributed to Shah Ismail beyond Diwan Shah Ismail. Within the Hikaylar tradition in Bulgaria, numerous poems incorporate a form of zikr, where a central chant, such as "Shah, Shah, Shah," is recited in circles. This zikr reveres Shah Ismail, not solely as a reigning monarch, but as a Seyyed—an individual attributed to Ahl al-Bayt, including Fatima Zahra (PBUH) and Hazrat Rasool (PBUH). In their view, the term "Shah" denotes a complete Murshid.

In the realm of Khatai tradition studies, our approach should involve cataloging the texts associated with this tradition and subsequently discerning the original content from the peripheral additions that have been appended to it over time. This separation process aims to reconstruct these texts, guided not by subjective assumptions, but by two foundational pillars: Firstly, the principles of The Gnostic Tradition, which hinge on the interplay between the Esoteric and Manifest Messengers. Secondly, the Diwan attributed to Shah

Ismail, whose authenticity has been affirmed. Despite these Diwan poems possessing a theoretical framework, their foundational elements have yet to be thoroughly explored. Pertinent inquiries include: 1) What are the theoretical underpinnings of Shah Ismail? 2) How does the Gnostic Tradition associated with Shah Ismail intersect with the Khatai tradition, prevalent beyond Iran but notably absent within its borders? 3) What connections exist between Shah Ismail's Gnostic Tradition and broader Islamic concepts such as Irfan, Sufism, and Hekmat or Gnosis? 4) How do Shah Ismail's foundational tenets, as encapsulated in Turkish literature (Diwan Shah Ismail and the Khatai tradition), relate to interpretations found in Persian and Arabic texts within Iran? Presently, the state of scholarship in this domain, while not at ground zero, remains close to it, with our inquiries still in their preliminary stages.

3        The Gnostic Tradition of Shah Ismail in Contemporary Studies

The theoretical Irfan and Gnosis that Shah Ismail speaks of are expressed in Turkish. Iranian identity is not confined to one language. The Khatai tradition, stemming from Shah Ismail's teachings, persists beyond Iran, flourishing among Anatolian, Balkan, Mesopotamian, and southern Mediterranean minorities, primarily in Turkish. Even in Bulgaria, adherents do not write in Bulgarian; instead, they continue the tradition in Turkish. This Gnostic Tradition, attributed to Shah Ismail, extends Iran's spiritual depth to the Balkans through the Turkish language. Shah Ismail did not solely innovate these concepts; predecessors like Fazuli, Habibi, and Murshid laid the groundwork. Many poet-sages, like Fuzuli, expressed themselves in Turkish, Persian, and Arabic, weaving a rich tapestry of linguistic and spiritual exploration.

The Gnostic Tradition, conveyed in Turkish, has been largely overlooked within Iranian discourse, including academic studies and literary analyses. One significant challenge in addressing its importance lies in the recurring need to authenticate its attribution to Shah Ismail. Skepticism about its provenance often overshadows meaningful engagement with its content. Additionally, when compared to the celebrated works of literary and spiritual luminaries such as Maulvi, Saadi, or Hafez, the texts associated with Shah Ismail appear less prominent, both in terms of recognition and scholarly examination. This disparity has led to questions regarding their relevance and authenticity, further marginalizing the Gnostic Tradition within the broader framework of Iranian intellectual and cultural heritage. However, these challenges underscore the necessity of rigorous scholarly efforts to authenticate and contextualize these texts, illuminating their potential contributions to the understanding of spiritual and literary traditions in the region.

This neglect highlights a disconnection from the diverse Gnostic Tradition expressed in various languages, particularly Turkish. Consequently, there is a notable absence of scholarly studies on Shah Ismail or the Khatai tradition in contemporary Iran. For instance, despite his reputation as a meticulous historian, Abbas Zaryab Khoei has not authored a single article on the Khatai tradition, despite his Azerbaijani background and significant contributions to Azerbaijani studies. Similarly, figures such as Seyyed Ahmad Kasravi, recognized for their scholarship in Iranian and Azerbaijani history, have portrayed Shah Ismail and the Safavid dynasty in ways that raise questions about the prevailing narrative surrounding their legacy. This narrative gap underscores a broader trend of overlooking the richness of the Gnostic Tradition across various languages, resulting in significant gaps in scholarly exploration and understanding.

During the same period as Seyyed Ahmad Kasravi's work, the Russian orientalist Vladimir Minorsky also engaged with topics related to Shah Ismail, offering insights shaped by his distinct cultural and academic background. Although Minorsky did not extensively explore the Khatai tradition, his studies included references to Shah Ismail and texts that shed light on his mystical worldview. Minorsky highlighted the presence of certain manuscripts and writings that delve into Shah Ismail's spiritual beliefs, noting their preservation in libraries across the Indian subcontinent. This observation underscores the geographical and cultural reach of Shah Ismail's influence, suggesting that his mystical legacy transcended regional boundaries, even if it remained less systematically explored in some contexts.

Over the past century, with the establishment of Iran's university system and the expansion of academic research, significant attention has been devoted to fields such as Theoretical Irfan and Safavid studies. Scholars from diverse backgrounds have contributed to these disciplines, exploring Iran's rich intellectual and historical heritage. However, despite its importance in understanding Shah Ismail's multifaceted legacy and its relevance to broader mystical traditions, the Khatai tradition remains conspicuously absent from scholarly discourse in Iran. This omission represents a critical gap in the study of Iran's spiritual and cultural history, as the Khatai tradition offers valuable insights into the synthesis of political authority and mystical thought that characterized Shah Ismail's contributions to the Islamic world. Addressing this lacuna could provide a more comprehensive understanding of Safavid history and the development of mystical traditions within the region.

Those who discussed Shah Ismail and the Khatai tradition outside of Iran often failed to contextualize the Khatai tradition within the broader Gnostic Tradition, and more significantly, they frequently neglected to connect these discussions to Iran. Azerbaijan emerges as the epicenter of this movement, with significant activity in Ardabil and other regions of Iran, intertwining these texts with the expansive movement of theoretical Irfan within the Islamic world. In the most favorable instances, scholars like Irene Markov attempted to frame this tradition within the Iranian context. However, many Sufis, mystics, and those who explore Irfan's perspectives beyond conventional Islamic discourse view such discussions as diverting attention from the primary discourse.

Markoff, alongside Alevi scholars such as David Shankland, expanded the scope of research on Shah Ismail by incorporating ethnographic methods in addition to textual analysis. Rather than limiting their focus to the texts themselves, they contextualized these writings within their broader social and cultural frameworks, treating them as dynamic components of a living tradition shaped by societal forces. This approach reframes Shah Ismail not merely as an author or a historical figure but as a vibrant legend deeply embedded in the collective memory of his followers across diverse regions. Recent monographs on Shah Ismail reflect this shift, prioritizing the exploration of his Diwan's cultural and societal significance over the mere authentication of his literary corpus. These works highlight how Shah Ismail's legacy transcends the boundaries of historical documentation, emerging as a potent symbol within the broader tapestry of Alevi and mystical traditions.

This evolving scholarship has redirected attention from Shah Ismail's role in religious rituals and literature to his broader cultural and social impact, particularly in regions such as Turkey, the Balkans, and Bulgaria. For example, Tord Olsson's "The Scripturalization of Alid-Oriented Religions" and David Shankland's "Anthropology and Ethnicity" in *Alevi Identity* (Olsson, et al., 1998) investigate Shah Ismail's role within the Alevi movement, emphasizing his influence on identity formation and communal practices. Shankland's work is particularly notable for extending beyond textual studies to include ethnographic research on Alevi communities, providing a nuanced understanding of their beliefs and practices in diverse sociocultural contexts. These studies underscore Shah Ismail's enduring relevance, not only as a literary and religious figure but also as a cultural icon whose impact resonates across multiple dimensions of Alevi identity and tradition.

While these interdisciplinary approaches have enriched the study of Alevis, Shiites, and the Khatai tradition, critics argue that such studies detach these communities from the broader intellectual and traditional Islamic context. Some view Alevis and others as outside the mainstream Muslim tradition, labeling them as syncretic or heretical. However, adopting a more nuanced perspective that places the Khatai tradition within the Gnostic Tradition challenges such categorizations, urging for a critical reevaluation of existing frameworks proposed by scholars like Shankland and Olsson.

4    The Criteria for Reconstructing the Gnostic Tradition of
     Shah Ismail

In examining the ongoing discourse surrounding esoteric movements, several key arguments emerge. Firstly, contemporary esoteric groups often hold distinct beliefs about themselves and their traditions, emphasizing secrecy, spiritual enlightenment, and the transmission of esoteric knowledge. Secondly, historically, Sunni Muslims have tended to view groups associated with esoteric traditions, such as Alawites, Qizilbash, Bektashi, and those linked with the Khatai tradition, with suspicion or even hostility due to perceived deviations from mainstream Sunni beliefs. Thirdly, a convergence between Shiism and Sufism has occurred over the past five centuries, with some Shiite scholars now viewing Sufism as compatible with their beliefs, although the exact stance of mainstream Twelver Shiites towards esoteric groups may vary. Finally, different traditions and societies hold diverse perspectives on the Khatai tradition, ranging from reverence to dismissal, prompting consideration of whether understanding the Khatai tradition can transcend societal biases for a more objective analysis.

It is conceivable to set aside the interpretations held by specific communities regarding the Khatai tradition and instead reconstruct it based on internal criteria. For example, when re-examining Ibn Arabi's works, one might analyze Ibn Arabi's "Conquests of Makkah" through the perspective of Shafi'i jurisprudence, taking into account the viewpoints of Shafi'i and Hanbali scholars who offer insights into the mystical interpretation of the Quran and hadiths. This approach involves distancing Ibn Arabi from conventional interpretations, potentially leading to a fresh understanding of his texts. Such analytical methods permit a new perspective free from preconceived notions, which may offer valuable insights into the Khatai tradition.

Examining figures like Maulvi and Shams Tabrizi through the lens of dominant jurisprudential views, particularly those of Ahl al-Tsan, necessitates their complete removal from the tradition. Shams Tabrizi, for instance, finds no place within this framework. Scholars seeking to reevaluate the tradition of Irfan (Gnosis) approach these texts critically, rejecting notions of heresy and recognizing the limitations imposed by jurisprudential perspectives on studying Khatai tradition texts. In Iran, Bulgaria, and the Balkans, the Khatai tradition primarily manifests in the Turkish language. However, within Turkey, the tradition has crystallized in three distinct languages: Turkish, Kurdish, and Zazaki. Each language community—Turkish-speaking Alawites, Kurdish-speaking Alevis, and Zazaki-speaking Alevis—contributes to shaping unique horizons of the Khatai tradition. It is essential to examine both the shared characteristics and distinctions among these groups, exploring the intersection of the Khatai tradition with each respective language. Furthermore, investigating the correlation between these languages and Diwan Shah Ismail, along with their possible associations with The Gnostic Tradition, provides valuable insights into the evolving dynamics of the Khatai tradition within varied linguistic and cultural frameworks.

## 5      The Gnostic Legacy of Shah Ismail: a Study Scheme

The interaction between the Shia religion, as the official faith in Iran since the Safavid era, and alternative practices formed through independent study of jurisprudence and religious beliefs, reveals a complex dynamic. In Iran, sects like Yarsanism and The Followers of The Right Path exist on the fringes of the religious society. These practices have been historically acknowledged by the state as part of Islam in a general sense, but there is typically limited interference in their specifics. This detachment has led to a lack of intellectual, religious, and societal interaction between these groups and the mainstream Shia establishment. Due to potential religious prejudices against them, these groups often adopt esoteric practices as a form of religious expression, akin to the restrictive measures seen in Ottoman, Bulgarian, and Turkish contexts. However, it is noteworthy that thinkers within these alternative traditions may choose to compose texts in the Persian language, thereby reflecting Iran's cultural and linguistic milieu.

One example of such groups, with which I have had firsthand interaction and conducted related research, is a community locally referred to as "Ali Elahi," who identify themselves as "The Followers of The Right Path." Their primary settlement is located near Rodhan, which has expanded and prospered over time and is now known as "Mehrabad." Historically, their spiritual leader was Seyyid Nizam al-Din. When I inquired about their ethnicity or language, they identified as Kurds; however, many members are not fluent in Kurdish and primarily speak Turkish, with their ancestors largely originating from Urmia. Notably, their religious texts are composed in Persian. Although these texts are not widely disseminated, they articulate beliefs regarding spiritual manifestation known as "don by don." According to this belief, the spirit of a mentor merges with the body of a newborn or fetus upon the mentor's departure from their physical form. This concept bears similarities to notions of reincarnation found in Buddhist and Hindu traditions.

In my encounters with The Followers of The Right Path in Rodhan, I did not observe Shah Ismail holding a significant position within their community.

Conversely, among the "Gorans" in Ilkhchi city, Shah Ismail occupies a special status, revered as a Pir (spiritual guide) and a complete mentor. While this designation was not exclusive to Shah Ismail—other Safavid kings, such as Shah Abbas, were also considered complete mentors—the perception of Shah Ismail significantly differs from that of Shah Abbas among groups like the Alawites or Qizilbash.

As Max Weber aptly notes, when charisma transitions into a bureaucratic institution, its charismatic essence diminishes. Shah Abbas sought to institutionalize the spiritual qualities and legacy of Irfan (Gnosis) through the bureaucratic role of complete mentor; however, it was evident that he lacked the spiritual charisma associated with Shah Ismail, embodying instead the role of a reformist ruler. Among the Safavid monarchs, only Shah Tahmasab may have approached the charismatic aura of Shah Ismail.

This book is dedicated to repositioning Shah Ismail within the context of the historical development of Hekmat (Gnosis) in the Islamic world. Thus far, Shah Ismail's significance has been overlooked within this narrative. For instance, Seyed Hossein Nasr, in his discussions on the evolution of Irfan (mystical wisdom) and Hekmat in Islam, typically mentions numerous historical figures, including Sheikh Safiuddin Ardabili, leading up to contemporary thinkers like Javadi Amoli, Allameh Hassanzadeh Amoli, and Imam Khomeini. However, Shah Ismail's name is conspicuously absent from Nasr's discourse. This book endeavors to rectify this omission and highlight Shah Ismail's pivotal role in the development of Hekmat within the Islamic world.

It is imperative to reposition Shah Ismail within this historical narrative. His inclusion alters our understanding of the historiography of Hekmat or Gnosis in the Islamic world and expands its dimensions within Iran. For instance, the historiography of ruling traditions need not be confined to the Persian language alone in our proposed reading. If Shah Ismail can be reconceptualized as a sage, theologian, mystic, and possessor of a judicial and theoretical framework, then the diverse facets of the Khatai tradition—forged under Shah Ismail's writings yet obscured in Iranian and Islamic history—can be revived and revitalized. In this scenario, the Turkish language assumes a critical role.

We can address the mechanism that has emerged within Iran, particularly within academic circles, known as "Persian language imperialism." This concept does not denote hostility towards the Persian language; rather, it represents a formulation wherein Iranian identity is perceived exclusively through the lens of Persian language and culture. When Iranian identity is predominantly associated with the Persian language, the Iranian academic and intellectual spheres may struggle to acknowledge and reconstruct Iranian identity beyond Persian linguistic boundaries. Shah Ismail's role becomes crucial in this context. As an Iranian, he not only founded a government but also espoused a distinct theoretical perspective, embodying his vision within a specific geographic context. This achievement was not solely through military might but also through intellectual prowess. Shah Ismail, an Iranian, communicated his ideas in Turkish. However, this tradition has waned within Iran, resulting in the marginalization of poets and mystics who wrote in Turkish after Shah Ismail. Figures like Hakim Hidji and Bayza Ardabili are relegated to the periphery of Iranian thought, as the center has been predominantly defined within a Persian framework.

Shah Ismail's ideas and influence extend far beyond the borders of Iran. Anatolia serves as a significant center for disseminating Shah Ismail's thoughts. However, due to the nationalistic lens of our historiography, regions like Anatolia or the Balkans are often disregarded. There exists a tendency to include regions within the historiography of Iranian identity only if Persian is spoken there, while disregarding regions where Persian is not the predominant language. For instance, the significance of Indian intellectuals who wrote in Persian is acknowledged in Iranian historiography, yet Shah Ismail, an Iranian who wrote poetry in Turkish, is often overlooked. The notion that Turkish is not "our" language, and the belief that Iran's borders are defined by the presence of Persian, has hindered our engagement with Shah Ismail's texts.

It is crucial to reinvigorate the human capacity for aspiration and vision. By revitalizing proficiency in languages such as Turkish, Arabic, Kurdish, and others associated with The Gnostic Legacy, the imaginative and intellectual horizons of the Iranian people can significantly expand. Consequently, Shah Ismail, acting as a conduit between Iran, Anatolia, the Balkans, and the Caucasus, can wield substantial influence. Contrary to prevalent beliefs in Iran that Shah Ismail's adoption of Shiism restricted Iran's cultural boundaries, a reinterpretation of Shah Ismail's legacy portrays him as a unifying force, forging connections among diverse global cultures.

Even today, we observe discussions regarding Shah Ismail's influence within religious and mystical trends, particularly in Anatolia, Turkey, and various regions of the Balkans, in recent studies. As an Iranian historian, founder, and sage, Shah Ismail continues to play a significant role in shaping Irfan (Gnosis) and religious movements in these regions. However, the extent of this influence and its potential implications for policy making are rarely addressed in Iran. Recent studies have primarily focused on the enduring significance of Shah Ismail's Diwan of poems as a crucial source of Irfan and Hekmat (Wisdom) outside of Iran. Nevertheless, there remains an absolute silence regarding the study of Irfan and Hekmat within Iran itself.

In Turkey, Bulgaria, the Balkans, and even among European and American scholars, there is significant interest in studying the Diwan of Shah Ismail as a governing text and its implications for Irfan (Gnosis). However, researchers in Iran who specialize in Sufism, Irfan, and Hekmat are often cautious about delving into this area. In the contemporary era, there is a growing focus on the message of Irfan and Hekmat within the Khatai tradition, which emphasizes concepts like love, compassion, and the elevation of humanity, rather than solely on the historical dimensions of Shah Ismail as the founding king of the Safavid regime.

New studies focusing on Shah Ismail's texts emphasize the importance of love and tolerance among individuals, viewing these qualities as central to spiritual enlightenment. The essence of Shah Ismail's message lies in the discourse of love and compassion. For instance, a notable study published in 1993 by Omar Olucay titled "Shah Khataei and Alaviism: Beliefs, Traditions, Elements, and Ethics" explores this theme extensively, despite the prevailing historical perspectives in Iran that often portray Shah Ismail as a figure of strength and military prowess. Unfortunately, within Iran, there has been a neglect of these new studies on Shah Ismail, with the intellectual climate largely disconnected from such endeavors. Addressing this trend requires fundamental changes. It is imperative to examine how the direction of these studies in Iran can be reshaped. This question is pivotal to our contemplations, emphasizing the necessity to prioritize this issue within Iran's academic sphere, especially within the realm of Gnosis studies.

The Turkish language transcends the boundaries of countries like Turkey or specific communities such as the Alevis in the Balkans or the Qizilbash in Bulgaria. Instead, it is also a language spoken by the Iranian people. Shah Ismail took great pride in this language and expressed his Irfan, Sufism, and Gnostic beliefs in Turkish. This aspect warrants theoretical consideration and deserves acknowledgment. In the Islamic world, particularly in regions like Iran, Turkey, and the Caucasus, many intellectuals and scholars did not convey their ideas and philosophies through conventional books. Instead, they adopted roles such as "poet-thinker," "poet-Sufi," "poet-mystic," or "poet-sage," often compiling their manifestos and theses in the form of Diwan poems.

A thorough examination of the Diwan of poems and their subsequent interpretations is essential. The oral transmission of numerous primary texts and poems among devotees of Shah Ismail's poetry, counsel, and anecdotes has culminated in the formation of the Khatai tradition. This oral tradition should not be overlooked. Initially recorded in Bulgaria in the early 20th century, it was later translated into Bulgarian and English. Lovers of Shah Ismail's poetry interpreted his poems and advice in their own verses and sayings, and these interpretations are now available. However, there exists a significant paradigmatic gap between these interpretations and our understanding, and we have yet to translate these texts into Persian or Arabic in Iran. Perhaps by reconstructing the central themes of Shah Ismail's Diwan of poems, we can unveil one key theme: The Gnostic Tradition of Ahl al-Bayt. Within Shah Ismail's poems, Ahl al-Bayt holds a unique and central position. Surrounding this focal point are various elements, including "love," "nature," "humanity," "suffering," "enlightenment," "music," and more. At the heart of these components lies Shah Ismail Khatai, the central symbol of The Gnostic Tradition and Ahl al-Bayt.

Without a doubt, the Gnostic Tradition of Irfan Maulvi and Shah Ismail intersect at a pivotal juncture. Various Sufi traditions encompass distinct practices; one tradition emphasizes spiritual intoxication, another prioritizes the pursuit of knowledge, while yet another focuses on asceticism, exemplified by figures like Qas Ali Hazoo. Despite these differences, numerous similarities exist among the styles of Irfan. The fundamental and defining disparity between Irfan Maulvi and Shah Ismail's tradition lies in their respective jurisprudential backgrounds. Maulvi initially adhered to Sunni jurisprudence but gradually distanced himself from it under the influence of Shams Tabrizi, ultimately aligning himself with the Tariqat dynasty's devotion to Amirul Momineen Ali (a). However, Shah Ismail's tradition did not originate from a Sunni framework. When examining Shah Ismail's tradition, it is crucial to contextualize it within historical disparities and the socio-cultural environment in which he operated. This analysis must acknowledge the connections between Shah Ismail and figures such as Sheikh Junaid, Sheikh Haider, and Sheikh Safiuddin Ardabili, who promoted Shiism and advocated a Shiite perspective of Irfan.

Undoubtedly, the Gnostic Tradition of Irfan Maulvi and Shah Ismail converge at a crucial intersection. Different Sufi traditions embrace distinct practices; one emphasizes spiritual intoxication, another prioritizes the pursuit of knowledge, while yet another focuses on asceticism, exemplified by figures like Qas Ali Hazoo. Despite these disparities, numerous similarities exist among the styles of Irfan. The fundamental and pivotal difference between Irfan Maulvi and Shah Ismail's tradition lies in their respective jurisprudential backgrounds. Maulvi initially adhered to Sunni jurisprudence, gradually distancing himself from it under the influence of Shams Tabrizi, ultimately aligning himself with the Tariqat dynasty's devotion to Ali ibn Abi Talib. However, Shah Ismail's tradition did not originate from a Sunni framework. In discussing the tradition of Shah Ismail, it is crucial to contextualize it within historical disparities and the socio-cultural environment of his era. One must acknowledge the connections between Shah Ismail and figures such as Sheikh Junaid, Sheikh Haider, and Sheikh Safiuddin Ardabili, who promoted Shiism and advocated a Shiite perspective of Irfan.

Indeed, the Gnostic Tradition of Irfan Molvi and Shah Ismail converge at a pivotal juncture. Various Sufi traditions exhibit diverse practices; one tradition may emphasize spiritual intoxication, while another may prioritize knowledge, and yet another may focus on asceticism. Despite these divergences, numerous parallels exist among the traditions of Irfan. The fundamental and crucial distinction between Irfan Molvi and Shah Ismail's tradition lies in their jurisprudential affiliations. Molvi initially adhered to Sunni jurisprudence but gradually distanced himself from it under the influence of Shams Tabrizi, ultimately aligning himself with the devotion to Ali ibn Abi Talib prevalent among all followers of Irfan in the Tariqat dynasty. However, Shah Ismail's tradition did not originate from a Sunni framework. When recounting Shah Ismail's tradition, one must consider the historical disparities and the socio-cultural context in which he evolved. It is impossible to overlook the association between Shah Ismail and figures like Sheikh Junaid, Sheikh Haider, and Sheikh Safiuddin Ardabili, who were Shiite preachers and espoused a Shiite perspective of Irfan.

In my research outlined in "Caucasus Developments and Their Impact on Iran's National Security," I encountered a distinctive Tariqat in the North Caucasus region, affiliated with the Qadiriya tradition. This branch, known as the Shiba of Qadiriyah Tariqat, was led by Sheikh Batal Haji until his demise in 1916. Today, his grandson, Sheikh Yaqub, assumes leadership within this spiritual lineage. Despite identifying as Shiite, the group opted for a discreet stance amidst the evolving landscape of the Caucasus, particularly following the emergence of Salafism in the aftermath of the Chechen wars. In response, they embraced a covert identity as practitioners of Esoteric Shiism, as discussed by Miri (2012). Notably, this classification diverges from Ismaili Shia doctrine, instead emphasizing adherence to the belief in the twelve imams, the fourteen infallible, and the pivotal Hadith of Saqlain, recognizing Imam Ali (a)'s dual role as successor and caliph. However, these convictions remain concealed, reflecting the nuanced interplay between religious identity, geopolitical dynamics, and cultural context, resonating beyond the confines of the North Caucasus to illuminate broader global perspectives on religious expression and adaptation amidst shifting socio-political landscapes.

In contemporary discourse outside Iran, Diwan Shah Ismail holds a notable place as a living text resonating with the intricacies of daily life. Much like "Masnavi-ye-Ma'navi" or "Divan-e Shams-e Tabrizi," it is revered for its spiritual depth and relevance, captivating audiences in Iran, Turkey, and America alike. However, within Iran itself, Shah Ismail's legacy and the Turkish language have been marginalized, relegated to obscurity within their own homeland. The phenomenon of Shah Ismail's diminished presence in Iranian public discourse raises poignant questions about the erasure of Turkish language and culture from the Iranian consciousness.

For years, scholars and intellectuals have pondered over the reasons behind this cultural alienation. Jalal Al-Ahmed's seminal article, "On the Service and Betrayal of Intellectuals," nearly seventy years ago, stands as an early exploration of this issue. Al-Ahmed illuminated the gradual expulsion of Turks from Iran's cultural sphere, shedding light on the gradual disappearance of texts and traditions crystallized within the Turkish language from the Iranian collective consciousness.

This historical trajectory underscores the intricate interplay between politics, identity, and cultural hegemony. The marginalization of Shah Ismail and the Turkish language within Iran reflects broader dynamics of power and nationalism, perpetuating a narrative that distances Iranian culture from its rich and multifaceted heritage. As scholars continue to grapple with these complexities, the legacy of Shah Ismail serves as a poignant reminder of the enduring impact of cultural exclusion and the imperative of reclaiming diverse narratives within the Iranian landscape.

Scholars have noted a clear distinction between the historical Shah Ismail, the founder of the state, and the Shah Ismail constructed within Khatai tradition. On one hand, Shah Ismail's establishment of a historical government holds significance, with attention drawn to the mechanisms employed in forming his governance. On the other hand, Shah Ismail embodies a figure laden with human emotion and profound thought within the Khatai tradition. His theories, poetry, intuitions, and beliefs have been imbued with the essence of Khatai tradition, capturing the essence of his spiritual and philosophical journey. This duality highlights the multifaceted nature of Shah Ismail's persona, serving as both a historical figure of political significance and a symbol of spiritual depth within the rich tapestry of Khatai tradition.

This book diverges from a narrow examination of Shah Ismail's governance, recognizing that his significance extends far beyond his role as a ruler. Similar to the risk of reducing Imam Ali (a) solely to his political tenure, such an approach could oversimplify Shah Ismail's multifaceted essence. Instead, the text delves into Shah Ismail's broader dimensions within the Khatai tradition, emphasizing the richness of his philosophical insights, beliefs, and literary contributions. By reframing our understanding of Shah Ismail's legacy in a comparative context with other philosopher-emperors, we uncover the depth of his intellectual contributions and spiritual journey. This holistic approach enables a nuanced exploration of Shah Ismail's worldview, transcending simplistic historical narratives to reveal the enduring significance of his thought and philosophy.

Shah Ismail's significance transcends mere historical narrative; rather, his legacy embodies a profound reservoir of Hekmat or Gnosis awaiting rediscovery. Despite the scholarly pursuits within the academic community and the realm of Tariqat, Irfan, Hekmat, and Sufism, the acknowledgment of Shah Ismail Khatai as a sage remains a topic yet to be fully explored. Central to our endeavor in this book is to cultivate an environment where these essential inquiries can surface organically.

This book serves as a scaffold, guiding the trajectory of research endeavors and projects toward the emergence of these fundamental questions. Through this exploration, we aim to illuminate the foundational tenets of Hekmat or Gnosis within the Khatai tradition and its intricate relationship with our broader Gnostic Tradition. When we speak of "we," we refer to the collective entity of the Gnostic Tradition in the Islamic world—a tapestry woven with dimensions, diversity, and complexity deeply intertwined with the profound realms of Hekmat or Gnosis.

Within this context, Shah Ismail Khatai's teachings and insights assume profound significance, beckoning us to delve deeper into their wisdom and illumination. Thus, our collective pursuit is to navigate these depths, unveiling the luminous heritage of the Khatai tradition and its resonance within the broader tapestry of spiritual enlightenment. This journey leads us to the earthly realm abundant with goodness, as articulated in the Quran, and revered as the light of knowledge within the Gnostic Tradition of Ahl al-Bayt, as expounded by Imam Sadiq (a).

Certainly, our discussion may seem to stray from the main topic at times, but it is essential to address peripheral points to contextualize the complexity of examining Shah Ismail and the Gnostic Tradition within the Islamic and global spheres of thought. Understanding the essence of Shah Ismail's poetry and deciphering the dialectic between the author's intent and the interpreter's understanding necessitates a nuanced approach. The texts within the Khatai tradition, including those attributed to Shah Ismail, beckon us to reevaluate them, acknowledging the concept of the "death of the author" and its implications on interpretation.

One crucial aspect is the language in which Shah Ismail's works were crystallized and realized. If we acknowledge Turkish as the language of Shah Ismail's expression, the subsequent inquiry delves into the significance of this language within the Iranian context. The term "official language" carries nuanced connotations beyond its constitutional definition, encompassing themes of identity, tradition, and societal norms. Shah Ismail's utilization of Turkish implies a dialectic between author and audience, situated within the broader Iranian linguistic landscape.

Drawing parallels with Wittgenstein's notion of private language, Shah Ismail's use of Turkish transcends individual expression, becoming ingrained within Iranian identity and personality. Moreover, the Turkish language emerges as a vessel for conveying Hekmat or Gnosis, enriching our Gnostic Tradition in Turkish. This parallels the evolving linguistic dynamics evident in the Russian language's integration into the Islamic world, exemplified by the utilization of Russian by Caucasian mystics and scholars.

Thus, the crystallization of the Turkish language within Shah Ismail's tradition underscores its significance as not merely a linguistic medium but as a cornerstone of Iranian identity and a conduit for transmitting spiritual wisdom. This seemingly simple observation carries profound implications, shedding light on neglected facets of our cultural and linguistic heritage, essential for understanding the interconnectedness of language, identity, and spirituality within the Islamic world and Iran specifically.

# CHAPTER 5

# Sociology of Knowledge and Its Relationship with Diwan Shah Ismail

## 1 Introduction

This chapter delves into the intriguing intersection between the sociology of knowledge and the literary corpus of Diwan Shah Ismail. However, for scholars entrenched in the field of literature, the connection between these two realms may not immediately resonate. Approaching the text of Diwan Shah Ismail solely through the lens of Turkish literature might obscure any perceived relevance to the sociology of knowledge. Similarly, those immersed in the sociology of knowledge might question its applicability to Shah Ismail's poetry, particularly when considering him as a "poet-sage" rather than the historical founder of the Safavid dynasty. Consequently, this inquiry prompts a crucial question: what is the relationship between the sociology of knowledge and Shah Ismail's literary oeuvre? Overcoming this cognitive obstacle, often termed "cognitive prejudice," demands a defamiliarization of entrenched perspectives within both literary and sociological frameworks. By transcending disciplinary boundaries and fostering interdisciplinary dialogue, scholars can uncover the nuanced connections between the sociology of knowledge and Shah Ismail's poetry, enriching our understanding of both fields in the process.

This chapter's subject matter necessitates a process of defamiliarization. Engaging with the sociology of knowledge in relation to the text of Diwan Shah Ismail presents inherent challenges. Scholars attempting to bridge these disciplines encounter obstacles that collectively contribute to what can be described as cognitive prejudice. This cognitive bias is not merely psychological but is ingrained within educational systems, higher education institutions, academia, and cultural organizations. It impedes a genuine phenomenological encounter with the text, rendering the audience unable to grasp the author's foundational principles and assumptions accurately. Overcoming this bias requires transcending disciplinary boundaries and fostering an environment conducive to interdisciplinary dialogue. By doing so, scholars can pave the way for a more nuanced understanding of the relationship between the sociology of knowledge and Diwan Shah Ismail's literary work, enriching both fields in the process.

In the realm of Persian literature and Iranian sources, one is unlikely to encounter terms such as "Sociology of Knowledge and Diwan Shah Ismail" or "Sociology of Knowledge and Turkish Gnostic Texts." Moreover, locating an article that not only explicates the foundational concepts of the sociology of knowledge but also applies these principles to Turkish literature, particularly focusing on legal texts in Iran and their relationship with Shah Ismail's ideology, presents a significant challenge. The dearth of scholarly discourse on Shah Ismail's Diwan from a sociological perspective underscores the presence of cognitive barriers and biases that impede the natural connection between researchers or authors and their audience.

In such a complex environment, a strategic approach becomes imperative. First, it is essential to define and formulate the sociology of knowledge, establishing a framework for analysis. Subsequently, elucidating how Diwan Shah Ismail ought to be interpreted using sociological methods becomes paramount. Notably, Turkish editions of Diwan Shah Ismail in Iran, as well as the Khatai tradition and related anecdotes within the Alawi/Bektashi/Qizilbash tradition outside of Iran, remain largely unexplored through this lens. This approach seeks to break through existing barriers and enrich scholarly discourse by offering a novel perspective on the intersection of literature and sociology within the context of Shah Ismail's work.

In essence, the endeavor to explore the multifaceted dimensions of Diwan Shah Ismail within the Gnostic tradition through the lens of sociology of knowledge transcends the capabilities of a single individual. It represents a comprehensive project that demands collaborative effort and interdisciplinary engagement. While notable works exist within the realms of Hekmat, Gnosis, theoretical Irfan, and Sufism, Shah Ismail's role as a sage, mystic, and the influential founder of a significant Islamic dynasty remains relatively uncharted territory. Moreover, Diwan Shah Ismail, a pivotal text in his legacy, has yet to undergo thorough examination from a sociological perspective. This observation underscores the need for concerted scholarly attention to shed light on this important intersection of literature, mysticism, and sociological inquiry.

## 2      What Is Sociology of Knowledge?

It is imperative to investigate the precise scope of the sociology of knowledge. This field encompasses diverse definitions and viewpoints articulated by prominent scholars such as Karl Mannheim and Anthony Giddens. In Iran,

Seyyed Mohammad Amin Qaneirad has made substantial contributions to this discourse through his doctoral thesis and subsequent publications on the sociology of knowledge. Qaneirad's research explores the historical progression of science, knowledge, and intellectual thought in the Islamic world, providing valuable insights into the sociological foundations of intellectual development (Qaneirad, 2000).

It is notable that Qaneirad's work includes critical examinations of Irfan as a model for knowledge formation, highlighting substantial criticisms of Irfan's approach. Simplifying the definition of the sociology of knowledge, it can be characterized as the examination of the interaction between "human thought" and the "social context" from which such thought arises.

It is crucial to acknowledge that when individuals articulate ideas or formulate thoughts, these expressions can originate from various levels, including intuitive, inspirational, or metaphysical realms such as dreams or subtle states of existence. However, when these ideas, dreams, or intuitions seek expression and conceptualization, they inevitably intersect with social contexts.

For instance, a person in Lhasa, Tibet, within the Buddhist tradition, would not articulate their heartfelt import or intuitions in Arabic, nor would they reference figures like Gabriel or Michael or describe God sitting on a throne. The social context, as a historical phenomenon, evolves gradually rather than instantaneously, shaping language over a series of historical developments and evolutions. This process results in the creation of a "network of concepts" within a language. Even individuals with profound thoughts are bound by this framework, as concepts and words emerge not solely from one individual but from the collective historical context.

The debate surrounding the relationship between human thought and its social context has received comparatively less attention for several reasons. However, within the sociology of knowledge, there is a focus on studying the impact of dominant ideas on societies. This field seeks to analyze how prevailing ideas shape societies and influence individual thinkers, sages, and mystics. When these individuals articulate ideas, they do so within the framework of the dominant ideas prevalent in their social context. In essence, they engage with and formulate their opinions in relation to these dominant ideas.

Moreover, the sociology of knowledge delves into theoretical frameworks and fundamental questions regarding the extent of social influences on individual lives, as well as the cultural and social principles that shape our understanding of the world. This multidimensional inquiry encompasses discussions on the limits of social influence on individual thought and the cultural and social underpinnings of our knowledge about the world.

3     Diwan Shah Ismail from the Perspective of Sociology of Knowledge

Many contemporary Iranian critics and thinkers scrutinize the Gnostic Tradition from which Shah Ismail emerged and the text he produced, often suggesting that Shah Ismail's poetry was a product of individual taste and circumstance, rather than a deliberate creation. However, from the perspective of the sociology of knowledge, it becomes evident that Shah Ismail's text cannot be viewed in isolation, as a solitary star or meteorite in the galaxy. Instead, it is intricately connected to both preceding and subsequent texts, and Shah Ismail's work did not emerge in a vacuum.

Acknowledging the relationship between social context and human thought, particularly in the case of figures like Shah Ismail, leads to significant implications. One such consequence is the inquiry into how the conceptual network of Diwan Shah Ismail was formed. Even with biased perspectives, it is apparent that Shah Ismail cannot be solely credited with the creation of the complex and meaningful conceptual networks present in his work. It is implausible to suggest that Shah Ismail single-handedly developed literary metaphors and conceptual frameworks in the Turkish language in Iran without drawing from predecessors and influencing successors.

Yet, many who encounter the general text of Diwan Shah Ismail's poems tend to overlook this crucial point. They may erroneously perceive Shah Ismail's text as a sudden arrival on earth without any continuity or influence beyond Shah Ismail's lifetime.

When exploring poetry, wisdom, Gnosis, philosophy, and Theoretical Irfan within Turkish literature studies, a distinct atmosphere emerges. Scholars well-versed in the Gnostic Tradition, Theoretical Irfan, and Sufism in the Turkish language are keenly aware of the rich tradition and historical depth inherent in every language. They understand that behind each language lies a robust tradition and history. However, in Iran, the prevalence of a nationalist perspective on culture and cultural achievements has led to the neglect of these critical axioms in scholarly discourse.

In every scholarly investigation, certain foundational principles are acknowledged. Take, for instance, the nature of language: no one attributes the creation of the Persian language, or any language for that matter, solely to individuals like Ferdowsi or Hafez. Instead, it is widely understood that language evolves over time, shaped by historical processes and cultural influences. The Persian language, spanning from the eastern regions of Iran to the borders of China, has a rich and complex history. Moreover, within Persian language studies, Hafez's poetry, for example, is not merely attributed to Hafez himself; rather, it is appreciated within the broader context of Persian literary tradition.

However, in Iran, a concerning trend has emerged regarding the Turkish language and Shah Ismail in particular. This issue stems from a failure to recognize the historical and cultural context in which Shah Ismail's poetry emerged. Sadly, this oversight has led to a reductionist view, wherein Shah Ismail's text is solely attributed to him as an individual creator. This obvious oversight has been largely ignored, hampering the ability of many researchers in Iran to engage in a meaningful scientific dialogue about Shah Ismail's text. While understanding this issue from a scientific standpoint is straightforward, cognitive prejudices have regrettably led many Iranian researchers to approach this phenomenon in a primitive manner. Consequently, they are unable to initiate a comprehensive and scholarly discussion about the text of Shah Ismail.

Viewed through the lens of the sociology of knowledge, it becomes apparent that attributing Shah Ismail's words solely to him is inadequate. These words exist in a more nuanced and interconnected manner within the broader literary landscape, resonating through the works of poets like Hafez, Saadi, and Nasser Khosrow. The sociological perspective highlights that such attributions do not occur within a vacuum but are influenced by historical and cultural contexts. Therefore, reducing Shah Ismail's words to his individual expression overlooks the intricate network of influences shaping his poetry.

In scientific research, the text itself holds significance as a subject worthy of reflection, validation, and thorough examination. It serves as a vital source for research and discussion, offering insights into the cultural, social, and intellectual milieu in which it emerged. Thus, by embracing a sociological approach, scholars can engage in a more comprehensive understanding of Shah Ismail's text within the broader context of literary tradition and cultural discourse.

The theoretical framework of the sociology of knowledge introduces a paradigm shift, altering our approach to study. Today, what we require in our scholarly endeavors is a revised strategy, one that reshapes the playing field. As we successfully navigate and redefine our strategies, our inquiries evolve, departing from previous paradigms set by Mahmoud Afshar, Seyed Ahmad Kasravi, Abbas Iqbal Ashtiani, Engineer Naseh Natiq, Javad Sheikh Al-Islam, and Seyed Javad Tabatabai. Their perspectives have illuminated the notion that the general text of Diwan Shah Ismail, known as Khatai, is not inherently his own creation; rather, it has been attributed to him.

It is proposed that Azerbaijan originally bore the name "Azerabadan," with its principal language being "Azeri." The Azeri language, in turn, is understood to be a branch of the Tati, Talshi, or Fahlavi languages. This perspective challenges conventional assumptions about the origins and linguistic heritage of the region, prompting a reevaluation of historical narratives and linguistic classifications.

Shifting the focus to the sociology of knowledge prompts a departure from discussions solely centered on language or texts in a broad sense. Instead, from this perspective, it becomes evident that any text is intricately intertwined with the cultural context from which it emerges. This cultural field is not the result of a singular event or conquest, such as the Mongol, Seljuq, or Ghaznavid invasions, nor is it solely shaped by Turanian and Iranian conflicts. Rather, it is a product of ongoing cultural evolution spanning thousands of years.

Our scholarly endeavor should therefore be to dissect and understand the components of this cultural field. This involves identifying the cultural language, defining cultural criteria, and elucidating the frameworks of cultural studies. By doing so, we gain deeper insights into the rich tapestry of cultural development and transformation that underpins the creation of any text.

## 4     The Gnostic Tradition of Shah Ismail in the Context of Islamic Studies

Of paramount importance is understanding how these cultural developments intersect with the fundamental tenets of wisdom (Hekmat) or Gnosis in the Islamic world. The poetry and discourse in the Turkish language, as well as in other languages predating Islam, had their own foundations. Similarly, Pahlavi language poetry may have been based on distinct principles. However, in the case of the Persian language, there exists a profound connection between wisdom, Gnosis, and the teachings of the Quran and the Sunnah of Ahl al-Bayt.

The historical context in which this connection between the Persian language and the Gnostic Tradition of Ahl al-Bayt emerged is significant. It is essential to explore how Persian language and culture became intertwined with the teachings and spiritual insights of Ahl al-Bayt, particularly within the historical period following the advent of Islam. Understanding this relationship sheds light on the deep-rooted connection between Persian language and culture and the spiritual heritage of Ahl al-Bayt, offering valuable insights into the synthesis of Islamic wisdom and Persian cultural expression.

The Masnavi-ye-Ma'navi, often regarded as a Quranic masterpiece in Persian literature, holds a unique position in the Islamic intellectual tradition. Incorporating over two thousand prophetic hadiths alongside broader Islamic teachings, it serves as a bridge between spiritual exegesis and literary expression. This integration of scriptural themes into Persian poetry underscores the depth of its religious significance and its enduring influence across Islamic societies. The Masnavi's synthesis of Quranic wisdom with the poetic and philosophical nuances of Persian tradition reflects its profound historical importance, enabling it to resonate with diverse audiences and fostering its recognition as a cornerstone of Islamic mysticism.

The interplay between cultural identity and nomenclature can be observed through the historical example of the Tungusic and Ionki peoples of Siberia. The Tungusic, originally referred to by this derogatory term by the Ionki, eventually adopted it as their own identifier within the Russian Federation. This phenomenon illustrates the dynamic nature of identity formation and the influence of external perceptions over time. Additionally, the linguistic and cultural heritage of the region underscores its historical richness. Siberia, as the cradle of the Turkish language, exhibits linguistic imprints in its river names and reveals deep-rooted connections in the customs, rituals, and religious practices of its inhabitants, including the Tungusic, Ionki, and Eskimos. These traditions, shaped by the Arctic and Siberian geography, highlight the intricate relationship between historical migrations, cultural evolution, and linguistic development.

For those delving into the study of the Turkish language within the Gnostic Tradition, particularly as crystallized in the text of Diwan Shah Ismail, historical considerations take on a different significance. Rather than focusing solely on broader historical contexts, attention is directed towards understanding how Shah Ismail was able to forge a connection between the ideas of the Gnostic Tradition of Ahl al-Bayt and the Azerbaijani Turkish language during his relatively short lifespan from 1490 to 1520.

It is evident that Shah Ismail did not undertake this task in isolation, nor did he initiate this connection. Instead, this link between language and tradition bears a specific historical date, one that is inscribed in the Turkish language itself. Therefore, the focus of study lies in uncovering how Shah Ismail, within the constraints of his temporal and linguistic context, was able to articulate and embody the teachings of the Gnostic Tradition of Ahl al-Bayt through his poetry in Azerbaijani Turkish.

For instance, preceding Shah Ismail, there existed mystics such as Sheikh Haider, Sheikh Junaid, and Sheikh Safiuddin Ardabili, as well as poet-sages like Fozuli and Habibi. Similarly, following Shah Ismail's era, figures like Nasimi emerged. This historical continuum underscores the fact that language and the development of concepts evolve overtime. This interconnectedness warrants thorough study.

Our contention is that in Iran, the relationship between the Gnostic Tradition and the Turkish language remains largely unexplored from the perspective of the sociology of knowledge. It seems that this topic has not even been considered within academic circles. Consequently, when broached, it tends to elicit discomfort and may spark debates framed within political or ideological contexts. Alternatively, it is often met with silence, perhaps to avoid stirring controversy within the scientific community.

When examining the connection between Shah Ismail's thought and its social context through the lens of the sociology of knowledge, it becomes evident that this relationship is not merely mechanical; rather, it is organic. This organic relationship is imbued with historical dimensions that evolve and expand over time. Each historical fact, whether it be periods of growth, contraction, or transformation, influences this relationship in significant ways.

However, within the historiography of literature, wisdom (Hekmat), Gnosis, poetry, Sufism, and Irfan in Iran, particularly in the last century, there is a noticeable absence of exploration into the Gnostic Tradition and its intricate connections, developments, and evolutions. This raises an important question: Is Shah Ismail an exception? While he may be considered exceptional from a historical standpoint, from the perspective of the sociology of knowledge, even with a biased view, the formation and evolution of ideas and concepts are not inherently exceptional and warrant further examination and explanation.

## 5    Sociology of Knowledge and Removal of the Gnostic Tradition of Shah Ismail

How are concepts and ideas formed within language? Do they emerge gradually or all at once? When we view language as a system of signs, it becomes apparent that language encodes and formulates a spectrum of ideas, providing them with structure, before decoding them and expanding their presence within the realm of signs. From this perspective, it is evident that while individuals may speak a language, it is their knowledge of that language that truly opens up their linguistic capabilities, allowing them to encode and decode concepts within the linguistic framework.

Similarly, in the context of Shah Ismail's text within the Gnostic Tradition of Ahl al-Bayt in Iran, it is not Shah Ismail who created the Turkish language within his text; rather, he emerged within the existing framework of the Turkish language within this tradition. In essence, Shah Ismail's linguistic expression is shaped and guided by the pre-existing linguistic and conceptual landscape within the Gnostic Tradition.

Why do we continually disregard a tradition that is not only Iranian but also a foundational aspect of the Gnostic legacy? The deliberate use of the term "permanent" underscores the logical principle of continuity, where every essential statement remains enduring. So, logically, what prompts the exclusion of the Turkish legacy, and by extension, the Gnostic legacy of Shah Ismail Khatai, from the Iranian narrative?

The challenge of disregarding the Gnostic Tradition in Turkish and its ongoing continuity presents a significant dilemma. Speaking out against this prevailing approach and questioning its strategies often leads to criticism. Yet, the fundamental question remains: What prompts this need for removal? Specifically, within what framework has necessity been invoked, and what are the underlying foundations of this imperative to continually erase this tradition?

Logicians have delineated five types of necessity: Permanent, Essential, Descriptive, and Temporal. However, it is striking that there has been little rational discourse regarding the necessity of removing the Gnostic Legacy of Shah Ismail Khatai or its relationship with these forms of necessity within the Iranian academic discourse. The enduring lack of discussion leaves us unaware of the permanence and necessity behind ignoring this crucial aspect.

It is important to recognize that the reluctance to accept these strategies is not a matter of mere will; rather, these strategies undermine Iranian identity and erase a vital part of the Iranian people's collective memory.

Consider the analogy of patients experiencing a stroke, wherein one of the initial effects may involve partial loss of memory or speech. Similarly, when we employ a nationalist framework as the criterion for defining Iranian culture, we unwittingly strip away elements of our collective memory and expressive capacity. Consequently, both consciously and unconsciously, segments of our cultural texts are discarded. Today, when we attempt to examine these texts, such as the Diwan of Shah Ismail Khatai, whether on a public or academic platform, we are met with vehement resistance. The prevailing belief suggests that such texts are irrelevant to us and should not be engaged with. Consequently, this collective "we" has suffered a loss of memory and cultural heritage.

Addressing this hostility towards engaging with these texts cannot be resolved solely by delving into psychological realms. Rather, it necessitates an exploration of why we have failed to develop theoretical frameworks to preserve and integrate our historical, cultural, and literary periods within Iran.

When examining the text of Diwan Shah Ismail, we observe that the poems are written in Turkish. Within every language lies a set of concepts, prompting the question: What processes are involved in concept formation? The construction of any concept typically unfolds in three stages: Firstly, there is the process of generalization, allowing for the possibility of broadening a concept's scope. Secondly, there is differentiation, which involves creating distinctions and nuances within the concept. Lastly, there is abstraction, which empowers language with the ability to conceptualize ideas at a higher level.

Some argue that the Turkish language lacks the power of abstraction or generalization, contributing to its neglect in Iran. However, when we examine Shah Ismail's text as a quintessential example of Turkish within The Gnostic Tradition, we find it encompasses both generalization and differentiation dimensions. Generalities are crystallized within it, along with the ability to differentiate between categories and the power of abstraction, even extending to the creation of metaphorical expressions. These dimensions, including the capacity for metaphorical creation, exist within the Turkish language and are evident in the text of Diwan Shah Ismail. However, these aspects have not been thoroughly explored within the humanities in Iran.

If we incorporate the texts of the Khatai tradition and Hikailar (a collection of anecdotes attributed to Shah Ismail Khatai) into this analysis, we encounter a substantial project. This endeavor offers an opportunity to explore not only the theoretical dimensions of the Turkish language but also The Gnostic Tradition, and how Shah Ismail adeptly integrated these three stages within The Gnostic Tradition.

Viewing these texts through the framework of sociology of knowledge reveals their intrinsic importance as integral components of the evolving thought and development within The Gnostic Tradition in Iran, conveyed through the Turkish language. They represent not anomalies but rather vital elements of a historical trajectory ripe for scholarly scrutiny and analysis. Yet, their marginalization within academic discourse reflects a deeper cognitive bias rooted not in psychological predispositions but in prevailing discursive paradigms.

Put simply, within the framework of nationalistic discourse, the concept of "Iranian" has been narrowly defined, with the Persian language assuming a central role. Consequently, any linguistic tradition other than Persian is often viewed as a competitor or adversary, perpetuating a state of conflict. Sociology of knowledge aids in deconstructing this conflictual dynamic, offering a platform to engage in discussions and analyses of the diverse array of texts within the Iranian context.

## 6      Islamic Hekmat or Gnosis in Persian Form

Corbini's perspective, notably embraced by Carbon, posits that the preservation of the Persian language within Islam is essential to safeguarding the essence of Iranian Islam and its associated wisdom. This viewpoint, often linked to nationalism discourse, equates "Ras Iranica" with Shiism and the Persian language. However, it oversimplifies the complex interplay between language, culture, and religious identity, disregarding historical and linguistic nuances within Islamic traditions.

He further contends that Shiism aligns with Iranian identity, contrasting it with Sunnism, which is portrayed as an Arab phenomenon. However, this narrative overlooks the historical reality that many eminent poets and scholars in Persian literature were Sunni Muslims. Moreover, none of the Shia Imams were of Iranian descent, nor did they speak Persian. For instance, Imam Ali ibn Musa al-Rida, revered in Shia Islam, was neither Iranian nor a Persian speaker.

These beliefs are due to the influence of nationalism discourse, which deprives us of a critical view even in the field of thought, and we face historical phenomena fanatically and nationalistically instead of phenomenologically. It does not lead anywhere, and it was Iranian Hekmat or Gnosis (as crystallized in Persian language and rooted in Pahlavi and earlier Pahlavi) that brought us to our destination. The fact is that Islam was not only formed in Iran but also in the Indian subcontinent. Although a part of the Indian subcontinent spoke Persian, an important part of it was influenced by the Hekmat or Gnosis of Dharma or Hindi; So, can we say that if Hekmat or Gnosis was not Dharma, Islam would have been reduced to something like ISIS?

The notion that Islam's global flourishing owes significantly to its association with Iran and the Persian language can potentially lead to a distorted historical interpretation. This approach resembles an analysis of historical events through a contemporary lens, projecting present concerns and frameworks onto past contexts. When utilizing primary sources from the first century of the Hijri calendar, such an approach risks interpreting them through the biases and perspectives of today. As a result, the focus of the study may shift towards addressing current concerns and sensitivities rather than achieving an accurate comprehension of historical circumstances.

Many discussions on Hekmat or Gnosis overlook a crucial point: the pervasive influence of nationalism, which may even affect high-ranking Shiite clerics without their awareness. Escaping the grip of nationalism, a mindset fostering a sense of belonging, is no simple feat. Orientalism, an enduring tradition shaping the theoretical underpinnings of our thinkers for over a century, continues to exert its influence. Consequently, even theologians and sages often view philosophy as Greek, contrasting it with the Quranic origins of Hekmat or Gnosis. However, if Hekmat or Gnosis is rooted in the Quran, its language should logically be Arabic, not Persian.

The sociology of knowledge provides valuable insights into the evolution of religious concepts, such as "Allah." Contrary to simplistic beliefs, the concept of "Allah" predates Islam and had various manifestations in Semitic cultures. For instance, in Abyssinian, "Lob" signifies "heart," resonating with the deeper connotations of "Ulul Albaab" in Semitic languages, which implies more than just "wisdom owners" but conveys a sense of "hearty devotion".

These concepts were not sudden creations but evolved over time within Arabic, Hebrew, Ethiopian, and Abyssinian cultures. Even terms like "Ulul Albaab," used in the Quran, carry rich semantic layers that transcend simplistic

translations. While the language of the Quran reflects the Messenger's revelations, it does not imply the Prophet constructed these intricate networks
of concepts.

Regarding the relationship between Hekmat or Gnosis and the Persian language, viewing Persian as equal to the Quran creates problematic dualities.
This perspective, influenced by thinkers like Henry Corbin, associates Shiism
with Ras Iranica, linking it to pre-Islamic Iranian culture. However, such views
have faced critique, notably from figures like Seyyed Musa Sadr, who challenged them in the 20th century. These debates underscore the complexity of
religious and linguistic intersections, urging a nuanced understanding beyond
simplistic dichotomies.

# CHAPTER 6

# Language and Religion in Iranian Thought in Relation to the Gnostic Legacy of Shah Ismail Khatai

## 1    Introduction

When addressing the dearth of theories concerning language, religion, and theology in Iranian intellectual discourse, it is important to distinguish our focus from the everyday understanding prevalent among the populace in their daily interactions in streets and markets. While this absence significantly affects their perception of Iran's historical and civilizational trajectory, our primary concern in these discussions and debates centers on the absence within the domain of scholars, historians, philosophers, sociologists, and other intellectuals who have studied Iran's societal development over the past five millennia. These scholars strive to articulate these transformations within theoretical frameworks.

In *Iran in Five Narratives* (Miri, 2019), a segment of this discourse is addressed, while in *The Idea of Language and National Unity* (Miri, 2018), I approach the topic from a distinct angle. Additionally, in the introduction to *General Theory of Religious Reform* (Miri, 2021), I touch upon the absence and deficiency of theoretical frameworks. Now, let us seize this opportunity to delve into the dimensions of this theory as we delve into the Gnostic Tradition of Shah Ismail.

In the past century, as academic discourse on Iran's religious developments has emerged, the question of how Islam took root, expanded, and evolved over approximately 1450 years in Iran has been a focal point. Two major narratives attempt to address this question. One narrative seeks to simplify the process, suggesting that Iranians, disillusioned with Sassanid rule, found resonance in Islam's justice-centered rhetoric. This narrative portrays Islam as offering a new political framework for Iranians amidst Sassanid oppression, thereby facilitating their acceptance of the faith. Within this discourse, the emphasis remains on theological interpretations of historical events, avoiding challenges to established religious boundaries. In essence, proponents of this narrative construct the story of Islam's introduction to Iran within a theological framework, shaping discussions on religious evolution in the country.

In contrast, the second narrative diverges from theoretical or theological perspectives, reflecting an antiquarian and nationalist inclination. Influenced by orientalist accounts and the archaeological findings of the 19th and

20th centuries, often propagated by Western European, American, and occasionally Russian scholars, proponents of this narrative delve into excavations in Iran, Mesopotamia, Central Asia, and the Caucasus. They seek to reconstruct pre-Islamic Iranian civilization, drawing attention to its achievements. According to this viewpoint, the conversion to Islam in Iran was coerced solely through Arab conquest, with Islam being imposed through force, pressure, and massacres. Advocates of this narrative cite historical sources such as Tabari's history to support their claims.

## 2    Religious Transformation in Iran

It is widely held that Zoroastrianism constituted the dominant religion in ancient Iran prior to the ascendancy of Islam. However, a more detailed exploration of historical events presents a more nuanced perspective. The idea that Iranians adhered exclusively to Zoroastrianism throughout their history does not align with broader historical developments in the region. Even during the periods of the Persians and Medes, it is suggested that Zoroastrianism was not the sole religious practice. Accounts indicate that the Parthians and Medes had their own distinct religious beliefs, while the Mughans adhered to a different faith altogether. The term "Magi," which finds its root in Latin languages and has evolved into "Magic" in English, hints at the magical and shamanistic elements present in the Mughan religion. Religious studies suggest that the Mughan religion placed a greater emphasis on magical practices compared to Zoroastrianism. Thus, it appears that the religious landscape of ancient Iran was more diverse and complex than commonly assumed, encompassing a range of beliefs including those with mystical and shamanistic undertones.

In the realm of religious studies, a clear distinction is drawn between religion and magic, despite their shared similarities. Religion typically offers a structured and rational framework for understanding existence, often positing that a divine entity created the world and established its order. Conversely, magic operates on the belief that certain individuals, such as shamans or sorcerers, can spiritually ascend to become intermediaries between the spiritual and material realms. These individuals are believed to wield supernatural powers, enabling them to influence and enact changes within the world. Such practices are observed among various tribal cultures in regions like the Amazon and Polynesia, as documented by renowned anthropologists.

Indeed, the Mughan religion stood apart from Zoroastrianism. During the Sassanid period, while Zoroastrianism was established as the official religion of the government, Buddhism flourished in Iran. In the eastern and northeastern regions, including Khorasan and Nishapur, Buddhist temples, known as "Bahar," were prevalent. The presence of large Buddha statues in Bamyan, now located in Afghanistan, signifies the penetration of Buddhism into Iran from the northeast, reaching the heart of the Sassanid Empire. Consequently, Buddhism found a following among Iranians, alongside other faiths like Mehr religion or Mithraism, indicating the religious diversity within Iranian society.

In his book *Mutual Services of Iran and Islam*, Shahid Motahari raises a compelling argument suggesting that had Islam not spread to Iran, Christianity would likely have become the predominant religion in the region. Motahari highlights the historical context, noting that areas such as Armenia, Georgia, and large parts of the Caucasus, which were once part of the Iranian Empire, were among the earliest to embrace Christianity. Even within Iran itself, figures like Tirdad II, a Parthian prince, played a role in the early adoption of Christianity, with its influence spreading to regions like Urmia through Tirdad's church.

Moreover, Judaism found a foothold in regions associated with the Khazarian Empire, which sometimes had ties to or rivalries with the Sassanids. Alongside Christianity and Judaism, various other belief systems like Mazdakianism and Manichaeism coexisted within Iranian territories during that era. This historical reality challenges the simplistic notion that all Iranians adhered solely to Zoroastrianism before the arrival of Islam, indicating a rich religious diversity.

Furthermore, the influence of Islam in Yemen, a part of the Iranian Empire at the time, was substantial. Iranians residing in Yemen, spanning from nobles to commoners, embraced Islam even before its spread from the central regions. Contrary to the popular narrative centered on individuals like Salman Farsi, this demonstrates a broader and more complex process of religious conversion. Motahari's analysis thus underscores the importance of delving into historical complexities rather than relying on oversimplified myths to understand the religious dynamics of the time.

The expansive reach of the Iranian Empire during its zenith included territories extending as far as Jalalabad in Afghanistan and encompassing regions such as Kazakhstan, Samarkand, Bukhara, and Uzbekistan. Over a span of approximately five hundred years following the emergence of Islam, its influence gradually extended into these areas. For instance, historical records indicate that Islam reached northern Caucasus regions, including among the Chechens, around the 1400s, 1500s, and even as late as the 1600s AD. This gradual expansion unfolded over nearly eight centuries, reflecting a process of organic growth rather than abrupt imposition.

It is essential to differentiate between political upheaval and religious transformation. While governmental changes may occur, the spread of religion operates on a separate trajectory. However, misconceptions often arise when these two processes are conflated. Some narratives attribute Islam's dissemination solely to Arab conquests, framing it as a coercive imposition enforced through violence upon the Iranian populace. Such oversimplified perspectives over-look the intricate historical narratives and fail to grasp the nuanced interplay of factors driving religious evolution. This lacuna in theoretical understand-ing results in a flawed interpretation of religious development, underscor-ing the necessity for a more comprehensive framework that accounts for the multifaceted nature of religious dynamics and historical transformations.

## 3      Language Status in Pre-Islamic Iran

Before the arrival of Islam in Iran, the linguistic environment was character-ized by remarkable diversity, mirroring the vast extent of the Iranian Empire. Unlike the homogenized languages associated with modern nation-states, there was no single standardized language spoken across this expansive ter-ritory. Instead, a multitude of languages and dialects flourished, reflecting the diverse ethnic groups and cultures within the empire. For example, while some regions may have predominantly spoken Persian, others might have used lan-guages such as Parthian, Median, or Elamite, among others.

The absence of an "official language" in ancient empires contrasts sharply with contemporary concepts of linguistic uniformity. Even within bureaucratic circles, where a prestigious "Diwani language" was utilized for administrative purposes, such as Mandarin in China, linguistic variation persisted among different social strata and geographic regions. This linguistic heterogeneity underscores the complex and multifaceted nature of pre-Islamic Iranian soci-ety, challenging simplistic narratives that portray linguistic unity across vast imperial domains.

Before the modern era, elite cultures across civilizations often maintained a distinct "High Culture" or "elite language" among the privileged classes. For instance, in Western Europe prior to the Reformation, Latin served as the lan-guage of intellectual discourse and administration for the elite, with figures like Descartes producing significant works in this language. However, as time progressed, local languages gradually emerged as standardized languages, supplanting Latin. This process of linguistic evolution, particularly evident in the 17th and 18th centuries, saw vernacular languages gaining prominence and becoming standardized, challenging the notion of a single, universal elite language. Thus, historical developments reveal a dynamic linguistic landscape characterized by the emergence and evolution of standardized languages across different societies, rather than a uniform linguistic hegemony.

Attributing the emergence of the Turkish language in Iran solely to the Mongol invasions, as suggested by Mahmoud Afshar and echoed in nation-alist narratives, oversimplifies the complex process of linguistic evolution.

While the Mongols did have their own language, Mongolian, which influenced regions they conquered, linguistic transformation in Iran is shaped by a myriad of factors over millennia, including migration, trade, conquests, and cultural exchanges. While languages may share common roots, such as Mongolian, Turkish, Korean, and Chinese, they have diverged significantly over time. Mahmoud Afshar's discourse, often linked to archaic nationalism, lacks a comprehensive theoretical basis for understanding linguistic evolution, risking a distorted interpretation of history. To understand linguistic changes in Iran, it is crucial to consider diverse historical dynamics and cultural interactions beyond singular events or invasions.

Language evolution entails a complex interplay of various factors, necessitating a coherent theoretical framework to comprehend its nuances. While no definitive theory is presented here, an exploration of studies spanning the last seventy years and observations of immigrant experiences offer valuable insights. Consider, for instance, immigrants from Iran or Turkey to Sweden: the first-generation grapples with learning Swedish, often resorting to their native language for emotional expression and familial communication, despite facing challenges conveying complex emotions in Swedish. However, the second generation, exposed to Swedish language and culture from childhood, navigates between their parents' heritage and the dominant Swedish culture, often mastering Swedish while their proficiency in their native language diminishes. By the third generation, ties to the ancestral language may further weaken, influenced by societal integration and intergenerational dynamics, potentially resulting in its eventual disappearance in subsequent generations.

This gradual language transformation illustrates the dynamic interaction between time, social space, and societal demands. Language, far from being static, reflects the evolving needs and dynamics of society. In contexts like Iran, including regions such as Azerbaijan, similar processes of linguistic evolution unfold, albeit shaped by distinct historical, cultural, and social factors. Understanding language change in these regions requires a nuanced examination of societal dynamics, migration patterns, and intergenerational shifts in language use and identity. Such complexities underscore the multifaceted nature of language evolution, challenging simplistic narratives of linguistic change as solely driven by coercion or external forces.

## 4 Linguistic Evolution in Iran

In Iran, there is a center known as "Afshar Mowqofat", of course the apparent name of this center is Mowqofat, but in reality, it is a center for studies and publication and expansion of antiquarian nationalism in Iran, and with one credit, this center can be considered a place for propaganda and even a kind of the office of the party of antiquarian nationalists took into account. In the last hundred years, this center has taken a narration from Mahmoud Afshar and highlights it until today. According to this narrative, in all past centuries and in all ages, the language of Iranians has been Persian, and if any impurity has been created in it, it is either the result of the invasion of Arabs, Turks, and desert wandering Mongols, or today it is the result of modern Western and foreign civilizations. It is that each of them has somehow caused the linguistic unity in Iran to disappear.

The narrative propagated by the Afshar Endowments over the past century deserves scrutiny, particularly in two key areas: religion and language. While the architects of this narrative refrain from direct attacks on Islam, they vilify Arabs and the Arabic language as a proxy. Following the 1979 revolution and the establishment of the Islamic Republic, direct competition with Islam became untenable, prompting a shift away from overt criticism of Arabic. However, in the realm of language, particularly regarding Turkish, more aggressive efforts to implement rejectionist policies are evident. Turkish is often portrayed as a relic of the Mongol legacy in Iran, targeted for erasure. Figures like Engineer Naseh Natiq and Javad Sheikh Al-Islami have authored numerous works focusing on Azerbaijan, yet they fail to offer substantive theories explaining the linguistic and cultural dynamics of Turkish presence in Iran. Questions regarding the origins of the Turkish language in Iran, its relationship to Mongolian, and the criteria for Iranian identity remain unanswered, exposing a glaring lack of theoretical underpinning in this discourse.

The concept of Iranian identity and its linguistic evolution raises fundamental questions regarding fixed criteria versus fluidity influenced by historical, social, and civilizational contexts. Has there truly been a singular "mother-language" in Iran, with all Iranians speaking the same dialect prior to external influences? The narrative suggests a disruption of linguistic unity by Arab, Turkish, Mongol, and Persian invasions, yet fails to address the complexities of language change over time. Critically, the absence of comprehensive answers to these questions underscores a profound deficiency in theoretical understanding, hindering the development of a nuanced and historically grounded discourse on language and identity in Iran.

Contrary to past notions of human racial uniformity, modern understanding rejects the concept of a single human race, acknowledging instead the vast diversity within humanity. This perspective suggests that there was a period of linguistic unity in human history, gradually followed by divergence driven by factors such as geographical separation, historical experiences, and cultural development. The Quran offers a narrative aligning with this view, portraying humanity as initially unified before gradually diverging into distinct nations with their own languages and cultures. Linguistic evolution and diversity in Iran are not exclusive to the Islamic era but have roots in pre-Islamic times and persist into the present and future. These linguistic changes reflect broader shifts in society, demonstrating the dynamic nature of language and culture over time.

Even in contemporary times, linguistic variations persist between closely situated cities like Ardabil and Tabriz, where terms such as "son-in-law" or "sister-in-law" are referred to as "Yazneh" and "Korakan," respectively. Considering the relatively slow and limited communication networks of a thousand or two thousand years ago, it is reasonable to infer that even greater distinctions existed in terms of language, habits, rituals, and customs during that era. The slower pace of communication would have allowed for more pronounced regional differences to develop and endure over time, highlighting the evolving nature of language and cultural practices across different regions.

Language is intricately linked to the environment in which it develops. Different environmental conditions, such as desert agriculture versus agriculture in vast plains, can shape vocabulary related to elements, tools, and natural products. It is conceivable that all languages originated as dialects, sharing historical roots in a common ancestral language that progressively diverged into distinct languages over the course of time. For example, English and German share a common root but have evolved into distinct languages with notable differences. Similarly, Scandinavian languages like Norwegian, Swedish, Danish, and Icelandic trace their origins to a common root, yet have diverged significantly, with mutual intelligibility diminishing over time. Iceland's geographic isolation has contributed to unique linguistic developments, resulting in a dialect or language that diverges from its mainland counterparts. While external forces like the Mongol invasions may have influenced regional changes, attributing all linguistic evolution to foreign imposition oversimplifies the complex processes at play. While historical events like the Mongol invasions may have accelerated changes, linguistic geography is shaped by a multitude of factors and cannot be altered significantly by the actions of a single individual or group.

If we perceive Persian language to have remained unchanged since the time of Ferdowsi until now, it signals a stagnation in our historical development. The ability to converse with the likes of Ferdowsi today reflects a slow evolution in our emotional and intellectual landscape throughout history, contrasting unfavorably with the dynamic progress seen in languages like English and French. This underscores a deficiency in our theoretical framework regarding language, preventing us from effectively encompassing the linguistic and religious diversity present in Iran. While linguistic and religious diversity have historically shaped our identity, the archaic narrative, whether pre- or post-Islam, espouses a singular notion, advocating for linguistic and religious purity while seeking to eradicate perceived impurities. However, the crucial question remains: What defines purity in this context?

## 5      Religious Transformation in Iran

Another pivotal moment in Iran's history is the religious transformation towards Shiism. While Shiism had been present in various regions since the early days of Islam, including areas beyond the boundaries of contemporary Iran such as Yemen, Egypt, parts of Lorestan and Khuzestan, Basra, parts of Khorasan and Mazandaran, parts of the Caucasus and Azerbaijan, and portions of Anatolia, it was during the Safavid period that Shiism became centralized and institutionalized on a grand scale. The Safavids established an expansive Shiite empire and wielded significant influence over religious affairs. While traces of Shiism were evident during the al-Buyeh era, it was under Safavid rule that Shiism became the dominant religious force, shaping the trajectory of Iran's religious and political landscape.

The notion that Iran's religious transformation to Shiism occurred solely through coercive means, such as the force of the sword, oversimplifies a complex historical process. This perspective fails to account for the nuanced dynamics of religious evolution within Iranian society. The religious landscape of Iran was shaped by a multitude of factors, including the influence of various religious sects such as the Aqaba movement, the Ilkhans, Al-Buyeh dynasty, as well as the presence of Alawites, Marashis, Mashashites in Lorestan, and the emergence of Sufism. Additionally, it disregards the impact of religious trends on the elite and popular spheres, which played a significant role in shaping religious identity.

The idea that Iran abruptly transitioned to Shiism as if by pressing a button neglects the gradual and multifaceted nature of religious evolution. This highlights a lack of theoretical framework in understanding religious transformation. Today, studies on religious conversion shed light on the complexity of this phenomenon. Factors such as personal experiences, encounters with different belief systems, and environmental influences contribute to individuals' decisions to change their religion. Examples like the conversion of individuals like Muhammad Ali Kelly or Malcolm X during their imprisonment illustrate how personal experiences and spiritual quests can lead to religious transformation, challenging the notion of religious change being solely driven by external coercion or force.

Malcolm X's critique of Christianity stems from its portrayal of Jesus (PBUH) as a white figure with European features, which he believes marginalizes and alienates black people. This perception leads to a sense of disconnect for black individuals who seek spiritual solace and guidance. For Malcolm X, converting to a new religion represents a rejection of the dominant semantic system that perpetuates white supremacy. By embracing a new faith, individuals like Malcolm X can find empowerment and a sense of cultural identity to fuel their socio-political activism. Malcolm X's criticism extends to figures like Martin Luther King Jr., whom he accuses of perpetuating the narrative of white dominance within the civil rights movement, thereby hindering the liberation of black communities.

While numerous studies have explored religious conversion, there remains a notable gap in our understanding of the psychological, anthropological, sociological, and philosophical dimensions of this phenomenon. Existing research often focuses on conversions between specific religious denominations, such as from Catholicism to Protestantism or from Sunni Islam to Shia Islam, without delving into the broader theoretical frameworks that could enrich our comprehension. By neglecting to incorporate insights from psychology, anthropology, sociology, and the philosophy of religions, our understanding of religious conversion remains incomplete. To formulate a more comprehensive understanding of religious transformation, it is imperative to explore diverse perspectives and interdisciplinary approaches that shed light on the complex interplay of individual beliefs, social dynamics, and cultural influences.

## 6 The Relation of Religious, Madhhab and Linguistic Developments with Shah Ismail

The significance of discussing issues related to Shah Ismail lies in his role as a symbol of religious transformation in Iran. However, our lack of theoretical foundations regarding religious evolution leads to cognitive biases and misunderstandings when attempting to explain or interpret Shah Ismail's religious shift. This cognitive bias is evident in two main areas: religion and language. Contrary to popular belief, some studies suggest that Shah Ismail was not the sole monarch who pursued poetry; other kings and princes also composed poetry, as documented in works like "Labab-ul-Labab."

For instance, Zahir al-Din Muhammad Babur, who reigned from 1526 to 1530, was not only a king but also a poet and author of his biography. Similarly, Sultan Selim I, who ruled from 1512, was unique among Ottoman sultans for his prowess in Persian and Turkish poetry, earning him the epithet "Mohibi." While some scholars argue that Shah Ismail's poetry may not match the metaphorical and literary depth of his contemporaries, what sets him apart is his profound influence on the public and masses, a legacy that endures to this day.

The absence of robust theoretical foundations regarding linguistic and religious evolution contributes to cognitive biases surrounding Shah Ismail's impact on the Turkish language and religious transformation in Iran. Cognitive prejudice simplifies complex issues, leading to superficial understandings of human phenomena and facilitating demagoguery. This bias is evident in the case of Shah Ismail, where his role in shaping the Turkish language and religious landscape is often oversimplified. Unlike his successors, Shah Ismail did not solely engage in poetic endeavors for personal reasons; rather, he strategically utilized poetry to further political, cultural, social, and religious objectives, allowing him to connect with a broader audience on multiple levels.

The question arises: Why did Shah Ismail choose to write poetry in Turkish, a language not widely understood by his Iranian audience? Despite his Aq Qoyunlu ancestry, Shah Ismail deliberately distanced himself from the linguistic tradition of his predecessors for political reasons, opting to express his thoughts and ideas in Turkish. This decision was strategic, as it allowed him to communicate directly with his Turkic-speaking supporters, forging a strong cultural and linguistic connection with his base. While Safavid sheikhs like Sadr al-Din, Khwaja Ali, and Safi al-Din predominantly used Persian or its dialects, Shah Ismail's preference for Western Turkish, distinct from the Eastern Jaghatai Turkish, was notable. Historical sources often refer to the Turkish used in Shah Ismail's Diwan as Turkmen Turkish, while contemporary sources may label it as Qizilbash Turkish, distinguishing it from Ottoman or Roman Turkish.

In formulating Shah Ismail's linguistic tradition, it becomes apparent that his poetic language aligns with the Nasimi tradition, which also includes figures like Jahanshah from the court of Aq Qoyunlu, who passed away in 1467 AD. Shah Ismail's conscious literary shift is noteworthy, especially considering his familiarity with Persian and potentially other languages, given his mother's Roman and Greek background, which suggests a possible knowledge of Greek or its dialects. However, Shah Ismail deliberately chose Turkish as his medium of expression to effectively communicate with his audience, demonstrating the deep-rooted connection of Turkish language within Iran's cultural fabric. Contrary to misconceptions, Turkish language in Iran predates events like the Mongol invasions or the Seljuks' departure, and has been integral to Iran's identity throughout its history. Even Ibn Khaldun, in "Al-Abar," refers to Persia as the homeland and refuge of the Turks, highlighting the enduring presence and significance of the Turkish language within Iran's historical narrative. Thus, the confusion surrounding Shah Ismail's linguistic tradition arises from cognitive prejudices and the absence of theoretical frameworks to comprehend linguistic and religious evolution in Iran.

# CHAPTER 7

# Jalal Al-Ahmed and the Theory of Expelling the Turkish Language from the Public Sphere

## 1    Introduction

Jalal Al-Ahmed is a multifaceted figure often hailed as one of the pivotal intellectuals of the 1940s in Iran. Born into a family with a prominent clerical background, Jalal briefly pursued studies in the Najaf seminary before delving into political activism by joining the Tudeh Party of Iran. However, he did not remain tethered to any one ideology, later shifting allegiance to the "Third Front" before ultimately departing. His journey took a significant turn after the passing of Khalil Maliki, leading Jalal to explore Islamic internationalism, a trajectory reflected in his notable work *A Straw in Mecca*. Jalal's complex character has sparked numerous discussions, particularly regarding his affiliations and ideological shifts, epitomized by the polarizing reception of his book *On the Service and Treachery of Intellectuals*. Beyond his political engagement, Jalal's literary prowess earned him recognition as a significant figure in contemporary literature, with his impactful writings leaving a lasting imprint on the literary landscape.

Jalal Al-Ahmad's intellectual legacy extends beyond his political engagements and literary contributions, encompassing his profound insights into Iranian social dynamics and collective identity. Despite this, Jalal's theoretical contributions in these realms have received comparatively less attention. The title and structure of his seminal work, *On the Service and Treachery of Intellectuals*, may have contributed to this oversight, as it predominantly focuses on the historical role of intellectuals in Iran. However, a crucial chapter within the book titled "Where Is Iranian Intellectualism?" delves into themes related to Shah Ismail's Gnostic Tradition and the Turkish language, shedding light on Jalal's nuanced perspectives. Despite this chapter's relevance, it has been largely overlooked. While I have explored aspects of this discourse in a chapter of my book *Iran in Five Narratives*, the neglect of Jalal's thought-provoking theories persists. It is essential to recognize and engage with Jalal's intellectual legacy in shaping our understanding of Iranian social affairs and collective identity.

In the fifth chapter of *Iran in Five Narratives*, titled "Where Is Iranian Intellectualism?" Jalal Al-Ahmad introduces a thought-provoking theory regarding the "collective identity of Iranians." He gradually unfolds what can be termed as "the theory of expelling the Turkish language from the public domain."

This theory elucidates how languages can be systematically marginalized and excluded from the public sphere, thereby impacting culture, identity, and ultimately the very essence of existence for individuals or segments of the Iranian populace. Jalal's perspective underscores both the notion of language expulsion and the lens of colonialism. It highlights the deliberate institutionalization and organization of language—or languages—in a manner that restricts their presence and development within the public realm, thus limiting the expression and evolution of cultural and national identity.

In light of Jalal Al Ahmad's expulsion theory, which stands as a significant conceptual framework, we can embark on two crucial theoretical formulations:

1.      Firstly, we can construct a theoretical model that acknowledges national identity as inherently diverse and pluralistic. This model would emphasize the multifaceted nature of identity formation, recognizing the myriad cultural, linguistic, and historical influences that contribute to shaping a nation's collective identity. By embracing diversity as a foundational aspect of national identity, we move away from monolithic interpretations and instead embrace the richness of varied cultural expressions and perspectives.

2.      Secondly, drawing from Jalal's expulsion theory, we can theoretically address language diversity in Iran in a manner that transcends political, ideological, or security-driven paradigms. Instead, our theoretical approach would focus on understanding language diversity as a dynamic and integral aspect of societal evolution. It would explore the historical processes and power dynamics that have shaped language usage and representation within Iran, while also highlighting the importance of preserving linguistic pluralism as a cornerstone of cultural heritage. By reframing the discourse around language diversity in theoretical terms, we can foster a deeper understanding and appreciation of linguistic plurality, moving beyond divisive political rhetoric and fostering inclusive dialogues within society.

## 2       The Theory of Expelling the Turkish Language from the Public Domain

Over the past four decades, figures like Seyyed Javad Tabatabai have consistently criticized Seyyed Jalal Al Ahmad and Ali Shariati, expressing disdain for the diversity and pluralism of languages in Iran. However, attributing all of Iran's calamities and afflictions in the last seventy years to Jalal Al-Ahmad seems unjustified. Jalal lived only 46 years and passed away in 1969, well before many significant events unfolded in Iran. So why does a right-wing statist like Seyyed Javad Tabatabai continue to target Jalal when discussing Iran's issues? This raises questions about the motivations behind such attacks and underscores the need for a more nuanced understanding of Iran's complex socio-political landscape.

Jalal Al-Ahmad has often been analyzed through various lenses, such as literature, Islamic internationalism, his affiliation with the Tudeh party, and his role as a writer and intellectual in the public sphere. However, amidst the onslaught of antiquarian nationalisms, one aspect of Jalal's work has been largely overlooked: his contributions as a thinker and theoretician in the realm of social issues and the collective identity of Iranians. Jalal's discourse in the fifth chapter of *On the Service and Treachery of Intellectuals* is essentially a theoretical exploration of Iranian collective identity. Here, he gradually formulates what could be termed as "the theory of the expulsion of the Turkish language from the public sphere." This theory, however, is not a product of personal invention or an imposition of interpretation onto Jalal's text. Instead, it emerges as a critical analysis rooted in Jalal's own writings and observations.

In the fifth chapter of *On the Service and Treachery of Intellectuals*, Jalal Al Ahmad underscores the distinction between a Persian-speaking intellectual and an Iranian intellectual. He argues that the fundamental attributes of an intellectual, namely philanthropy and free-thinking, transcend borders and nationalistic ideologies. He emphasizes that the notion of Iran as a unified nation from its inception is a recent construct, emerging as a facet of urbanization. Jalal further elucidates that an Iranian intellectual may hail from regions like Azerbaijan, where Turkish is the mother tongue. He critiques the efforts of archaic nationalisms, which seek to equate the Turkish language with Azeri, exposing the distortions generated by such discourse. He questions the efficacy of governmental policies aimed at linguistic and cultural homogenization following the constitutional revolution, highlighting both the advantages and drawbacks. Notably, he explores the consequences of expelling the Turkish language from educational and cultural spheres, a topic he delves into in subsequent pages (Al-Ahmad, 2016: 381–382).

The neglect of texts in non-Persian languages, such as Turkish, particularly in the realms of education and culture, highlights a significant and persistent trend. Even the works of influential figures like Hakim Hidji and Shahriar's Turkish poems were overlooked in the 1960s. But what led to the dismissal of the Turkish language in these crucial domains? The emergence of the school system, a relatively recent institution dating back only two hundred years, played a pivotal role. Despite this, scholars of the past were adept in Persian, Arabic, and Turkish, engaging in debates, reproducing texts, and fostering intellectual discourse. During the Qajar era, the influence of the French Revolution prompted the adoption of French as a key language in Iran's academic sphere, serving as a mediator or *lingua franca* in scientific endeavors. Consequently, alongside Arabic, Persian, and Turkish, many Iranian elites also embraced French. This phenomenon was not unique to Iran; nobles in Russia, Turkey, and elsewhere also pursued French education. Notably, Naser al-Din Shah himself was proficient in French and employed tutors to teach his children the language.

Jalal highlights the consequences of expelling non-Persian mother tongues, particularly Turkish, from the cultural sphere, shedding light on the challenges faced by intellectuals who wrote in languages other than Persian. Despite its significance, few intellectuals have dared to openly discuss the expulsion of the Turkish language from the public domain. According to Jalal, a prevailing assumption among intellectuals, writers, and subsequently, the general public, is that Iran is a monolingual nation. This belief, perpetuated by politicians and policymakers, including those at the Persian Academy of Literature and Languages, emphasizes the preservation of monolingualism as a fundamental aspect of Iran's identity, deserving protection from harm. But Jalal says:

> My purpose of this introduction was that I didn't want to allow myself to say Persian-speaking intellectuals, as we might and should, considering that Iran is a multi-lingual nation—and not monolingual.
> AL-AHMED, 2016: 384

Iran is undoubtedly a multilingual nation, a fact that becomes apparent through simple field studies from various perspectives including ideological, nationalist, ethnographic, anthropological, and sociolinguistic lenses. Despite this straightforward reality, the acknowledgment of Iran's multilingualism has been neglected and often actively suppressed. While some assume Iranians speak only one language, framing Iran as a monolingual nation, the reality is far more complex. Over the past 150 years since the establishment of the nation-state in Iran, various powers and institutional interests, including schools, universities, and media, have orchestrated efforts to marginalize other languages from the public sphere. This policy is not unique to Iran but is observed in countries like Turkey, Iraq, Arab nations, emerging Central Asian and South Caucasus states, and even in European countries. Consequently, diverse linguistic manifestations have been systematically eradicated, as linguistic diversity and pluralism inherently embody ontological aspects of language.

The policy of marginalizing languages from the public sphere in Iran has resulted in the expulsion of the Turkish language. An intriguing aspect highlighted by Jalal Al Ahmad, yet often overlooked by researchers, is the nature of the relationship between languages. Al Ahmad boldly suggests that the relationship between languages in Iran is essentially colonial—a statement that few in Iran have dared to make besides him. This raises the question: Has the historical relationship between languages in Iran always been colonial, or did it assume a colonial character primarily in the contemporary era? It is essential to consider whether the institutionalization of languages and the implementation of interventionist policies within the framework of the nation-state led to the expulsion and marginalization of certain languages, effectively subjecting them to colonization.

Throughout history, especially in Iran, the relationship between languages has not been inherently colonial. Rather, it has often involved mutual assistance and support among languages existing before the advent of modern institutions. However, Jalal Al Ahmad highlights a shift in the contemporary era, where politicians, policymakers, and influential figures in the public sphere have propagated an ideological assumption that Iran is a monolingual nation, with Persian as the mother tongue of all Iranians. This perspective, endorsed by figures like Mahmoud Afshar and Mohammad Reza Batani, suggests that achieving national unity hinges on standardizing Persian as the language of all Iranians. In contrast, Jalal contends that attempting to achieve national unity by erasing other languages is both a flawed notion of unity and an unattainable goal. Moreover, he argues that this approach exacerbates cultural divisions among Iranians instead of fostering unity. Contrary to Mohammad Reza Batani's idea, Jalal says:

> Before the advent of cultural institutions such as schools, the press, and widespread literacy, language differences were not as pressing of an issue among the common people. Except for discussions on Sharia and religious matters, where the use of Turkish was permissible, literacy and schooling were not common activities for the masses. However, with the emergence of post-constitutional governments and the recognition of minority languages as seen in the October Revolution in Russia, efforts to enforce national unity policies intensified. Despite attempts by Iranian governments over the past four decades to restrict and erase the Turkish language, renaming cities and neighborhoods in Azerbaijan and relocating Turkish-speaking individuals to non-Turkish areas, these efforts have largely failed. Despite such endeavors, the Turkish language has persisted, defying attempts at eradication.
>
> AL AHMAD, 2016: 415

In the footnote, Jalal refers to one of his ethnographic studies entitled "The Tatneshins of Zahra Block" where he says:

I even witnessed the spread of the Turkish language, which, although
it has been expelled from the field of culture and school, but with the
play it has in the territory of the street, market, and village, there is
nothing to prevent it except the spread of culture, school, and means of
communication.

AL-AHMAD, 1402: 117

Despite the efforts of government authorities during the reigns of Reza Shah
and Mohammad Reza Pahlavi to suppress the Turkish language using symbols
of modernity such as schools and communication tools, Turkish has persisted
in Iranian society, asserting itself in streets, markets, and public spaces. Despite
the adoption of archaic nationalism as the government ideology aimed at eliminating linguistic diversity and specifically targeting the Turkish language, this
approach has not resulted in achieving national unity as envisioned by figures
like Mohammad Reza Batani, Mahmoud Afshar, and Seyed Javad Tabatabai.
These individuals argue that national unity cannot be attained without linguistic
uniformity. According to Jalal, linguistic unity does not lead to national unity:

The situation has reached a point where instead of fostering national unity,
it has led to a sense of national pride, which our governments exploit to
maintain their order, often at the expense of justice. They do so by enforc-
ing directives that prioritize government interests. This is evident in the
practice of deploying Persian officials and soldiers to Turkish-populated
areas, and vice versa. The outcome of this approach is striking: throughout the country, whether they are officials, soldiers, or gendarmes—the
last link between the government and the people—they are perceived
as outsiders by the local population. Their conduct reflects a form of
colonial behavior rooted not in mutual understanding, but in fear and
estrangement.

AL-AHMED, 2016: 416

In essence, the endeavor of antiquated discourse aimed at achieving national
unity through linguistic uniformity, positing that this unity could be attained
by eliminating the Turkish language. However, what we have actually realized
is not national unity, but rather a sense of national pride—a misguided notion
that Iranian identity can be solidified by eradicating the culture and language
of a segment of the Iranian populace. A portion of Iranians' collective memory, notably the Shiite Gnostic Tradition of Ahl al-Bayt, has been enshrined in
the Turkish language. Despite the efforts of antiquated nationalism spanning
the last century and beyond, these endeavors have resulted in the erasure of a

segment of Iranians' collective and historical memory. Today, as we endeavor to revive this faded tradition after more than a century, we encounter various obstacles, as elucidated by Jalal Al Ahmad. He says: "Given all these consequences, hasn't the day come when our government considers a higher and broader concept of national unity policy?" (Al Ahmad, 2016: 422).

In his writings and public discussions in the 1990s, Seyyed Javad Tabatabai sought to discredit Jalal, accusing him of undermining Iran's national unity due to his leftist background and introduction of socialist, communist, and Stalinist concepts. However, Jalal's writings precisely address the concerns he raised. Contrary to the accusation that Jalal aimed to sow national division, his texts do not support such claims. Additionally, assertions suggesting that Jalal employed deceitful tactics to undermine the Pahlavi regime and foment discontent find no validation in his writings.

Jalal's question about the "higher and broader concept of national unity policy" in this text prompts us to consider the deeper dimensions of national unity beyond conventional approaches. While every government formulates policies to reinforce national unity, Jalal suggests that Iran needs to elevate its understanding of national unity beyond mere surface-level policies. He questions whether there are still those who fail to recognize the necessity of adopting a more expansive and inclusive approach to national unity.

When Seyyed Jalal Al-Ahmad poses the question, "Has the day not come when our government considers a higher and broader concept of national unity policy?", he urges us to reconsider the approach towards national unity in a more comprehensive manner. This question becomes particularly pertinent when we observe the dynamics of language classification and politicization in Iran, as highlighted by thinkers like Abbas Iqbal Ashtiani. The security-based classification of languages, especially those with cross-border speakers like Kurdish, Arabic, and Turkish, reflects a narrow approach to national unity that prioritizes containment rather than inclusivity. This approach, influenced by geopolitical tensions and historical events, has persisted through different regimes and continues to shape policy decisions. However, Jalal's question challenges this paradigm by suggesting the need for a more expansive understanding of national unity that transcends security concerns and embraces diversity.

In Chapter Three of *Language and National Unity*, I discuss Abbas Iqbal Ashtiani's analysis. Abbas Iqbal Ashtiani delves into his categorization of languages in Iran through a security lens. He outlines a classification system where languages with co-speakers and neighboring communities across Iran's borders are deemed security languages. Ashtiani suggests a politicized approach to these languages, advocating for measures to limit their proliferation to prevent

potential threats. For instance, languages like Tabari and Gilani, lacking counterparts across the Caspian Sea, are considered less hazardous. Conversely, languages such as Kurdish, Arabic, and Turkish are flagged as more perilous in his
security classification.

Abbas Iqbal Ashtiani's discussions align with a tumultuous period marked
by the aftermath of the Democratic sect uprising and subsequent political
events. Iran becomes embroiled in conflicts with Iraq, while broader tensions
simmer in the Arab world under the leadership of Gamal Abdul Nasser. The
Pahlavi regime faces staunch opposition from a significant portion of the Arab
world, exacerbated by its alignment with Israel. To counterbalance pressure
from Arab nations like Egypt and Iraq, Mohammad Reza Pahlavi establishes
diplomatic ties with Israel. In a strategic move, Iran collaborates with Israel
to support Iraqi Kurds against the central government. This sets the stage for
the formation of Iran's foreign policies during Pahlavi II's reign, profoundly
influencing the perspectives of Iranian thinkers and policymakers like Abbas
Iqbal Ashtiani and those who follow him. Consequently, languages such as
Kurdish, which shares linguistic ties with Iraq and Turkey, along with Turkish
and Arabic, are heavily scrutinized, politicized, and classified within the realm
of security concerns.

This perception and ideology persist beyond the revolution, echoing in the
minds and discourse of certain policymakers since the mid-1980s to the present
day. While these policymakers may not align with the foundational tenets of
archaist nationalism, remnants of its discourse have influenced their thinking.
Though they may tread cautiously around discussions concerning the Arabic
language due to its association with Islam, they openly express concerns about
the Turkish language. When Syed Jalal Al-Ahmed poses the question, "Has
the time not come for our government to adopt a broader and more inclusive
approach to national unity policy?", he refers to this discourse and specifically
to people like Abbas Iqbal Ashtiani and says something that still exists,

> and take actions more suited to the demands of the 20th century in
> these realms, particularly in fostering a more encompassing and forward-
> thinking concept of national identity. Especially now that the political
> and ideological threat of transcendent attraction has dissipated, leaving
> only its linguistic allure. It would be simple, for instance, to transform
> the University of Tabriz into a center for the study of Turkish language,
> science, and culture. Across the border, Turkish is officially written in
> Cyrillic, while on the Turkish side, it is in Latin script. With the collapse
> of the Soviet Union, Turkish in the Republic of Azerbaijan is no longer

written in Cyrillic but predominantly in Latin script, albeit with some variations from Turkish Latin. Yet, barriers persist, such as the refusal to allow Rashid Behdaf, a Caucasian singer, to perform in Tabriz, or restricting Russian Azerbaijani football players to Tehran matches only. Even Russian orientalist Aliov faces obstacles in spending time in Tabriz. However, it is essential to interrogate the core of this attraction, which elicits fear and negative reactions from the government. If governments acknowledge that the primary draw of the Azerbaijani community towards the neighboring region is language-based, and if they prioritize the mother tongue as the principal language in the province while mandating Persian as a secondary language, many of these issues could potentially be mitigated. It is not unfounded to propose that, regardless of other factors such as climate, geography, or international policies, the language issue fundamentally underpins all crises in Azerbaijan.

AL-AHMAD, 2015: 422–423

Jalal's words, spoken six decades ago, have yet to manifest as a guiding policy or a comprehensive theory of national unity. Remarkably, for sixty years, this theory has remained sidelined in the discourse, notably absent from texts like *On the Service and Treachery of Intellectuals*. Despite this, figures like Hamid Ahmadi, along with many active within the University of Tehran, particularly in political science and history, persist in asserting that Farsi should be the mother tongue of all Iranians. However, another crucial aspect highlighted by Jalal aids in comprehending the theory behind the exclusion of the Turkish language from the public sphere:

At the end of this chapter, in which I have listed intellectual problems in Iran, I want to be more clear and say that since the beginning of the concept of nationality, that is, from the time of constitutionalism until now (unlike Mohammad Ali Eslami Nadushan or Seyed Javad Tabatabai, who say that Iranian nationality has existed for 2700 years), nationality is a new construction. It is not merely a matter of people inhabiting Iran historically, but rather the concept of nationality entails identification with a specific nation defined by language and supported by institutional mechanisms, such as possessing a distinct passport and affiliations with various governmental bodies and ministries. These are new phenomena: the Tehran government considers Azerbaijan as its colony, if not from a political and economic point of view, but certainly from a cultural point of view, and the first bad result of this cultural colonization is the killing of Turkish culture in Azerbaijan, and on this occasion, I would like to say to Ume Caesar that He is a black poet and what pains he has in his heart in this context: After stating the discussion, M. Sezer says that this is in a way related to our understanding and theoretical formulation of the theory of expelling the Turkish language from the public domain, and then he says: For every culture to flourish, it needs a framework and a structure; But it is certain that the elements that make up the cultural life of the colonized people are either destroyed or corrupted in the colonial regime. Of course, these elements are primarily political organizations ... another element is the language that the people speak with. Language has been called (frozen psychology). Since the native language is no longer the official language, the administrative language, the school language, and the language of thought, it is regressing, and this regression hinders its growth and sometimes even threatens it with extinction ... when the French do not accept that the Arabic language in Algeria and Malagasy language to be the official languages, they prevent these languages from realizing their full potential in the conditions of the modern world, and in this way, they attack Arabic and Malagasy culture.

AL-AHMED, 2015: 424

One complication arising from language expulsion is a form of cultural colonization. Cultural colonialism entails the belief, mindset, and assumptions that establish a linguistic hierarchy, with the Persian language occupying the highest position, relegating other languages beneath it. This hierarchy is so entrenched that some individuals now openly claim, even within academic and public spheres, that there is no distinct Turkish language in Azerbaijan. Instead, they assert that what is spoken is "Azeri," a blend of Persian and Azeri, with any Turkish influence being merely incidental. According to this perspective, Azeri lacks the capacity to formulate concepts.

The question arises: Is this linguistic hierarchy a product of inherent linguistic structures, where one language naturally rises above others, relegating them to mere dialects? Or is it the outcome of language policies driven by political and ideological discourse? Arguably, the logic behind this linguistic hegemony, which marginalizes certain languages or excludes them from the realm of linguistics altogether, is not inherent to language itself. Rather, it stems from an ideological logic rooted in a particular interpretation of the state and nation. As Jalal suggests, in the eyes of proponents of this perspective, the Iranian nation is perceived as monolingual. Any move towards bilingualism or multilingualism is viewed as a threat that could unravel the constructed national identity.

3    The Relationship between the Expulsion Theory of the Turkish
     Language and the Gnostic Tradition of Shah Ismail

The discussion surrounding the expulsion of the Turkish language from the
public domain intertwines with our exploration of The Gnostic Tradition
and Diwan Shah Ismail Khatai. One notable connection lies within the realm
of educational institutions, particularly universities. While schools hold significance, universities play a more pivotal role in shaping our contemporary
understanding and contextualizing it within historical frameworks in academic discourse.

However, when Iranian universities succumb to antiquated nationalist
rhetoric, they restrict the study and analysis of texts beyond those in Persian,
effectively marginalizing other literary traditions. Over the past two decades,
academic works dedicated to the history of poetry and literature in Iran have
overwhelmingly overlooked the development of the Turkish language and poetry
within the country. This institutionalized neglect has become so ingrained that
even well-educated individuals question the existence of Turkish language texts
suitable for academic study.

Today, discussing Diwan Shah Ismail and The Gnostic Tradition of Ahl al-Bayt
(a) in Turkish requires an initial hurdle: establishing the authenticity of such a
figure. While historical evidence affirms Shah Ismail's existence, there are
attempts to detach him from certain texts, contending they are not attributable
to him. This phenomenon, consistent with Jalal's theory, extends beyond Shah
Ismail to encompass texts in languages like Armenian, Georgian, Kurdish, and
others, all of which have been effectively expelled from the public discourse
in Iran.

Remarkably, scholarly exploration of the Armenian language and its literary
developments within Iran remains conspicuously absent. This neglect is exacerbated by the colonial narrative imposed by Russian, English, and French historians, portraying Armenians and Georgians as inhabitants of foreign lands
later liberated by the Russians. Despite their deep historical roots within Iran,
Armenians, Georgians, Arabs, Turkmens, and Turks find their texts and contributions sidelined in the Iranian academic milieu. For instance, a significant Armenian poet, possibly contemporaneous with or following Jalāl al-Din Muḥammad
RumiRumi, remains virtually unknown outside Armenian circles, with no sum-
maries or translations of his work accessible to non-Armenian audiences.

It is not coincidental that even in contemporary times, scholars and experts
rarely engage in discussions about the Gnostic Tradition of Shah Ismail, and
its acknowledgment remains sparse. This neglect stems directly from deliberate policies rooted in the rhetoric of antiquated nationalism. Essentially,

this nationalist discourse concerning Iran was not grounded in cultural perspectives but rather in a narrow nationalistic framework. This reductionist approach has led to the suppression and concealment of a diverse array of texts and languages. Without a comprehensive theoretical framework to address the expulsion of the Turkish language in Iran, our discussions devolve into mere arguments and verbal sparring, hindering meaningful dialogue. However, Jalal's conceptualization of national identity and collective affairs in Iran transcends these limitations, offering a more nuanced and inclusive perspective.

Jalal's theory did not emerge fully formed; it was shaped by his complex background. With deep roots in Shiite traditions, religion, and a conservative upbringing, Jalal's family ties further enriched his perspective—being the cousin of Ayatollah Seyyed Mahmoud Taleghani, a pivotal figure in the Islamism movement with a democratic bent. Additionally, Jalal's father, a renowned cleric, contributed to his religious and traditional upbringing.

Yet, Jalal's journey was multifaceted. He also delved into leftist ideologies, ascending to high ranks within the Tudeh Party, which employed various tactics. Fluent in French, he absorbed the influences of both Russian and French leftist movements, translating works like Dostoevsky's *The Gambler* from French to Persian. Hence, he was imbued with the progressive ethos of the European left tradition.

Moreover, Jalal navigated the complexities of Iranian politics, aligning with the "third stream" during the Dr. Mossadegh and Darbar dispute. His understanding of Iranian nationalism was thus characterized by civic nationalism—a stance that did not seek to subjugate or oppress Iranians of different linguistic or cultural backgrounds. Instead, he advocated for inclusivity, rejecting repressive policies against those whose culture and language did not align with the dominant Persian culture and language.

Jalal contends that the pursuit of language unity, championed by figures like Mohammad Reza Batani and Mahmoud Afshar, should not be achieved at any cost. While not formally trained as an anthropologist or ethnographer, Jalal collaborated with the Social Studies Research Center, founded by Ehsan Naraghi and others in 1951, contributing to the book *The Inhabitants of the Block of Zahra*. Engaging in field studies in his father's village in Taleghan, Jalal highlighted critical points often overlooked by academics.

In *The Inhabitants of the Block of Zahra*, Jalal draws attention to a significant fact: in the 1940s, nearly seven million Turks resided in Iran. Considering Iran's population of about 22 million at the time, these Azerbaijani Turks constituted roughly a third of the country's populace. Jalal emphasizes that denying such a sizable minority their fundamental human rights, including the freedom to use any language, cannot be justified. He prompts readers to contemplate the repercussions of depriving millions of Iranians of such basic rights, underscoring the urgency of addressing this issue (Al-Ahmad, 2022: 410).

Jalal's perspective stands in stark contrast to figures like Afshar, whose ideology centers on a vision of authenticity linked to Zoroastrianism and the Pahlavi language. While Afshar and proponents of archaism advocate for a return to Persianization and ultimately a revival of Zoroastrianism, Jalal's approach is firmly rooted in ethnographic observation rather than ideological constructs. He rejects the notion of imposing abstract ideals onto reality, opting instead to analyze the existing social and linguistic landscape. For Jalal, understanding comes from observing and engaging with the lived experiences of diverse communities, a methodology that shapes his inclusive and nuanced perspective on Iranian identity and language.

Jalal's ethnographic inquiries are evident in his extensive collection of travelogues, such as "A Journey to the Land of Israel" (The Land of Azrael), documenting his travels to Israel (Al-Ahmed, 2011), as well as his journeys to America, the Soviet Union, France, and beyond. He was attuned to global developments of his time, benefiting from his familial ties to prominent intellectuals and travel writers. Notably, his wife was a student of Fatima Sayah, whose nephew, Ferdowsi, was a contemporary intellectual and fellow travel writer. Fatima Sayah, with her Russian heritage and contributions to comparative studies, is regarded as a pioneering figure in Iran's social sciences, fluent in six languages including French, Russian, Turkish, and Farsi. Similarly, Simin Daneshvar's influence underscores Jalal's engagement with the complexities of linguistic diversity and the dynamics between center and periphery within the discourse of colonialism. This interconnected network of influences and relationships shaped Jalal's insightful exploration of these themes.

Another noteworthy aspect to consider is Jalal's eloquence and appreciation for beauty, which adds depth to his discussions of Shiism, the Safavid era, and the Turkish language. Jalal posits that Iran's cohesive and integrated identity, particularly under the umbrella of Shiite Islam, owes much to the Turkish language. This perspective sheds light on the intricate relationship between language, culture, and religious identity in Iran's historical narrative. Jalal articulates this phenomenon as follows:

> Irrespective of speculative scenarios, it is apparent that Azerbaijan served as the birthplace of the Safavid movement, consequently facilitating the widespread adoption of Shiism within the region and beyond. Given the historical backdrop, one may inquire whether the prevalence of the Turkish language in Azerbaijan contributed to the swift acceptance of Shiism in the province. Comparatively, many Kurds have yet to embrace

Shiism. Furthermore, tracing the migration of Turks from Ahar to Qazvin, then Isfahan, and finally Tehran during the Safavid to Qajar periods, raises the question: Did the linguistic differences between Persian and Turkish contribute to the establishment of Shiism in Azerbaijan and its subsequent proliferation throughout Iran? Additionally, despite centuries of conflict, Turkish failed to dominate the province from the east, encountering resistance from Khorasan with its rich history, geography, and cultural heritage. Thus, from Azerbaijan's historical perspective, whether acknowledged or not, the influence of Turkish remains undeniable.

AL-AHMED, 2016: 412–413

Understanding Iran's national identity is incomplete without acknowledging the pivotal roles of the Turkish language and Shiism. Indeed, Shiism, particularly under The Gnostic Tradition of Ahl al-Bayt, is intricately linked to the Turkish language. Historically, the Turkish language has served as a conduit for the dissemination of Shiism, contributing significantly to Iran's unity. However, some have attempted to marginalize and expel the Turkish language from the public sphere. Nevertheless, the textual evidence of Shiism within the tradition of Ahl al-Bayt is readily available in Turkish today, highlighting the enduring connection between Shiism and the Turkish language.

While Jalal's texts may not explicitly engage with the theory of the "linguistic turn," his exploration of the "expulsion of language" theory emerges as a crucial aspect within the current discourse. This theory, which should rightfully be attributed to Jalal, delves into how a language, and consequently, a culture and identity, are systematically removed from the public sphere through institutional and organizational mechanisms. By examining how certain languages are marginalized, Jalal sheds light on the emergence and perpetuation of power dynamics. This issue is framed within the context of colonialism, emphasizing the parallels between linguistic suppression and colonial control.

According to Jalal's theory, the quest for national identity is inherently flawed due to several misconceptions. Firstly, the notion that Iranians constitute a monolingual nation is erroneous. Secondly, the belief that preserving national identity necessitates the suppression of other identities is equally misguided. Jalal advocates for a broader perspective that embraces the cultural diversity inherent within the Iranian nation. He emphasizes the importance of engaging with the rich tapestry of language, literature, and culture that characterizes Iran's pluralistic society. Such encounters should not be dismissed as separatist; rather, they are essential for fostering a more inclusive and nuanced understanding of Iran's heritage. Those who propagate narrow definitions of national identity, such as Mahmoud Afshar, Seyyed Javad Tabatabai, Abbas

Iqbal Ashtiani, and Mohammad Reza Batani, are, according to Jalal, the true cultural separatists. They obscure the truth of Iran's diverse and millennia-old cultural legacy, reducing it to a simplistic nationalist construct.

In his book *Emergence of Iranian Nationalism*, Reza Zia Ebrahimi discusses Ali Akbar's perspective on the expulsion of Arabic language and Islam from Iran:

> Ali Akbar's stance on Islam becomes apparent when he reflects on Iran's connection, or lack thereof, with Imam Ali (a): While acknowledging Imam Ali's piety and martyrdom, Ali Akbar asserts, 'He was an Arab, and therefore, I hold no interest in him. Anyone who is not from my country, who is not Iranian, cannot be my favorite'.
>
> ZIA EBRAHIMI, 2018: 290

It appears that Ali Akbar's political agenda aims to diminish Shiism by associating it with Arab influence. In his manifesto, Mahmoud Afshar identifies two main obstacles hindering the growth, continuity, and stability of Iranian identity: Islam and Shiism. Unable to directly address Islam, he symbolically targets Arabic language, and similarly, he veils his criticism of Shiism by referencing Turkish language. Afshar views the institutionalization of Shiism during the Safavid era, alongside the prevalence of the Turkish language in Iran, as factors inhibiting the development of a cohesive national identity.

It appears that among intellectuals of advanced modernity, a division of labor has emerged. For instance, despite being born into a Muslim family, Pordawood's endeavors aimed to equate Iranianness with Zoroastrianism. This inclination was so pronounced that upon Pordawood's passing, Indian Zoroastrians sought to bury him according to Zoroastrian customs. However, the Purdawood family declined this request. These intellectuals operated within distinct spheres: some focused on expelling Islam, while others concentrated on revitalizing Zoroastrianism and institutionalizing its resurgence in Iran. Abdullah Shahbazi's seven-volume work, *Jewish and Persian Monarchs*, highlights the ties between Zoroastrian Persians in India and the first Pahlavi dynasty, extending to some extent to the second Pahlavi dynasty (Shehbazi, 2004). For instance, certain Persians in India played a significant role in Iran's cinema industry during the Pahlavi era, influencing the societal metaphors and imagination. Surprisingly, Iranian cinema and Persian films have received relatively less scholarly attention from this perspective.

Aref Qazvini stands out as a prominent figure striving to expel both the Turkish language and Islam from Iran. His poems and compositions are dedicated entirely to this endeavor. During advanced modernity in Iran, intellectuals and certain politicians pursued similar projects, aiming for the cultural disintegration of the country. While they achieved some success in certain aspects and generated societal contradictions, their overall impact remained limited.

In simpler terms, Jalal's theory of expulsion can help us understand how and through what methods the text of Diwan Shah Ismail and The Gnostic Tradition, originally composed in Turkish language in Iran, became inaccessible to us. This exclusion was not merely a result of personal preferences, but rather, these authoritative texts in Turkish were systematically and linguistically kept beyond our reach. To understand this process of eviction, it is essential to discern the discursive signals and reconstruct the dialogues from a discursive perspective. This entails placing less emphasis on individual or collective intentions in the reconstruction process, and instead focusing on the dominance or non-dominance of the discourse, which ultimately dictates the potential outcomes of expulsion or annexation.

# CHAPTER 8

# The Gnostic Legacy of Shah Ismail Safavi

## 1    Introduction

In the realm of journalism, we often engage with societal issues by scrutinizing daily events and offering analyses rooted in the pulse of the present moment, while also anticipating tomorrow's developments. Amidst the ever-evolving landscape of Iran's social fabric, a recurring inquiry persists: What defines our collective identity? How do we achieve and sustain unity amidst diversity? What unifies disparate individuals and societal strata, weaving them into a cohesive "we"? Delving deeper, we ponder the origins of our collective and national identity, exploring the threads that bind us together and the fault lines that threaten division. Which policies hold the potential to mend our fractured community, fostering solidarity and inclusivity? Conversely, what approaches yield no tangible results, perpetuating discord and disunity? These questions linger as we navigate the complexities of Iranian society, seeking pathways towards greater cohesion and understanding.

To effectively tackle these issues, it is crucial to acknowledge that humans are shaped by their historical contexts, influenced by various factors such as practices, customs, beliefs, languages, and geography. These elements gradually intertwine to define the distinct identity of a nation and its populace. A comprehensive understanding requires moving beyond the immediacy of the present and delving into the historical origins and significant events that have molded our shared identity. By revisiting these turning points, we gain valuable insights into the complex interplay between history, culture, and societal development, providing a deeper understanding of contemporary challenges and avenues for meaningful progress.

Throughout the annals of a nation's history, pivotal events emerge that, while rooted in distant origins, crystallize into transformative turning points. In the context of Iranian society, two such moments stand out: the introduction of Islam and its subsequent encounter with Shia Islam. These encounters, previously referred to as the "Jafari" and "Imāmiyya Ithnā ʿAshariyya" religions, respectively, marked significant shifts in Iran's cultural and religious landscape. These encounters reshaped societal norms, beliefs, and identities, leaving an indelible mark on the trajectory of Iranian history.

These two events in the history of Iran have marked fundamental changes in the mind, language, life and collective identity of Iranians. But the why and how of this change and transformation and its effects on our present and here have been less theoretically addressed. Those who are close to Islam or to Shiism, have a religious interpretation of these developments. For them, it is well known that Islam is a final and noble religion and as God promised, Islam is the highest religion, therefore it has been able to overcome other competitors and spread among different ethnic groups and shape historical developments.

Iran, as a prominent center of civilization, has undoubtedly been impacted by these global developments, much like other regions. However, differing ideological perspectives exist regarding the influence of Islam within Iran's civilizational context. Some argue that Islam has not introduced any fundamentally new elements to Iranian identity, viewing it instead as an occupying force that has distorted the Iranian mindset, language, and civilization over the past fourteen centuries. According to this viewpoint, an authentic Iranian identity is rooted in Aryan Iranian heritage and the Zoroastrian religion. Advocates of this perspective advocate for a return to the pre-Islamic era as a means of reclaiming an untainted Iranian identity.

Over the span of fourteen centuries, Islam's institutionalization has deeply influenced the greatest thinkers not only within Iranian and Islamic history but also within the broader realms of philosophy and global thought. These thinkers, operating within the framework of Islamic semantics and revelation, have generated rich philosophical, theological, jurisprudential, mystical, and literary systems. Yet, what were the foundational principles and components of this religious transformation? While Islam expanded into regions such as Spain, southern France, and southern Italy, its presence gradually waned due to military pressures from the Franks, Spaniards, and Italians. However, in Eastern Europe and the Balkans, Islam endured even after the expulsion of Muslim Turks. If military or coercive force were solely responsible for religious transformations, why do we observe varied outcomes across different regions of the Islamic world and Eastern Europe? What other factors influenced these developments? Neither proponents nor opponents of Islam have rigorously theorized the turning points of Iranian identity; instead, they often construct their understanding of Iranian identity based on personal convictions and aspirations.

The ideological debates surrounding Islam in Iran extend beyond historical discourse; they hold significant sway in contemporary political and intellectual spheres. One camp, often aligned with the government, advocates for the Islamization of various facets of Iranian society, including sciences, social structures, and individual mindsets. Conversely, opposition factions, whether inside Iran or in diaspora communities like Paris, London, Washington, or Tel Aviv, challenge this narrative. According to their perspective, a substantial portion of Iranians, both within and outside Iran, are deemed impure and inau-thentic, necessitating a process of purification to restore their "true" Iranian identity. This ideological divide essentially manifests as a clash between those advocating for the "Islamization" and "Aryanization" of Iranian society. These contrasting currents reflect deeper tensions and aspirations within Iranian society, shaping its trajectory in the modern era.

This discussion regarding Islam in Iran encompasses not only historical analysis but also pertains to our present circumstances and future trajectories. Approaching the topic from a historical perspective allows us to understand the factors and dynamics that led to Islam's emergence in Iran, including the collapse of the Sassanid dynasty and the subsequent rise of the Muslim caliph-ate within and beyond the Iranian realm. However, solely focusing on the past would be limiting, as it fails to address the contemporary realities and future implications of these historical developments. Similarly, discussing the pres-ent without acknowledging the historical context would be incomplete. Thus, a comprehensive understanding requires us to intertwine historical analysis with considerations of current circumstances and future prospects.

Indeed, the study of history, comprehension of historical processes, and logical analysis of developments provide invaluable insights for envision-ing the future of Iran within the modern and post-modern world. However, a critical question arises: Can the Iranian identity be solely defined through an Islamic lens? Is it possible to reduce the multifaceted Iranian identity to merely an Islamic interpretation? Conversely, can Iranian identity be encapsu-lated within an Aryan or ancient framework? Furthermore, is there a neglected aspect of Iranian history that has engendered a distinct component within contemporary Iranian society?

Neglecting this latter component could hinder our understanding of the broader Iranian identity and impede efforts to synthesize a vision for its future. Moreover, the formulation of religious evolution necessitates not only his-torical perspectives but also ideological considerations. By integrating these diverse viewpoints, we can hope to gain a more comprehensive understand-ing of the complexities inherent in Iranian identity and chart a more nuanced course for its future trajectory.

## 2     Important Developments in the History of Iran

It could be argued that Iranian history, as recorded, has witnessed four trans-formative trends or turning points that have captured the attention of Iranian intellectuals and impacted the lives of ordinary people. However, the analyses offered regarding these turning points often fall short of providing satisfactory answers. These four developments are:

1) Religious transformations in Iran;
2) Madhhab transformations in Iran;
3) Linguistic shifts within Iranian society;
4) Changes resulting from encounters with modernity and Western civiliza-tion, as observed in the works of figures such as Akhundzadeh, Mirza Agha Khan Nouri, Talebov, Mirza Malkum Khan, and Seyyed Jamal Din Asadabadi, who referred to advanced nations, a concept now synony-mous with developed modern societies.

Even though nearly 118 years have passed since the signing of the constitu-tional decree in 1906, discussions surrounding Iran's evolution and entry into the modern world remain contentious. Some attribute the constitutional rev-olution to the activities of Freemasons, while others view Iran's embrace of modernity as a loss of identity and existence. Still, there are those who argue that Iran lacked positive components prior to the modern and constitutional era, asserting that Iranianness and Iranian identity emerged only with the advent of modernity.

Yet, none of these perspectives offer a comprehensive understanding or the-oretical framework for Iranian modernity. Addressing these four milestones in Iran's history necessitates a robust theoretical apparatus that can accom-modate the complexities and nuances of Iran's historical evolution. Such an approach would provide a deeper understanding of Iranian modernity and its implications for contemporary Iranian society.

Scholars like Abdul Hossein Zarinkoub, Mahmoud Afshar, Ebrahim Pourdawood, Javad Sheikh Al-Islami, Iraj Afshar, Shahrokh Moskob, and others delve into Iran's religious development during the modern and medieval eras, yet their analyses often lack a cohesive theoretical framework. Instead, their narratives often rely on simplistic and flawed dichotomies, portraying Iranians as noble and Arabs as primitive. To offer a more balanced perspective, some acknowledge the corruption within the Sassanid government as a contribut-ing factor to religious transformation and the Arab conquest. They speculate about alternative historical outcomes, such as a Sassanid victory at Qadisiyah and Nahavand, which could have altered the course of history.

It is noteworthy that Islam's spread did not solely rely on military con-quest, as evidenced by its acceptance in regions like Kazakhstan, Kyrgyzstan, Uzbekistan, and Tajikistan centuries after the fall of the Sassanids. Furthermore, some areas in the Caucasus, such as Chechnya, Ingushetia, Balkaria, and parts of Dagestan, did not adopt Islam until much later, despite their historical con-nections to the Iranian Empire during the Sassanid era. These observations suggest that our theoretical understanding of Iran's religious evolution remains imprecise. In essence, there is a need for a more nuanced and comprehensive theoretical framework to elucidate the religious dynamics shaping Iran's history and identity. Such an approach would facilitate a deeper understanding of the complexities inherent in Iran's religious evolution.

For a period of 700 years, the majority of Iranians were somewhat integrated under Sunnis. Around the year 1500, when the Safavid dynasty was established, the Shiite religion also spread in Iran. There are two dominant currents regarding the religious evolution of Iranians. A trend that, from the point of view of belief and belief, is of the opinion that because Shiism was the true religion, all Iranians accepted it with open arms, just as they accepted Islam. The intuition and Irfan of Iranians was so deep that they easily accepted Shiism. On the opposite side, there are those who try to prove with historical documents that Shah Ismail and Qizilbash killed many Iranian people. Wherever they went, they started wars and bloodshed and even Qizilbash ate human flesh. Therefore, the religious transformation has taken place by force and sword; Because the Iranians had no other choice but to accept Shiism.

Is it truly possible to bring about religious change through the force of the sword? Historical records, not only within Islam but also across other religions, seem to contradict this notion. Consider Christianity's entrance into the Roman Empire: for 150 years, it faced persecution and severe suppression. Many Christians were executed or thrown to lions and leopards in efforts to deter conversions. Yet, after this tumultuous period, Constantine embraced Christianity. His conversion was not a sudden epiphany or spiritual awakening; rather, it was a pragmatic decision. Constantine found himself at a crossroads, caught between competing ideologies. On one side, the nobility and elites leaned towards Mithraism, a religion also practiced in the rival Sassanid Empire. This inclination towards Mithraism posed significant challenges for Rome. In such a precarious position, Constantine had little choice but to align himself with Christianity, a move that ultimately altered the course of history.

While the Iranian Empire did not embrace Christianity, Constantine found himself at a crossroads where he perceived one path as bad and the other as worse. In his view, choosing Christianity was the lesser of two evils for his empire. However, attempts to forcibly change people's religious beliefs through coercion, wealth, and violence often proved ineffective. In fact, history shows that such efforts often backfired, with increased resistance leading to strengthened adherence to the targeted religion.

The comparison between the Roman Empire and the Arab powers is intriguing. Despite the Arab powers not surpassing the military might of the Roman Empire at the time, the method of using force and coercion to impose religious change yielded different outcomes. This raises questions about the complex dynamics at play in religious transformations and the role of various socio-political factors.

Examining the history of Islamic developments in Iran reveals a diverse array of anti-Islamic movements. If those coerced into converting to Islam had turned to these movements, the course of history might have been different. However, this scenario did not unfold as expected, highlighting the inadequacy of existing theories to explain these pivotal moments.

In scholarly discourse, there is a noticeable absence of comprehensive theories regarding religious transformations in Iran. The lack of theoretical frameworks leaves room for interpretations that either view religious transformation towards Shiism as an intra-religious phenomenon or adopt simplistic, oppositional perspectives devoid of theoretical depth, as seen in the writings of figures like Kasravi. This gap underscores the need for nuanced and rigorous theoretical formulations to better understand the complexities of religious transformations in Iranian history.

The discourse surrounding linguistic evolution in Iran presents a paradoxical narrative. Scholars like Shahrukh Moskob, Mahmoud Afshar, and Abbas Ashtiani, who explore Iranian identity, frequently portray the Persian language as an unchanging constant amid significant societal transformations. It is depicted as a persistent medium of communication, seemingly unaffected by linguistic shifts. This perspective implies a perception of a static linguistic landscape, were Persian reigns supreme without variation or modification.

However, a closer examination reveals a different reality. While Persian has served as the primary means of communication among Iranians, the linguistic diversity within Iran tells a more complex story. Even in the past century, Iran has been home to numerous languages and dialects, each with its own unique characteristics. These linguistic variations have not only coexisted alongside Persian but have also played crucial roles in various aspects of Iranian life.

Despite this evident linguistic diversity, a comprehensive formulation of this evolution remains elusive. The absence of a coherent theoretical framework seems to hinder our understanding of this complex phenomenon. It is as though the discussion of linguistic evolution in Iran is plagued by a fundamental flaw, akin to Achilles' heel or Esfandiar's eye, stemming from the lack of a robust theoretical approach.

The discourse on modernity and Iran's transition into the contemporary era, while extensively explored in comparison to other cases, often overlooks whether Iran's shift was solely prompted by external factors or if intrinsic elements within its civilization also played a role. This neglect raises questions about whether the quest for a new historical and civilizational trajectory stemmed solely from external influences or if internal dynamics within Iranian society, and the wider Islamic world, were at play. Western civilization, in this context, could be perceived as a conduit through which Iranians sought to redefine themselves, not necessarily to emulate Western identity, but to integrate new models and components into their cultural identity. This nuanced approach acknowledges both the impact of external forces and the agency of Iranian society in navigating modernity while preserving its distinct cultural heritage.

Jalal Al Ahmad stands as a prominent figure who delved into the discourse surrounding national identity and the cultivation of unity within Iran. Following the demise of the democratic movement in 1946, a void emerged, prompting endeavors to redefine national identity and foster cohesion within the country. This effort led to the emergence of perspectives, exemplified by thinkers like Abbas Iqbal Ashtiani, who pondered the role of language in Iran. Ashtiani's exploration of language transcends the conventional inquiry into its nature as either a cultural or social construct. Instead, he boldly advocates for the politicization of language in Iran. For Ashtiani, politicization entails a dual significance: on one hand, it involves disciplining and harnessing language akin to taming a horse, enabling its effective use; on the other, it calls for the active engagement of language in the political sphere, where it becomes a tool for shaping and expressing socio-political realities (Iqbal Ashtiani, 1945: 3).

In the discourse surrounding language in Iran, a notable divergence arises wherein certain voices assert that specific languages pose a threat to national security, framing language not as a cultural or social construct but rather as a security concern. This perspective contrasts sharply with the philosophical musings of figures like Heidegger, who views language as the shelter of existence, and Chomsky, who emphasizes the innate linguistic capacity of humans. Unlike these philosophical approaches, Abbas Iqbal Ashtiani adopts a distinct stance, eschewing considerations of language as a universal trait inherent to human nature. Instead, he categorizes certain languages in Iran as potential security risks, proposing an atlas of languages wherein any language with linguistic ties beyond Iran's borders is perceived as a potential threat to national security. This viewpoint underscores Ashtiani's emphasis on the geopolitical dimensions of language and its perceived implications for national cohesion and stability.

For instance, languages like Tabari or Gilki, which lack speakers beyond the Caspian Sea, are not deemed threats to national security, allowing for their inclusion in media platforms like television and radio without concern. However, three languages within Iran—Kurdish, Turkish, and Arabic—are identified as significantly perilous. While Turkmen, despite bordering Turkmenistan or the former Soviet Union, does not evoke the same apprehension. Among these, Kurdish, although spoken by indigenous Iranians, is viewed with less alarm. However, Turkish and Arabic are perceived as particularly hazardous, requiring a strategic politicization to mitigate their influence. The imperative, as posited, is to strategically remove Turkish and Arabic from Iran's cultural landscape to foster a unified national identity.

Javad Sheikh Al-Islami, approximately 25 years later, advocates for a method aimed at ensuring that children born in Turkic-speaking regions are relocated to areas where Persian is the primary language. He emphasizes the necessity of Persian becoming the predominant language. Sheikh Al-Islami draws parallels with student exchange programs in Europe, where individuals immerse themselves in a new language and culture; however, he proposes a one-way exchange, wherein Turkic individuals would solely learn Persian. Unlike the reciprocal cultural exchange typical of student programs, Sheikh Al-Islami's approach prioritizes Persian language acquisition without corresponding exposure to Turkic languages.

About two decades later, Mohammad Reza Batani extends the discourse initiated by Sheikh al-Islami in his book on language. Batani argues that to achieve national unity, it is imperative to eradicate languages deemed threats to security, particularly Turkish. By eliminating these languages, Batani contends, Iran can attain both national and linguistic unity, thereby fortifying national security. However, it seems that these authors may not fully grasp the historical significance of their proposals. They inadvertently target the role of Shiism and Shiite unity, historically fostered through the Turkish language during the Safavid era, based on Ahl al-Bayt theology. Their recommendations operate within a complex historical and cultural landscape, potentially overlooking the intricate dynamics at play.

Jalal Al-Ahmad presents an overlooked perspective on the historical and national identity developments in Iran, albeit one open to criticism and questioning. According to Jalal, Iran's religious transformation took root during the Safavid dynasty, particularly under Shah Ismail, with significant implications for the Turkish language. He argues that Turkish served as a unifying force among the Turkic tribes settled across regions like Azerbaijan, Anatolia, Ardabil, Astara, and Zanjan. This linguistic cohesion fostered solidarity among these tribes. Additionally, Jalal highlights the mystical interpretation of Shiism, later termed as Qizilbash or Aleviism, and known in Persian regions as "The Followers of The Right Path" or "Ali-Illahism," which further bolstered religious unity among these tribes. Jalal suggests that linguistic unity facilitated the emergence of religious solidarity, underscoring the intertwined nature of language and religion in shaping Iran's collective identity.

In his analysis, Jalal Al Ahmad explores the interconnectedness between language and religion, suggesting that Iran achieved a degree of religious unity partly due to linguistic cohesion, particularly during the Safavid era under Shah Ismail. He underscores the significance of the Safavid dynasty in strengthening national unity through the promotion of the Turkish language. Jalal posits that throughout history, and notably following the establishment of the Safavid dynasty, the prominence of Turkish language contributed to the consolidation of Iran's national identity. Conversely, the decline of Turkish language usage in the public sphere correlated with a weakening sense of national unity among Iranians. Jalal Al Ahmad brought attention to this dynamic during the 1950s and 1960s, shedding light on the pivotal role of language in shaping Iran's collective identity.

During the Pahlavi II era, a cohort of intellectuals spearheaded a campaign to challenge the dominance of Islam, particularly Shiism, in the public sphere. Figures such as Abbas Iqbal Ashtiani, Javad Sheikh Al-Islami, Mahmoud Afshar, and Pordawood sought to subvert these religious institutions through a nuanced approach. Recognizing the formidable obstacle posed by the deeply entrenched Islamic identity in Iran, they employed covert methods, avoiding direct confrontation. Instead, they directed their efforts towards undermining linguistic and cultural aspects associated with Islam. Arabic, as the language of the Quran and integral to Islamic tradition, became a primary target. By advocating for the purification of Persian from Arabic loanwords, they aimed to dilute the influence of Islam and reshape Iran's cultural landscape.

Simultaneously, this group also took aim at the Turkish language, with Seyyed Ahmed Kasravi emerging as a key proponent of this endeavor. By attacking linguistic ties to Shiism, they sought to weaken the religious and cultural bonds that bound Iran to its Shiite heritage. This concerted effort to challenge both Arabic and Turkish languages reflects a broader strategy to distance Iran from its Islamic roots. Despite facing resistance, their intellectual discourse laid the groundwork for ongoing debates surrounding language, identity, and religion in Iranian society.

Jalal highlights a crucial point regarding Shah Ismail's pivotal role in the elevation of Shiism as Iran's national religion, facilitated significantly by the Turkish language. Despite his undeniable influence, Shah Ismail often seems overlooked in scholarly examinations of these historical shifts. Unlike lesser figures such as Agha Mohammad Khan Qajar, whose literary impact is minimal, Shah Ismail's imprint on Iran's trajectory extends far beyond governance. Yet, his multifaceted persona remains largely unexplored, with little public discourse on the various dimensions of his character. This raises the central question: Why does Shah Ismail occupy such a peripheral position in both intellectual dialogue and broader societal consciousness? This persistent query underscores the need to delve deeper into historical narratives and cultural perceptions surrounding Shah Ismail, potentially yielding valuable insights into Iran's historical and cultural fabric.

Shah Ismail's absence from intellectual discourse contrasts starkly with his undeniable historical significance. While figures like Agha Mohammad Khan Qajar fade into obscurity due to their minimal impact on literary or intellectual realms, Shah Ismail's influence on Iran's religious and cultural landscape demands closer examination. Yet, despite his pivotal role in shaping Iran's identity over the past five centuries, discussions about Shah Ismail's character and contributions remain surprisingly sparse in Iranian public discourse. This omission prompts a critical inquiry into the underlying reasons for his marginalization. By addressing this "why," scholars and society alike may uncover deeper insights into the historical narratives, cultural dynamics, and ideological currents that have shaped perceptions of Shah Ismail in Iran.

Throughout history, civilizations have encountered the phenomenon of one culture dominating others, leading to a dynamic of cultural exchange where one culture becomes predominant. Seyyed Fakhreddin Shadman highlights the importance of navigating this exchange in a manner that preserves autonomy and identity, cautioning against merely reactive or politically and militarily driven responses. Engaging in this exchange requires thoughtful consideration, transcending mere translation or adoption of foreign works. Instead, it involves confronting entrenched historical patterns that shape our existence and have become ingrained in our cultural fabric. Thus, effectively managing cultural interactions necessitates a nuanced approach that encompasses both intellectual reflection and strategic foresight.

Seyyed Jamaluddin Asadabadi authored *Rebuttal to Materialism* in 1881, a significant work that remains relevant today. Over a century ago, Din and Danesh publishing house in Tabriz republished this book, underscoring its enduring importance. In the introduction, the publisher raised poignant questions about the pervasive influence of materialism, which has led many astray, particularly the youth. This situation prompts a crucial inquiry: Who can effectively counteract these ideological deviations? The publisher's note also highlighted the scarcity of paper at the time but emphasized the imperative of disseminating such critical texts, even at considerable cost, to reach a wide audience.

These reflections underscore a recurring theme in our cultural history: the imperative to defend our identity amidst evolving global currents. While European and American identities have undergone continual transformation, our own cultural landscape has often been marked by a reactionary stance.

Embracing the principle of development and acknowledging that change is inherent to our nature and existence, as proposed by Mulla Sadra five centuries ago, is essential for fostering meaningful cultural exchange. Rather than viewing development as an external imposition, we must recognize it as an intrinsic aspect of our being. By adopting a proactive approach to change and engaging in constructive dialogue, we can navigate cultural shifts and contribute to a richer, more dynamic global discourse.

Allameh Tabatabai introduced the concept of "edrakat-e etebari" in a concise seventy-page treatise, which Shahid Motahari later engaged with, expanding on Tabatabai's ideas in his comprehensive five-volume work titled *Principles of Philosophy and the Method of Realism* (Tabatabaei and Motahari, 1400). Motahari regarded Tabatabai's insights as novel theories deserving of greater attention, emphasizing their significance within philosophical discourse. However, Ali Asghar Mosleh suggests that Tabatabai's discussion of "edrakat-e etebari" has been overlooked, as both his audience and students, including Motahari himself, failed to grasp its depth and originality (Mosleh, 1400: 6). Despite this oversight, Tabatabai's exploration of "edrakat-e etebari" remains central to his philosophical contributions, focusing on how societies should navigate the changes and developments of the world.

"Edrakat-e etebari" delves into the question of whether societal developments are inherently negative or if their depth and value, as reflected in a culture's credentials, determine their significance. For instance, while the Amazon community may possess a succinct set of credentials, the American community's "etebariat" likely extends far beyond that. Etebariat symbolizes a civilization's cultural prowess, reflecting the collective achievements and values of its creators. The strength of a culture and civilization lies in the depth, breadth, and development of its "etebariat," enabling it to effectively engage in cultural exchange and withstand external influences. The degree to which non-Western societies may feel defeated in cultural exchanges with the West hinges on their level of intellectual sophistication, cultural credentials, and societal organization and institutional development.

From the late 19th century to the mid-20th century, the focus of anthropological discourse shifted from biogenetics and progeny to culture, particularly following the downfall of fascism and Nazism and the ascendancy of liberal capitalist ideologies. This transition led to a reevaluation of concepts like race, with differences in skin color being explained in terms of environmental factors rather than innate biological distinctions. Iranian texts produced during this period also reflected this shift, with increased attention given to the Iranian progeny from a genetic standpoint. Even interpretations of classical Persian literature, such as Ferdowsi's *Shahnameh*, and modern works like

Ali Shariati's *Recognition of Iranian Islamic Identity*, reflected this changing discourse. Shariati, for instance, attributes Iran's historical defeats to societal stagnation, citing examples from *Shahnameh* where fathers and sons engaged in fratricidal conflicts, leading to a loss of social mobility. He contrasts this with the early Islamic Arab society's social mobility, which he believes contributed to their victories over Iran.

These discussions underscore the enduring reality of cultural exchange throughout human history. However, the crux lies in how societies confront these changes and whether they possess coherent theories to guide them through linguistic, religious, and civilizational transformations. The absence of figures like Shah Ismail Safavi from religious and mystical studies cannot be fully understood without a theoretical framework. Thus, challenging Eurocentric interpretations of identity and analyzing Iran's historical identity transformations demand serious scrutiny. Perhaps revisiting discussions surrounding Shah Ismail could serve as a catalyst for this critical reevaluation and reconstruction of Iran's cultural and historical narrative.

# CHAPTER 9

# Truth in Shah Ismail Safavi's Thought

## 1    Introduction

In delving into the concept of truth as perceived by Shah Ismail Safavi, also known as Khatai, it is customary to situate his viewpoint within the context of his works and the broader intellectual tradition. For instance, just as the philosophical ideas expounded in Heidegger's "Being and Time" were cultivated within the rich soil of the German intellectual tradition before being disseminated and debated across various linguistic and cultural landscapes, so too did Shah Ismail Safavi's insights develop within their own historical and intellectual milieu.

In the non-Western sphere, a space has indeed emerged for engagement with Western philosophical currents. Many intellectuals, drawn to philosophical inquiry, have delved into the works of Heidegger, translating and studying them. In Iran, figures like Seyed Ahmad Fardid immersed themselves in Heidegger's writings, often encountering interpretations by scholars like Henry Carbone. These encounters sparked discussions among Iranian philosophers, professors, and thinkers, fostering networks and conceptual frameworks. Consequently, discussing truth from a Heideggerian perspective today does not startle audiences, as intellectual pathways have been paved.

Engaging with the ideas of Shah Ismail Safavi presents a unique challenge. His thoughts are not necessarily enigmatic; rather, the primary obstacle lies in the fact that his Diwan, composed in Turkish, has not been integrated into contemporary intellectual discourse for over five centuries. The task of presenting Shah Ismail's texts for scholarly discussion is complex, as each concept emerges from a dialectical interaction between the author and the audience, which in turn shapes a collective intellectual landscape. It is important to recognize that writers and thinkers do not operate in isolation; their works are directed toward specific societal contexts. However, the societal backdrop of Shah Ismail lacks a readily accessible mental framework, even among academics and thought leaders. This absence complicates efforts to analyze and interpret truth through his perspective.

In his exploration of the theoretical evolution of mysticism and Sufism in Iran, Seyyed Hossein Nasr extensively references contemporary thinkers like Ayatollah Javadi Amoli, Allameh Hassanzadeh Amoli, and Allameh Tabatabaei. However, spanning nearly a millennium in his studies, Shah Ismail Safavi remains conspicuously absent. Despite his significant contributions as a mystic, sage, theologian, and author within the Islamic and Iranian spheres, and his notable lineage tracing back to Sheikh Safi, Nasr's works do not include mention of Shah Ismail Safavi.

While Nasr acknowledges Sheikh Safiuddin Ardabili as a prominent mystic of Azerbaijan, the works and legacy of Shah Ismail Safavi remain largely overlooked within the academic community and among intellectual circles. Despite being a prolific writer and thinker, whose influence reverberated throughout the Islamic world and Iran, Shah Ismail Safavi's contributions have yet to find resonance within contemporary discourse.

To grasp the essence of truth through the lens of Shah Ismail, one must undertake a multifaceted exploration. First, it is essential to understand the prevailing perceptions and notions regarding Shah Ismail within the societal consciousness and linguistic discourse. Following this, these perceptions should be systematically categorized and analyzed, facilitating a process of deconstruction and reconstruction. This iterative approach enables the formulation of a novel understanding and representation of Shah Ismail. Engaging in this nuanced inquiry allows for the examination of various dimensions of the Khatai tradition and Shah Ismail's legacy. For instance, an exploration of the distinction between Shah Ismail, known as Khatai, and Shah Ismail, the founder of an influential Iranian ruling dynasty, emerges as a critical inquiry from this reconstructed perspective.

Although Shah Ismail Safavi and Shah Ismail Khatai refer to the same individual, there exists a considerable gap between these two identities. While the Iranian consciousness and language have some familiarity with Shah Ismail Safavi, recognizing him as the monarch and founder of the Safavid dynasty, Shah Ismail Khatai remains largely unknown. Adding to the challenge is the fact that Shah Ismail Safavi's texts are written in Turkish, a language that has undergone significant changes in Iran over the past century, as discussed in Jalal Al-Ahmed's theory on the marginalization of the Turkish language. Therefore, it is crucial to acknowledge the difficulty in engaging with Shah Ismail's texts and the concepts he introduced. In essence, diving into Shah Ismail's writings cannot occur abruptly, as the necessary conceptual infrastructure and implicit assumptions are not readily prepared for such an undertaking.

The life of Ismail Ibn Sultan Haydar Ibn Sheikh Junaid, known as Shah Ismail Khatai, spans from his birth on July 17, 1487, to his passing on May 23, 1524, marking nearly five centuries since his demise. He stands as the seminal figure in Safavid history, emerging during the reign of the Aq Qoyunlu. Understanding the context of Aq Qoyunlu, their territorial dominion, and their relationship with Shah Ismail Safavi is crucial. However, within the historiography of Iranian dynasties over the past century, there has been a selective focus on historical narratives. While the Samanid era resonates more strongly with the Iranian consciousness despite the temporal distance, the Aq Qoyunlu and Qara Qoyunlu periods, though temporally closer, remain distant in our collective memory.

The Aq Qoyunlu dynasty, which held sway over Iran, Iraq, Eastern Anatolia, modern Armenia, modern Azerbaijan Republic, and the South Caucasus from 1378 AD to 1508 AD, belonged to the Turkmen lineage. It is crucial to acknowledge that the term "Turkmen" in this context may differ significantly from its contemporary connotations. Historically, "Turkman" referred to a specific subgroup of the Oghuz Turks, as elucidated by prominent anthropologists such as Abu Rihan Biruni. These Oghuz Turks, who converted to Islam during the early period of its dissemination in Iran and the Eurasian regions, were identified as Turkmen. Consequently, it is important to avoid conflating the historical concept of "Turkmen" with the modern understanding of Turkmen identity in Iran.

The query may arise regarding the presence of non-Muslim Turks. Indeed, in regions like Central Europe near Moldavia, there exists the "Republic of Gagauzia," where Gagauz people, akin to Oghuz in Turkish and Moldavian languages, reside. While they hail from Turkic tribes and speak Turkish, their religious affiliation leans towards Christianity, particularly the Russian Orthodox Church. Hence, it is evident that not all Turks adhere to Islam; some follow Christianity.

Shah Ismail's birth in Ardabil during the reign of the Aq Qoyunlu dynasty links him intricately to this historical context, given that Uzun Hasan, Shah Ismail's maternal grandfather, held prominence within the Aq Qoyunlu realm. The prevailing languages within the Aq Qoyunlu territory were Turkish and Persian. However, Uzun Hasan's significant role in Iran's developmental history often receives less attention.

Furthermore, delving into the diplomatic ties between the Aq Qoyunlu and Safavid realms with European powers, particularly the Venetians, opens avenues for exploration. Safavid connections, including potential blood relations, with the Venetians, as well as their interactions with the Christian world, warrant thorough analysis. Notably, parallels and affinities between Safavid Shiites or Qizilbash and Catholic Christians, highlighted by scholars like Shariati and Motahari, add layers of intrigue to this historical inquiry.

Following in the footsteps of Seyedamaddin Nasimi, Ismail, known as Khatai, elevated Azerbaijani literature to global prominence. However, delving into Shah Ismail's literary corpus necessitates understanding its historical context. It is crucial to examine the role his works played in shaping Azerbaijani

Turkish and to identify predecessors and successors who embraced his literary style. Over the past five centuries since Shah Ismail Khatai's passing, has his mystical Divan been studied and interpreted? Has it remained a focal point for scholarly discourse amid the evolution of theoretical mysticism, diverse Sufi schools, and literary developments? Exploring these questions provides insight into the enduring legacy of Shah Ismail Khatai's literary and mystical contributions.

While Persian literature and scholarly texts show scant reference to the Diwan of Shah Ismail, it would be premature to conclude that his work has vanished from our intellectual history. Further investigation is warranted. Although mainstream intellectual and literary traditions within Iran may overlook the Diwan of Shah Ismail, it holds significant relevance within marginalized sects and religious movements that diverge from mainstream Shiism. Among these sects, including "The Followers of The Right Path," "Ali-Illahism," "Qizilbash," "Alawis," and "Bektashi," scattered references to Shah Ismail's Diwan abound. In some regions like Iran, Anatolia, the Balkans, Iraq, and the South Caucasus, Shah Ismail, known as Khatai, occupies a central and revered position within these religious communities. While these religions identify with Shiite principles, they diverge from the dominant Shiite movement. Thus, Shah Ismail's Diwan holds particular importance, almost akin to a sacred text, within these religious circles.

## 2    Truth in the View of Shah Ismail

The quest for truth stands as a cornerstone in the intellectual pursuits of philosophers, sages, mystics, and thinkers across ages. What constitutes truth? Is it a mere conceptual abstraction or does it transcend into a meta-conceptual realm? Shah Ismail, amidst his multifaceted identity as a monarch, mystic, and poet, undoubtedly grappled with such profound questions. Yet, unlike traditional philosophical or mystical discourses, his approach to truth might diverge, bearing the distinct imprint of his socio-political context and spiritual convictions.

In contemplating truth, Shah Ismail likely pondered its intimate relationship with humanity. Did he perceive truth as a force shaping the essence of individuals, and could resistance or indifference to it fundamentally alter one's nature? These existential inquiries, coupled with his role as a religious and political leader, might have prompted Shah Ismail to offer unique insights into the transformative power of truth upon the human soul.

Moreover, the methodological aspect of truth-seeking undoubtedly occupied Shah Ismail's reflections. While philosophers advocate empirical evidence and mystics extol intuition, Shah Ismail's approach might have been informed by a synthesis of practical wisdom, spiritual gnosis, and political exigencies. Thus, delving into Shah Ismail's conception of truth unveils not only philosophical musings but also a rich tapestry of socio-political and spiritual considerations, shaping his worldview and legacy.

Before addressing these questions, it is imperative to emphasize a critical aspect regarding the intricate formulation of Shah Ismail's text: its interpretation. Within popular Gnostic traditions, two prevailing approaches emerge: "sequential interpretation" and "thematic interpretation." Sequential interpretation, also referred to as "analytical interpretation" or "part-by-part interpretation" by scholars like Shahid al-Sadr, involves dissecting the text in its continuous composition. Here, the commentator scrutinizes each segment, such as a stanza or a verse, examining it meticulously word by word and sentence by sentence. In contrast, thematic interpretation adopts a broader perspective. In this method, the commentator gathers all verses or passages relating to a specific theme, treating them as a cohesive unit, and constructs interpretations based on this holistic understanding. These interpretive methodologies offer distinct lenses through which Shah Ismail's text can be analyzed and comprehended.

It is essential to recognize that the discourse surrounding interpretation, particularly within the human sciences over the past two centuries, has undergone significant transformations, especially in the last half-century. These changes have profoundly influenced how texts—ranging from the Quran to various mystical and governing writings—are approached within the Islamic world. For example, the relationship or dialectic between a text and its context, along with the numerous factors that shape this relationship in a polyglot environment, have emerged as critical areas of inquiry. Without addressing these complexities, discussions of interpretation remain inadequate. In light of this intricate landscape, how should we approach the text of Khatai?

"Khatai" served as the surname of Shah Ismail, derived from the Persian word meaning "sinner." Shah Ismail consistently portrayed himself as culpable and remorseful before the mercy and grace of God. In his poetry, he frequently laments his perceived shortcomings, particularly in relation to his obligations towards Ahl al-Bayt (the Family of the Prophet). In the closing verses of his poems, he expresses his sense of guilt, acknowledging his failure to fulfill his religious duties before God. This profound conviction of negligence towards the truth's grace weighs heavily on Shah Ismail's conscience.

The Diwan of Shah Ismail has historically received limited attention within Iran, resulting in a dearth of comprehensive interpretations. However, this lack of engagement does not indicate a complete abandonment of the work over the past five centuries. Rather, it has witnessed a resurgence of interest and reinterpretation within the Turkish literary tradition, as well as among various communities such as the Alevi, Bektashi, Qizilbash, and the Followers of the Right Path in Iran, Anatolia, and the Balkans. Despite its relative neglect within the Persian literary canon, the Diwan of Shah Ismail has undergone a revitalization, engaging a diverse array of communities and traditions across multiple regions over the centuries.

Currently, there is a pressing need for fundamental research to establish interpretive schools for Shah Ismail's text across a vast geographical expanse. It is imperative to delve into the theoretical underpinnings and frameworks of these interpretive traditions. What messages do they convey? What conceptual networks have they forged, and what are their predominant themes—mystical, Gnostic, Sufi, or folkloric? Such inquiries necessitate comprehensive research.

In this context, we will adopt an interpretive approach that considers each verse as possessing inherent meaning, independent of its connections to other verses. Each verse, akin to a standalone "house" of meaning, possesses its own message, themes, and concepts. While analyzing the entire Diwan and other works of Shah Ismail Khatai would yield comprehensive insights—especially concerning the concept of truth—our current approach involves interpreting individual verses or series of verses in isolation. This method allows for a nuanced exploration of each verse's inherent significance and its contribution to the broader thematic tapestry of Shah Ismail's writings.

Within the Diwan of Shah Ismail, a distinct section known as the "qoşma" or "couplet" stands out. This couplet form, typical in Turkish poetry, comprises five stanzas, occasionally extending beyond this count. Each stanza consists of four lines, each containing eleven syllables. Notably, the final line of each stanza rhymes with the concluding line of all subsequent stanzas. In the ultimate stanza, referred to as the "Mehrband," the poet includes his surname, marking a significant hallmark of this poetic tradition.

The poetic style characterized by couplets holds a significant place in literary tradition, renowned for its accessibility and versatility. This format enables direct engagement with the poet's inner world, fostering an intimate connection between creator and audience. Its blend of verbal and spiritual elements adds depth and resonance to the verses, appealing to a diverse range of sensibilities. Beyond mere written form, couplets often find expression through musical compositions and vocal performances, further enhancing their popularity among different segments of society. With themes ranging from love and mysticism to religious devotion and social commentary, couplets serve as a conduit for exploring complex emotions and philosophical concepts.

While some critics argue that this style is unique to Shah Ismail Safavi and lacks broader historical precedent, a closer examination reveals its enduring presence across centuries and cultures. Poets preceding and succeeding Shah Ismail Safavi, both within and beyond Iran, have embraced the couplet format in their works. Notable figures such as Molla Panah Vagif, Molla Vali Vidadi, Gasim bey Zakir, Nabati Qara Daghi, and A Sheikh Pari have contributed significantly to this poetic tradition. Moreover, influential Iranian poets like Shahriyar, celebrated for their national-level prominence, have further enriched this legacy with their compositions. Our study acknowledges the rich tapestry of couplet poetry, spanning diverse voices and perspectives, and seeks to explore its enduring relevance in contemporary literary discourse.

As noted earlier, our approach to understanding these verses, particularly when exploring Shah Ismail's perspective on the concept of "truth," involves examining individual verses or sets of verses rather than critiquing the Diwan as a whole. In couplet number 31 on page 478 of the poem, Shah Ismail expresses:

> Truth veiled, a mystery concealed,
> Seek its depths, if revelation's revealed.
> In disbelief, faith's kernel resides,
> Belief and doubt entwined, where truth abides.

Khatai's exploration of the cosmic relationship between disbelief and faith transcends cultural and religious boundaries, echoing universal themes found in various Gnostic traditions worldwide. Analogous to the complementary forces of yin and yang in Chinese philosophy, the interplay between disbelief and faith embodies a delicate balance crucial for the harmony of existence. This balance, when disrupted, unsettles not only individual beliefs but also societal and cosmic equilibrium. Khatai's perspective suggests that within disbelief lies the essence of faith, emphasizing the intertwined nature of these seemingly opposing concepts. This understanding forms a foundational aspect of Khatai's philosophy, shaping his interpretation of truth and the pursuit of spiritual connection. Next, Khatai continues his speech as follows:

> The gates of heaven swing wide, treasures untold,
> In a realm of precious stones, stories unfold.
> A path to Paradise, narrower than a hair's strand,
> Step forward if you dare, to the celestial land.

Our life finds its source in the kingdom divine, our bodies stemming from the pure root of Salman's lineage. The elixir we imbibe is crafted from the essence of milk, a sacred offering inviting those able to partake to step forth into its nourishing embrace. In the next verse, he concludes his speech as follows:

> Our essence akin to angels' grace,
> In Salman's frame our mortal place.
> Nourished by lion's blood, bold and pure,
> Step forth, if able, to partake, secure.

Our life, a gift from the kingdom, springs forth from celestial realms, while our earthly vessel finds its origin in the sacred lineage of Salman, imbued with purity. The sustenance we partake in, a beverage distilled from the essence of milk, offers nourishment to both body and soul. Should you possess the fortitude to partake in this divine elixir, step forth with courage and embrace its sanctified essence. In the next verse, he concludes his speech as follows:

> From my old man, counsel wise,
> From my teacher, lessons rise.
> Wings folded, poised in the sky,
> Step forth, if you can fly.

> In gardens and meadows, I bloom with grace,
> Nightingale's song in every space.
> A key to forty doors, mystical lore,
> Step forward, if a door you can explore.

This clause is the same clause in which the poet gives his last name in the couplet:

> I am Shah Khatai, akin to the month's light,
> Mountains veiled in mist, a mystical sight.
> Here lies the Bible, there the Quran,
> If you can choose, dare to understand.

In this verse, Shah Ismail, identifying himself as Shah Khatai, presents a profound choice symbolized by the presence of the Bible and the Quran. With the mist-covered mountains as a backdrop, he invites contemplation and decision-making. The juxtaposition of these sacred texts suggests a pivotal moment of personal and spiritual significance. By urging the listener to choose,

Shah Ismail underscores the importance of individual agency and the journey towards truth.

The poem examines the enigmatic nature of truth as perceived through Khatai's perspective. It posits that truth cannot be readily grasped or confined within the limitations of mere concepts; rather, it is intricately intertwined with existence itself, transcending the boundaries of human understanding. The ideas of faith and disbelief are closely linked to our comprehension of truth, profoundly influencing our spiritual journeys and actions. A central theme in this exploration is the concept of free will, which enables individuals to navigate toward truth—an elusive yet essential pursuit for the fulfillment of humanity.

Human existence, according to Shah Ismail's perspective, hinges on one's relationship, or lack thereof, with the truth, which manifests in multifaceted dimensions such as color, scent, and form. Unlike conventional notions, Shah Ismail contends that faith and disbelief are not merely products of superficial religious readings; they transcend mere conceptualization. He challenges the prevailing belief that one's interpretation holds absolute truth, noting that truth is elusive and hidden, requiring deep spiritual introspection and years of dedication to uncover. Despite the multitude of claimants asserting their possession of truth, Shah Ismail underscores that it is not readily attainable; rather, it necessitates profound existential contemplation and spiritual development. Truth should not be regarded as a mere possession to be wielded; instead, it represents a complex and profound entity that eludes simplistic notions of ownership.

Shah Ismail asserts the premise that truth is not an inaccessible enigma; rather, it is a concealed secret that awaits discovery through the exercise of one's free will and agency. He underscores the intrinsic connection between human existence and the truth, implying that every individual possesses the capability to attain it. However, like nourishment essential for life, accessing truth requires one to elevate themselves to a level capable of receiving it. This entails embodying qualities akin to a lion—courageous, ambitious, and resilient—unwavering in the face of truth's revelations. While scriptures like the Bible assert that "the truth will set you free," embracing truth entails forsaking comfort and security for the uncertainties of freedom. It necessitates forging a distinct path in interpersonal and societal realms, demanding deliberate choices and a steadfast commitment to living authentically.

In our cultural heritage, Al-Hurr ibn Yazid Al-Tamimi stands out as a vivid embodiment of this principle. He exemplifies how one, nourished by life's experiences, can swiftly align with truth, as demonstrated in his pivotal decision one fateful night. Shah Ismail eloquently articulates this existential bond between human existence and truth in couplet number 31 of his Diwan. Within this work, Shah Ismail synthesizes key themes from theoretical mysticism, Sufism, and the foundational principles of Islamic wisdom spanning centuries. His unique perspective encapsulates these themes, illustrating how truth, though shrouded in mystery, remains intricately woven into the fabric of our existence. For example, he says about love in couplet number 32:

> You appeared in our lives, unbidden,
> Welcome, dear, welcome.
> With love, you've filled our hearts, unhidden,
> Welcome, dear, welcome.
> Two souls entwined, our journey begun,
> Love's door opened wide, its warmth won.
> Grateful for this union, under the sun,
> Welcome, dear, welcome.

We were two souls, we joined each other or became one and found unity, when we found unity, then the door of affection and love was opened; That is, in order to reach love, affection and empathy—and in the language of sociology, solidarity—we need to bring our existential horizons closer together. Without love, the possibility of existential rapprochement and solidarity, or in Shah Ismail's own words, the unity of existence between God and man, the unity of existence between man and man, and solidarity in the macro-human society is impossible. In each of the key themes and concepts that have been studied during the last fourteen centuries and even more broadly during the history of mysticism and Hekmat or Gnosis and Gnostic traditions, Shah Ismail has a special look at them. And he has expressed an opinion that can be considered.

Shah Ismail's intellectual depth and spiritual inclination may seem unusual for a monarch, but they find resonance in the broader context of the era's poet-kings and philosopher-sage rulers. Across regions like Iran, the Ottoman Empire, India, and Central Asia, rulers such as Sultan Salim, Babur, and Shibak Khan were not merely political figures but also prolific writers. Babur, for instance, left behind a richly detailed book containing his poems and intellectual reflections on various subjects spanning politics, economy, and culture. Similarly, Akbar Shah of India distinguished himself as a philosopher-king, engaging with diverse religious and philosophical texts, shaping a syncretic religious ethos.

Shah Ismail's upbringing within the Safavid Sufi tradition profoundly influenced his worldview and intellectual pursuits. He descended from a lineage of Sufi elders, including his grandfather Junaid and father Haider, who were revered within the Safavid Tariqat. The convergence of the Safavid and Zahidiya Tariqats through his lineage provided him with a rich spiritual education. Born into this milieu, Shah Ismail received tutelage from various scholars in both the Safavid school and Gilan, nurturing a multifaceted personality that blended political leadership with spiritual insight.

While Shah Ismail's reign is often characterized by his political achievements and territorial expansion, his personal struggles and emotional turmoil are lesser-known aspects of his life. In his later years, he faced isolation and profound emotional distress when his wife was taken captive by the Ottomans and married off, causing him significant anguish. Despite these challenges, Shah Ismail's emotional depth and vulnerabilities reveal a human dimension behind the grandeur of his rule.

Interestingly, the absence of critical biographies on Shah Ismail in Iran raises questions about the historiographical treatment of his legacy. Legends surrounding his reign, such as the purported massacre of fourteen thousand people and his imposition of Shia Islam, persist but lack scholarly scrutiny. This absence of critical engagement leaves room for myth and legend to shape popular perceptions of Shah Ismail's reign, obscuring a more nuanced understanding of his rule and personality.

Outside Iran, particularly within mystical traditions like Bektashism, Alevism, and Qizilbashism, Shah Ismail is revered not merely as a king but as a spiritual guide or "vali." This transcendent reverence underscores the enduring impact of his spiritual teachings and legacy within these mystical communities. In these traditions, the title "Shah" carries connotations of spiritual leadership rather than mere political authority, emphasizing Shah Ismail's enduring significance as a sage and spiritual luminary.

In conclusion, Shah Ismail's life and legacy reflect the complex interplay between politics, spirituality, and intellectual inquiry in the early modern era. His intellectual depth, spiritual inclinations, and personal struggles enrich our understanding of his reign beyond conventional historical narratives. By exploring these dimensions, we can appreciate Shah Ismail not only as a formidable ruler but also as a complex human figure shaped by his cultural, religious, and emotional experiences.

# CHAPTER 10

# Mohabat in the Gnostic Legacy of Shah Ismail

## 1    Introduction

In this chapter, we delve into the theme of "Mohabat" in the writings of Shah Ismail, also known as Khatai. As discussed in previous chapters, a fundamental question emerges: Why is it significant to analyze the concept of "Mohabat" within the works of Shah Ismail? This inquiry highlights a notable phenomenon: the texts authored by Shah Ismail, who is esteemed as both a mystic and a sage, have, over the past five centuries, mysteriously diminished in prominence within historical discourse. The Diwan of Shah Ismail appears to have become a concealed enigma, seldom discussed or acknowledged within contemporary discourse.

A prominent example of scholarly inquiry into Persian Sufism is the book titled *Sufism of the Safavid Era and its Literature*, authored by Seyed Jalal Mousavi, a faculty member at Payam Noor University. Published in 2016 by Amir Kabir Press, this work primarily investigates Sufism during the Safavid period. It aims to trace the historical origins of Sufism and mysticism (Irfan) within Safavid Iran, delving into the lineage of these phenomena that extends back to the era of the Ilkhans and even earlier.

The author of this book embarked on a thorough examination of Sufi developments predating the Safavid era, spanning from the Mongol period to the establishment of Safavid rule. Subsequently, the author explored the Timurid epoch before delving into theoretical discussions. Among these discussions, the author scrutinized the factors that led to a notable convergence, particularly evident with Sheikh Heydar Amoli, a prominent mystic and Sufi figure within Shiism. This convergence between Shiism and Sufism culminated in a synthesis termed "the nexus of Sufism and Shiism." Throughout the Safavid era, this connection fostered the emergence of a distinctive brand of Sufism that resonated strongly with the Shiite faith and community.

At the cultural and social level, the author explores the lineage of the Sunnah and the Safavid Tariqat. This lineage includes notable figures such as Sheikh Safiuddin Ardabili, Sheikh Sadruddin Musa, Khwaja Ali, Khwaja Ibrahim, Junaid, Haider, and Sultan Ali (Mousavi, 2016). Furthermore, the author conducts an analysis of Sufi developments during the Safavid era, highlighting the convergence between the Nematollahi Tariqat and the Safavid Tariqat. The text also identifies significant individuals associated with this tradition (Mousavi, 2016: 75). Additionally, the author addresses the Nematollahi Tariqat's rebellion against the Safavids and elucidates the distinctions between the leaders of the Safavid Tariqat and those of the Nematollahi Tariqat (Mousavi, 2016: 80).

An intriguing aspect of this book, pertinent to our current focus, is the notable absence of Shah Ismail's significance within its pages. The author primarily addresses a facet of Shah Ismail's persona that historians often highlight: his ascent to power as a monarch. Within the section titled "Shah Ismail and harshness against opponents," the author portrays Shah Ismail as a ruler wielding power and the sword. His ambition is depicted as tinged with zealotry, leading to a disposition characterized by severity (Mousavi, 2016: 85).

This book exemplifies a broader trend within Iranian research methodologies, wherein Shah Ismail Khatai—also known simply as Shah Ismail—is conspicuously absent, despite his significant roles as a Pir, Murshid in the Safavid Tariqat, and a mystic of the Qalam. Throughout its 378 pages, there exists a notable silence regarding Shah Ismail's contributions as a sage within the Shia tradition, including his writings, poetry, and the ownership of his Diwan. This omission is not unique to Seyed Jalal Mousavi's work; rather, it reflects a prevailing pattern within Iranian scholarship.

Addressing this dominant discourse requires more than just sporadic interviews or academic gatherings; it demands fundamental revisions. Establishing a research center dedicated to Shah Ismail Khatai and organizing scholarly meetings centered around his texts could potentially reshape the cultural atmosphere in the country. Through such initiatives, there is a prospect of gradually revitalizing Shah Ismail's Diwan and rekindling interest in this tradition within the academic and theoretical realms of Iran.

## 2     Mohabat in the Gnostic Tradition and Theoretical Irfan

Before examining Shah Ismail's perspective on "Mohabat" and how he theoretically formulated and articulated it, it is essential to understand the foundational significance of Mohabat within the gnostic tradition, theoretical Irfan, and various Sufi "Tariqats". Investigating the role of Mohabat in these traditions provides critical context for comprehending its function as a governing principle in Irfan, particularly from Shah Ismail's viewpoint.

In the broader gnostic tradition and theoretical Irfan, as well as across different Sufi Tariqats, "Mohabat" holds a central position. It is revered as a fundamental concept that encompasses profound love, devotion, and spiritual connection, both towards the Divine and among individuals within the mystical journey. Various scholars and Sufi masters have expounded upon the significance of Mohabat, emphasizing its transformative power in shaping both the individual and society.

Before delving into Shah Ismail's exploration of Mohabat as a governing category in Irfan, it is important to recognize that his Diwan may not explicitly emphasize the significance of "Mohabat" in the formation of societal and individual identities. Instead, he was situated within the broader gnostic tradition and theoretical landscape of the Islamic world, where key themes of Irfan had been extensively discussed and developed over centuries. Thus, offering an introductory overview of Mohabat within these traditions establishes a foundation for a more profound understanding of its conceptualization in Shah Ismail's perspective.

As one of the esteemed sages of his time, Shah Ismail expressed his thoughts predominantly in the Turkish language. Disregarding this aspect of his tradition would lead to a flawed understanding, portraying him as an isolated figure who suddenly emerged and composed poems in the language of the "desert peoples" associated with the Mongol invasions, only to vanish thereafter. Such oversights perpetuate misconceptions regarding Shah Ismail, Shiism, and the Turkish language in Iran, often arising from ideological biases rather than from rigorous historical inquiry.

Throughout Iran's history, particularly during periods marked by ideological fervor such as the era of archaic nationalism, misconceptions regarding Shah Ismail's use of the Turkish language and its relationship with Islam in Iran have proliferated. Even following significant events like the martyrdom of Amir Kabir and into the early Pahlavi period, thinkers like Arif Qazvini, Mahmoud Afshar, and Ibrahim Pourdawood propagated an anti-historical narrative regarding the Turkish language and its role within Iranian Islam. Unfortunately, these narratives continue to linger in the collective consciousness, shaping perceptions despite lacking historical validity.

The subject of "Mohabat" has taken a high place in religious and Irfan literature; In addition to the special position of Irfan, this category is also one of the important pillars of moral concepts in religions. There is a difference of opinion in the definition of "Mohabat" among scholars, ethicists, and mystics, and these differences are to such an extent that some believe that "Mohabat" is the language of the present and not the future. Mystics and sages, inspired by Quranic and religious teachings and narratives, discussed the subject of Mohabat in their works and spoke about its meaning and effects. A scholar like Faiz Kashani, as an interpreter, researcher and sage, has given special attention to the subject of "Mohabat" in his works, influenced by the thoughts of some mystics and philosophers such as Ghazali, Ibn Arabi and Mulla Sadra.

The relationship between "Mohabat" and "knowledge" stands as a pivotal aspect in the discourse surrounding spirituality, particularly within the realm of Irfan. This connection holds significant importance for sages and practitioners, drawing inspiration from Gnostic teachings and profound Islamic traditions such as the hadiths of "A Hidden Treasure" and "Arova Navader." Influenced by the wisdom of mystics and sages, Irfan emphasizes the intertwined nature of Mohabat and knowledge, recognizing their mutual reinforcement in spiritual growth and understanding. Al-Sharif al-Jurjani further explores this profound relationship in his "Treatise on Existence," shedding light on how Mohabat serves as both a conduit and culmination of knowledge, guiding seekers along the path to deeper spiritual insight and enlightenment. He says:

> The Muhvahedah Sufi sect posits that beyond the realm of rationality lies a stage where truths are unveiled through direct observation and revelation, surpassing the limitations of mere intellectual comprehension. While some have mistakenly perceived a conflict between these two modes of understanding, the essence of their argument is that certain truths transcend the capacity of the intellect to grasp independently, yet they can be apprehended through the method of experiential discovery.
>
> JORJANI, 1402: 321

Ibn Turka elaborates on the notion that certain truths or monotheistic teachings transcend the grasp of reason; however, this does not imply that reason is entirely incapable of comprehending them. Rather, it suggests that the intellect alone may be insufficient for their understanding. Instead, such truths must be discerned through enhanced perceptual faculties, often referred to as the power of the heart (Ibn Turka, 2022: 384).

In the realm of Irfan and the broader Gnostic tradition, the discourse surrounding "Mohabat," "mavaddat," or "love" holds profound significance. While the Quran and hadiths utilize the terms "Mohabat" and "mavaddat," only the latter is specifically mentioned in hadiths. Within Sufism, distinctions have been drawn between these terms, with some asserting that "mavaddat" represents the lowest level of love, while "love" signifies the highest echelon. Sages and mystics contend that the essence of morality and Irfan is encapsulated in the "mavaddat" of God, viewing all moral virtues as either prerequisites for or outcomes of this divine love.

For instance, adhering to commandments such as refraining from gossip or lying can lay the foundation for the Mohabat of God, while engaging in acts like nighttime prayers can serve as both a manifestation of and a pathway to experiencing God's mavaddat. However, some hold the belief that love can only exist between entities of the same type and gender, suggesting that Mohabat arises from disparity. Contrary to this notion, the Gnostic Tradition posits a different perspective, emphasizing the multidimensional nature of human existence. As humans possess both a physical body and a soul, the soul, being singular and infused with the divine spirit, is capable of harmonizing with and loving the transcendent God. Therefore, the notion that the materiality of humans and the singularity of God preclude the possibility of love between them is challenged within the Gnostic Tradition, where mystics and sages offer theoretical elaborations that diverge from this viewpoint. As mentioned previously, the lowest level of this affection is termed "Mohabat". Here it is necessary to mention a few issues, which are: a) definition of Mohabat; b) the origin of Mohabat; c) means of strengthening Mohabat; and d) obstacles to Mohabat.

a)  **Definition of Mohabat:** Mohabat is perceived as the natural inclination towards pleasure inherent in human nature; hence, without comprehension, one cannot experience true love. An important aspect to consider here is the correlation between "understanding" and "Mohabat." Within the framework of the Gnostic Tradition and Irfan, three stages of understanding are delineated: sensory, imaginative, and intellectual. Correspondingly, one's level of understanding determines the depth and nature of their love. If one's understanding is limited to sensory perception, their love remains confined to material matters. Conversely, if understanding transcends to the realm of imagination, love likewise operates on the level of fantasies. Moreover, for those whose understanding reaches the intellectual level, their love takes on a more nuanced and complex nature. Ultimately, the extent and quality of an individual's pleasure and love are contingent upon their level of understanding and the depth thereof.

b)  **The Origin of Mohabat:** According to a narration attributed to Imam Ali (a), "Al-Insan Ubaid Al-Ahsan" (Tamimi Amadi, 2015: 69). While many interpret this phrase as "man is a slave of kindness," the phrasing of the hadith suggests that man is captivated and drawn to benevolence. Therefore, it can be inferred that the term "slave" could be replaced with "servant." In essence, when someone extends kindness to another, the recipient may naturally develop affection towards the benefactor, whether intentionally or not.

c)  **Means of Strengthening Mohabat:** Contemplation, reflection, and a sincere desire to perform good deeds are integral methods for fortifying Mohabat.

d)  **Obstacles to Mohabat:** The primary obstacle to Mohabat is opposition and defiance. When an individual acts contrary to the will of the beloved, their Mohabat towards the beloved diminishes.

Mystics and sages critique the varying degrees of Mohabat, asserting that it can exhibit both intensity and weakness, displaying degrees of affection. This understanding is often derived through introspection and conscience. Just as humans do not hold equal regard for all colors or individuals, Mohabat is perceived to fluctuate in its intensity. This notion finds resonance within the Gnostic Tradition and Irfan, with reference made to verse 165 of Surah Al-Baqarah, which speaks of loving others as if loving Allah (Al-Baqarah: 165). However, sages, mystics, and Sufi scholars diverge in their interpretations regarding the precise number of degrees of Mohabat.

It is evident that Mohabat did not emerge suddenly in Shah Ismail's discourse; rather, its discussion within the traditions of Irfan and Sufism, as well as among sages, boasts a profound and extensive history. When Shah Ismail speaks of Mohabat, he attributes it to the esoteric realm of human nature, emphasizing that without Mohabat and the attainment of a certain level of consciousness, awareness, and love, one cannot grasp the truth. This concept did not materialize abruptly in Shah Ismail's teachings; instead, it has undergone a historical evolution. In referencing the traditions of Irfan and the Safavid Tariqat, scholars such as Seyyed Jalal Mousavi highlight figures like Sheikh Safiuddin Ardabili, Seyyed Haider, and Seyyed Junid. However, Shah Ismail is predominantly portrayed as a Pir of the Tariqat, a mystic, and a sage, with insufficient emphasis placed on his theological contributions within the Safavid tradition. (Mousavi, 2016).

3      **Mohabat in the Thought of Shah Ismail Khatai**

Shah Ismail delves into the discourse of "Mohabat" in verse number 14 of the couplet section within his Diwan. These verses, spanning approximately 60 pages, hold a significant place in his poetic oeuvre. The specific poem concerning Mohabat within the couplet section carries a profound depth and resonance. It is worth noting that these poems are often enhanced when accompanied by music, as the fusion of poetry and melody creates a spiritually enriching atmosphere, heightening the emotional and intellectual impact of Shah Ismail's poetic expressions. He says:

Kindness echoed within Esoteric's embrace,
Who forsakes Mohabat, truth cannot trace.
Denying the hungry, withholding the bread,
Mohabat's path, from truth, they are led.
God's creation, through Mohabat's light,
Yet tolerates souls shunning love's might.
The breath of life, belief in one's heart,
Sacrifice given, never to part.
Cursed be the faithless, who falter and stray,
Mohabat abandoned, truth fades away.
Hazrat Muhammad, by love's essence born,
Hazrat Ali's guardianship, in one word sworn.
Intercession upheld, by twelve revered names,
To forsake Mohabat, truth's essence maims.
Four chapters, forty stations, a path divine,
Seventy-two levels, in Mohabat's shrine.
For believers and Muslims, advice holds sway,
Mohabat's path, from truth don't stray.
Without Mohabat, truth's light fades away,
No bond with truth, for those who betray.
O friend, heed this breath, Khatai's decree,
Through Mohabat's path, truth's light we see.

This poem delves deep into the essence of love. Shah Ismail articulates that through an esoteric revelation, he was made aware that one who disregards love inevitably forsakes truth. In essence, Shah Ismail's discourse on the interplay between truth and love suggests that without love, human existence remains stagnant. Love shapes individuals towards truth; it serves as the catalyst for the divine connection between humanity and God. Lack of love necessitates tolerance from those unaffected, for without it, relationships wither. In relationships devoid of love, if the parties are not contentious, they merely endure, anticipating their eventual dissolution, each veering onto separate paths.

Truth, often synonymous with the divine, serves as a focal point across philosophical traditions. Analytical philosophy dissects truth as a categorical concept, dependent on the alignment between mental representations and external reality. However, in mystical traditions like Irfan, truth transcends mere correspondence, intertwining with the essence of existence itself, particularly with the divine. Islamic philosophical schools such as existentialism, Hekmat, and Gnosis offer diverse perspectives on truth. Existentialism emphasizes subjective experience and individual authenticity, while Hekmat seeks harmony between reason and revelation. Gnosis delves into esoteric truths through spiritual intuition. These traditions expand the notion of truth beyond cognitive parameters, incorporating metaphysical, existential, and spiritual dimensions into its exploration.

Shah Ismail delves into the intricate relationship between goodness, human nature, and the profound concept of "Mohabat" or love. According to his perspective, the essence of religion, including the roles of prophets and messengers, stems from love. In Shah Ismail's view, the connection between humanity and these divine figures is rooted in love. He asserts that all authority was bestowed upon Imam Ali (a), and the lineage of the twelve Imams is founded upon the principle of "Intercession," which is essentially an expression of love.

Shah Ismail emphasizes that those who neglect love, fail to embody it, or obstruct its path are unquestionably misguided. Thus, he establishes a criterion linking love with truth. The greater one's affinity for love, the closer they align with the path of righteousness. This connection underscores the profound importance of love in human existence, transcending mere public discourse.

While Shah Ismail's discourse primarily emphasizes individual existence rather than societal matters, it is essential to recognize that his perspective does not negate the pursuit of justice in the public sphere. An individual seeking their rightful due may not necessarily embody love in that particular act; however, this does not render them unloving or ignorant in a broader sense, according to Shah Ismail's understanding.

According to Shah Ismail, "Mohabat" or love stands as a crucial pillar in the journey of existential transcendence. He elucidates on the framework of love and its fundamental role in the creation of existence and humanity. Shah Ismail extends this concept into the realm of Gnostic Tradition, asserting that even the esteemed figure of Prophet Muhammad (peace be upon him) is an embodiment of love. For Shah Ismail, love forms the bedrock of religion, intercession, guardianship, and the institution of Imamate. He contends that anyone disconnected from love in their pursuit of truth and righteousness cannot be considered truly aligned with the path of faith.

Shah Ismail elevates love to the highest echelon of existence, viewing it as the conduit through which the essence of being manifests. He questions with astonishment: How can one establish a genuine relationship with truth without love? He addresses believers and Muslims, emphasizing their identity as people of compassion and guidance. Shah Ismail iterates that to forsake love is to forsake truth itself.

Throughout his works, Shah Ismail consistently highlights the intimate connection between love and truth. He posits that those who tread the path of righteousness are invariably infused with love, and vice versa. In essence, Shah Ismail's philosophy revolves around the inseparable bond between love and truth, a theme that permeates his writings and poetry.

When grappling with existential matters, the human mind often inclines towards compartmentalization, seeking to dissect and isolate various aspects. However, the fabric of existence itself is concrete, characterized by a dialectical interplay between its components. Take, for instance, the age-old debate of whether thought precedes action or vice versa. Similarly, questions arise regarding whether action reflects character or character molds action. Yet, the reality is that thought influences action just as action shapes thought, engendering a dynamic dialectic between the two. Some philosophers even posit that thought itself can be considered a form of action, further blurring the distinction between the two realms.

Mohabat and truth share a symbiotic relationship—they are not diametrically opposed but intricately connected. It is not a matter of one being positive and the other negative; instead, they complement each other. Just as a fruit cannot simultaneously be sweet and bitter, a person who embodies knowledge inevitably harbors love and compassion. In the realms of Irfan and Sufism, the pursuit of "arresting" people is a central theme, signifying the seeker's quest for spiritual enlightenment. When Shah Ismail delves into Mohabat, he presupposes that those contemplating love are on a spiritual journey, while seekers are engaged in the pursuit of enlightenment.

However, a pertinent question arises: How do seekers ascertain their attainment of truth? The answer lies in the paradigm through which we perceive reality. Shah Ismail's worldview is not rooted in analytical philosophy; rather, it aligns with the tenets of theoretical Irfan and Sufism. While analytical philosophy may not serve as Shah Ismail's framework, there is no inherent contradiction between Irfan, Hekmat, and Gnosis. Instead, these traditions converge on the concept of Mohabat, underscoring its significance across various spiritual traditions.

The distinction between the traditions of Irfan and Sufism is often drawn, with Sufis or dervishes perceived as the practical manifestation of theoretical Irfan. However, when discussing the theoretical framework of figures like Ibn Arabi within the tradition of Irfan, it does not imply a negation of Hekmat or Gnosis in their intellectual systems. The Gnostic Tradition encompasses various perspectives, with each Pir (spiritual guide) or Murshid (teacher) offering unique insights specific to their Tariqat (spiritual path).

When Shah Ismail speaks of Mohabat and its correlation with knowledge, he illustrates a dynamic where Esoteric wisdom flourishes when nurtured by the waters of love. Here, Mohabat transcends mere theory; it embodies a practical dimension. When one encounters another being—whether human, nature, or even animals in the Bektashi tradition—they engage in Mohabat, entering the realm of practical application.

Mohabat extends beyond favoring those who align with our beliefs and resenting those who oppose us. True Mohabat, according to Shah Ismail, resembles the sun, radiating its warmth indiscriminately upon all, regardless of differences. It is the very essence of human existence, and one devoid of Mohabat, in Khatai's interpretation, remains disconnected from truth.

The term "Gnostic Tradition" encompasses a multifaceted spiritual lineage that extends beyond conventional religious frameworks. When Shah Ismail regards Muhammad (PBUH) as the product of Mohabat, he alludes to a dimension beyond the confines of organized religion. This perspective does not necessarily imply that Mohabat is superior to religion; rather, it suggests that religion itself is a manifestation and outcome of Mohabat. In this light, Mohabat serves as the foundational force that underpins religious experience and expression.

Addressing the first question, the Gnostic Tradition is not positioned in opposition to the Hellenic tradition. It incorporates elements of proof and taste, with the latter holding a distinct significance within its framework. However, these nuances find no place within the Hellenic tradition or analytical philosophy. The Gnostic Tradition embraces a holistic approach to spirituality, integrating experiential insights alongside rational inquiry, thereby transcending conventional philosophical paradigms.

In response to the second question, Shah Ismail's texts do not draw sharp distinctions between what lies within and outside the realm of religion. Rather, they emphasize the interconnectedness of spiritual concepts both within and beyond religious frameworks. Mystics and sages often discuss the duality of human nature—man as a being with both inherent spiritual essence and rational faculties. It is observed that many individuals neglect their primordial connection and fail to achieve the self-awareness essential for comprehending the truth. In such instances, divine intervention is often manifest, typically through the Exoteric Messenger, who serves to guide them back to their inherent nature and facilitate their spiritual journey toward truth.

The assertion that Muhammad (peace be upon him) is the product of Mohabat, leading to the existence of another principle beyond him, may appear somewhat ambiguous. However, within the framework of Gnosticism, the intellect of the Esoteric Messenger and the prophets serve as the visible conduits for divine guidance. In the eyes of mystics and sages, the Esoteric realm holds precedence over the Exoteric, as it embodies hidden truths and deeper realities. The phenomena of the Exoteric realm strive to mirror the noumenal or concealed Esoteric truths. Each phenomenon harbors layers of interpretation, seeking to unveil deeper meanings.

This perspective aligns with a hadith of the Prophet (peace be upon him) that asserts: "Every appearance has an Esoteric, and every Esoteric has seventy esoterics." This implies that existence is not merely a superficial and finite discourse but rather a complex and multifaceted phenomenon, containing layers upon layers of hidden truths waiting to be uncovered.

Shah Ismail's assertion that Muhammad (peace be upon him) is the embodiment of Mohabat implies that God's selection of messengers is rooted in divine love for His servants and creation. This love-driven relationship between God and humanity is a central tenet in mysticism, where the essence of existence is perceived as Mohabat. According to this perspective, prophets like Muhammad, Jesus, and Moses are sent by God as manifestations of His boundless love, serving to guide and uplift humanity.

In Gnostic thought, the role of saints extends beyond traditional prophets and imams. During tumultuous times, individuals recognized as saints of God may emerge to offer guidance and support to His servants. The Quranic narrative of encounters between prophets like Musa and righteous servants underscores the depth of insight possessed by these individuals, who may not be prophets themselves but are deeply attuned to the divine wisdom. This view emphasizes the primacy of Mohabat in the divine-human relationship, highlighting the profound love that underpins God's interaction with His creation. Shah Ismail says in poem number 13:

> I immersed myself in the bustling city, delving into its depths.
> How beautiful it is to encounter Mohabat,
> My focus unwavering, fixated on one singular pursuit.
> How beautiful it is to encounter Mohabat.

Embarking on a spiritual journey within the realm of my existence, I encountered Mohabat and Safa. In the intricate tapestry of human existence, the foundational concept is none other than Mohabat. Upon dissecting the intricacies of human life, one finds that Mohabat permeates every aspect of existence, from life itself to movement, being, and even non-being.

Now, one might wonder about the relevance of these discussions to our current situation in Iran. It must be noted that these topics hold significant relevance to our present circumstances. In times of turmoil, such as during World War II when Europe was ravaged by chaos and violence, existentialist philosopher Karl Jaspers penned a succinct, yet profound work titled *What Is Europe?*. Jaspers' endeavor in this book was to explore avenues towards realizing unity amidst the fragmentation and discord plaguing Europe. In the midst of bombings, massacres, and widespread brutality, Jaspers sought to foster solidarity among Europeans, recognizing the urgent need for unity to avert further decline and destruction.

The fundamental question arises: Can society truly coalesce without giving due attention to the foundational components of Mohabat, which in sociological terms is known as social solidarity? Discussions often revolve around the structuring of institutions and organizations to foster social cohesion, but before delving into such matters, we must address an existential concern: Do we genuinely desire to coexist as a collective?

As a community of individuals sharing a common space, the quest for happiness and the aspiration for a just society propel us forward. Can we navigate from our current reality towards an ideal society, leveraging both rationality and compassion, guided by the harmonies of the heart?

Viewing Shah Ismail's discourse through the lens that human existence is essentially Mohabat, we confront the question: Can human society exist devoid of Mohabat, the binding force that unites hearts? What is it that transforms the sum of individual "I"s into a collective "us"? Can a cohesive "we" emerge without social solidarity and the essence of Mohabat?

Shah Ismail's contemplation centers on the individual and their relationship with existence, where the ultimate meaning is found in the divine essence of "Allah" or "God." Through his lens, existence is inseparable from Mohabat. Can social existence truly be anything other than Mohabat, the force that binds hearts and forms the essence of collective unity?

Sufism delineates the spiritual journey into distinct stages: Sharia, Tariqat, and Truth, each contributing to the seeker's progression towards enlightenment. Sharia encompasses the principles and passions bestowed by God to guide individuals towards perfection. It represents the foundational framework for worship and righteous conduct, initiating the seeker onto the path of spiritual growth. Tariqat, on the other hand, involves selecting the most optimal and steadfast path and diligently following it. It signifies the commitment to embodying divine commandments and principles in daily life, moving beyond mere adherence to rituals towards genuine spiritual realization.

At the pinnacle of the journey lies Truth, the ultimate realization of existence attained through profound introspection and intuitive insight. It transcends conventional understanding, offering seekers a profound connection with the divine essence. The attainment of Truth is the culmination of the seeker's spiritual odyssey, marking the culmination of their quest for enlightenment. Throughout this journey, the seeker traverses these stages concurrently, with each phase complementing and reinforcing the others, rather than progressing linearly from one to the next.

The seeker embarks on this path propelled by love—a driving force that propels them forward through the spiritual realms. Love serves as the initial impetus, igniting the seeker's journey and guiding them through the stages of spiritual evolution. As the seeker progresses, their love deepens, propelling them from one stage to the next until they are consumed by the intense flames of divine passion. It is through this profound love that the seeker is drawn closer to the divine presence, ultimately leading to the annihilation of their ego and the realization of divine unity.

In the final stage of Fana, the seeker experiences the dissolution of the self, surrendering completely to the divine will. This state of annihilation marks the culmination of the seeker's journey, as they transcend their individual existence and merge into the eternal essence of God. In this state of Baqaa, the seeker's consciousness is united with the divine, experiencing the eternal bliss of divine union. Thus, the journey of the seeker concludes not with the mention of love, lover, and beloved, but with the transcendence of individual identity and the realization of divine oneness. Here, it may be interesting to refer to a phrase from Seyyed Hyder Amoli's words, which describes these words:

> According to mystics, knowledge is fundamentally intuitive, leading to variations in interpretation among them. These discrepancies stem from differences in comprehension, spiritual attainment, innate abilities, and the interpretation of evidence. Consequently, the count of knowledge bearers remains elusive, mirroring the unquantifiable nature of knowledge itself. However, a broad categorization reveals three levels of knowledge: Sharia, Tariqat, and Truth. Notably, when knowledge is grounded in the credibility of its seeker, it transcends into Islam, faith, and belief.
>
> AMOLI, 1368: 23

Mustafa Malekian argues that rationality and obedience are inherently incompatible, asserting that worship contradicts reason. However, Shahid Motahari offers a nuanced definition of worship, emphasizing the concepts of "Abd and Taabbud" and their historical lineage. Motahari posits that worship entails engaging with truths beyond individual comprehension, rather than blindly obeying an unassailable truth. In this context, worship involves traversing a unique path towards truth, a journey that demands both intellectual and emotional engagement. Motahari suggests that worship is a multifaceted process that provides the intellect with diverse elements to explore and discover its own path.

Contrary to contemporary perceptions, pre-modern reason did not inherently oppose worship. Instead, it was the form of reason characterized by subjectivism or self-centeredness that stood in opposition to worship. Motahari proposes that subjectivism represents just one manifestation of rationality, prompting consideration of alternative conceptualizations of reason. By reframing reason beyond subjectivism, it becomes conceivable to reconcile rationality with worship. Thus, the apparent conflict between rationality and worship in contemporary discourse may stem from a narrow understanding of reason, rather than an intrinsic opposition between the two concepts.

Shahid Motahari highlights that diverse facet of human existence present varying demands and pathways. In his work on Irfan, Motahari suggests that within the concept of "Allah," there lies a perception of existence, yet humans often fixate on worldly attachments. Although the term "love" may not be explicitly mentioned in the Quran, its essence permeates its teachings. Motahari emphasizes that relying solely on the Quran for understanding religious concepts is insufficient. In Shiite literature, both the hadiths of the imams and the Prophet are regarded with equal importance to the Quran, extending the scope of Quranic comprehension beyond its revelation period. A system known as "ilm ar-rijāl and ilm aldraya" discerns between authentic and fabricated hadiths, illustrating the expanded significance of religious sources beyond conventional understanding, as discussed in the book *Beyond Secular Knowledge and Religious Knowledge.*

# CHAPTER 11

# Sojourn in the Gnostic Legacy of Shah Ismail

## 1    Introduction

Human beings possess a unique capacity for spiritual sojourn, setting them apart from other forms of life on Earth. While some philosophers historically defined humans as "talking animals," emphasizing linguistic abilities, a deeper ontological perspective suggests that humans excel in transcending themselves through inner exploration. Unlike other beings limited to physical existence, humans harbor rich inner worlds, providing a gateway to spiritual journeys. This inner journey, central to Irfan, Sufism, and Gnostic traditions, allows individuals to move beyond surface-level realities and tap into deeper dimensions of existence.

Central to this spiritual Sojourn is the concept of Tariqat, where individuals embark on a path of self-discovery and transcendence. Within Islamic teachings, extensive texts have explored the intricacies of traversing the Tariqat Valley, with over three thousand texts dedicated to guiding individuals through this transformative process. Stepping into the realm of Tariqat signifies more than mere self-awareness; it is a profound realization of one's existential status and position, extending beyond social and geographical boundaries to encompass ontological understanding. Through Tariqat, individuals gain insights into their inner selves and embark on a journey towards spiritual enlightenment.

The Sojourn through Tariqat unfolds in stages, each representing a deeper level of self-awareness and spiritual evolution. Salik, or the seeker, navigates through these stages, gradually transcending worldly concerns and delving into the depths of their inner being. This journey is not merely intellectual or theoretical; it is a deeply personal exploration that requires dedication, introspection, and spiritual discipline. As the seeker progresses, they move beyond the confines of external reality and enter into a realm of spiritual enlightenment and self-realization.

Ultimately, the concept of spiritual sojourn underscores the profound depth of human existence and the limitless potential for inner exploration. Through the path of Tariqat, individuals awaken to the true essence of their being, transcending the boundaries of the physical world to connect with the divine. This journey towards self-discovery and spiritual enlightenment is a testament to the unique capabilities of human beings to explore the depths of their inner worlds and embark on a transformative quest for truth and understanding.

In the diverse landscape of Gnostic tradition, Irfan, and Sufism, mystics and Piran Tariqat have articulated profound insights into various conceptual realms, formulating intricate semantic systems. Shah Ismail, within his Diwan, delves into these realms, expressing them poetically and offering conceptual formulations. One such exploration is found in poem number 33 on page 480 of *Diwan Khatai*, where Shah Ismail addresses the theme of the "sign of sojourn" through the lens of poetic couplets. This poem, nestled among a collection of verses, serves as a focal point for examining Shah Ismail's perspective on the concept of spiritual sojourn.

## 2      Sojourn in the Traditions of Irfan and Sufism

The Sojourn badge, according to Shah Ismail, symbolizes the distinctive essence of a dervish within the mystical tradition. While Shah Ismail, as a revered Pir and Murshid within the Safavid Tariqat, undoubtedly provided his own definition of Spiritual Sojourn, exploring its broader understanding in the traditions of Irfan and Sufism sheds light on his perspective.

Despite the absence of references to Shah Ismail's conceptual framework in existing literature on Sufism and Irfan, his poetic work in *Diwan Khatai* offers insights into his understanding of Sojourn. Delving into the characteristics and ideals embodied by dervishes in Sufi and Irfan traditions can provide valuable context for interpreting Shah Ismail's views on the Sojourn badge, revealing the spiritual attributes he deemed essential for those traversing the path of enlightenment.

In the exploration of conduct signs within the works of Jalāl al-Din Muḥammad Rumi, a vast literature has emerged over the past seven centuries. Beyond Rumi's own texts like the Masnavi-ye-Maʿnavi, Divan-I Kebir, and Fihi Ma Fihi, subsequent interpretations have further enriched this discourse. However, the case of Shah Ismail presents a distinctive scenario. In Iran, our primary reference is his own text, which has received comparatively lesser attention. Fortunately, the *Diwan Khatai* remains intact, affording us the opportunity to grasp Shah Ismail's perspective on the journey through life by delving into his poetry and its interpretations.

In "Risala-yi Lubb al-Lubab dar Sayr wa Suluk-i Ulul Albab," Seyyed Hossein Tehrani defines sojourn as walking the path, which entails observing the works and features of the houses and the steps along the way (Tehrani, 1366: 25). However, Allameh Hasan Hasanzadeh Amoli, in his work "Fusus al-Hikm," proposes a different perspective. He suggests that sojourn is a journey towards Allah and an ongoing journey towards Him. According to Amoli, this journey has no ultimate end; rather, it entails transitioning from negative words, actions, and morals towards goodness and divine enlightenment (Hassanzadeh Amoli, 1986: 309).

In contemporary terms, we might describe Spiritual Sojourn as a journey of self-discovery and self-awareness. Attaining this state can lead to liberation and a sense of unity with oneself, existence, and the world at large. Essentially, Spiritual Sojourn represents a mystical path—an inward journey toward self-realization and understanding. Ultimately, it culminates in the states of Fana (annihilation of the self) and Baqaa (permanence or subsistence) after Fana. While some view Fana as the ultimate goal of Spiritual Sojourn, others see it as a step towards Baqaa.

While Spiritual Sojourn finds practical application within the realm of Irfan as a dynamic movement, its foundation lies in theoretical understanding. In essence, spiritual sojourn in Irfan represents a practical manifestation rooted in theoretical principles. In the Quran, synonyms for spiritual sojourn include terms such as escape, emigration, and travel. Travel, in this context, signifies the journey of the heart towards God—a profound attentiveness of the heart to the Divine. The ultimate goal of spiritual sojourn is to draw near to God Almighty. Despite God's lack of physical or spatial proximity, closeness to Him is attainable. This closeness necessitates the removal of veils and obstacles, symbolizing the purification of the soul and the acquisition of divine attributes and names. Ultimately, the culmination of Spiritual Sojourn is the realization of monotheism—Tawheed—where one becomes united with existence and truth, transcending self-awareness and reaching a state of oneness with God. However, a crucial question arises: What are the signs of Spiritual Sojourn? In other words, how does one recognize this profound self-awareness?

Shah Ismail uses the concept of "Darwish" or "Sufism" in couplet number 33. This concept has had a long and tumultuous history in the context of Irfan, Hekmat or Gnosis, and Gnostic traditions in both the East and West. Therefore, it is worth exploring further. "Darwīsh" means "poverty" and is figuratively used to refer to "Sufism." Some people believe it derives from the word "dar pish" meaning "at the door," while others believe it comes from the combination of "dar" meaning "door" and "vihin" meaning "beggar," resulting in the overall meaning of "beggar at the door." However, in Pahlavi, the word "Darwīsh" means "poverty" and "destitute," and in Persian literature, it is always used in this sense or in the specific context of Sufism. The question of what Sufism and Darwīsh are and what their characteristics and essence are, is an ongoing one. In the book *Asrar al-Tawhid fi Maghamat al-Sheikh Abusaid*, a question is posed about the meaning of Darwīsh. A question has been raised about what Darwīsh is. It is stated in Asrar al-Tawhid:

One of those present approached the Prophet Muhammad (PBUH) and said, "Do you have five Dirhams?" The man replied, "Yes, I do." The Prophet said, "Then you are not a Darwīsh." He called another man and asked him, "Do you have five Dirhams?" The man replied, "No, I do not." The Prophet asked, "Do you have anything worth five Dirhams?" The man replied, "Yes, I do." The Prophet said, "Then you are not a Darwīsh." He called another man and asked him, "Do you have five Dirhams?" The man replied, "No, I do not." The Prophet asked, "Do you have anything worth five Dirhams?" The man replied, "No, I do not." The Prophet asked, "Do you have space for five Dirhams?" The man replied, "Yes, I do." The Prophet said, "Then you are not a Darwīsh either." He called another man and asked him, "Since you do not have any Dirhams, do you have anything worth five Dirhams?" The man replied, "No, I do not." The Prophet asked, "Do you have the ability to earn five Dirhams?" The man replied, "Yes, I can." The Prophet said, "Get up, for you are not a Darwīsh." He called another man and asked him, "Do you possess anything from all that I have mentioned?" The man replied, "No, I do not." The Prophet asked, "If five Dirhams were to appear, would you say that they belong to me and that I have a share in them?" The man replied, "No less than that." The Prophet said, "Get up, for you are not a Darwīsh either." He called another man and asked him, "Do you possess anything from all that I have mentioned?" The man replied, "No, I do not." The Prophet asked, "If five Dirhams were to appear, would you think about taking them?" The man replied, "No, I would not, O Messenger of God." The Prophet asked, "What would you do then?" The man replied, "I would abide by the judgment of the Darwīsh, and I would have no share in it." The Prophet Muhammad (PBUH) said, "You are truly a Darwīsh. A Darwīsh should be one who possesses nothing of these things." When the Prophet said this, the others present began to weep and said, "O Messenger of God, everyone calls us Darwīsh, and this is what a Darwīsh should be according to what you have shown us. Who are we then?" The Prophet replied, "He is the Darwīsh, and you are all his dependents."

In simpler terms, our sheikh explained, "Darwīsh is more than just a title; it represents the ultimate state where nothing remains except God ... Therefore, Darwīsh is not merely a person; if you were to embody the qualities of Darwīsh, you would become one." Darwīshhood is not external; it resides within oneself. Thus, anyone seeking the path of truth must traverse the inner journey of Darwīshhood, for Darwīsh resides within each seeker.

IBN MUNAVAR, 2021: 239–247

According to Abu Said Abul-Khayr, Darwīshhood is characterized by poverty, and a Darwīsh is recognized by this attribute. However, we may wonder: Does Shah Ismail offer his own perspective on Darwīshood? How does he define terms like Spiritual Sojourn, Darwīsh, and Sufi?

### 3 Sojourn in the Thought of Shah Ismail

Shah Ismail employs the notion of Darwīsh in developing Salek, asserting that Darwīsh is a destination rather than an inherent trait. He contends that not everyone is inherently imbued with this morality, and to attain the status of Darwīsh, one must traverse various stages and steps. On page 480 he says:

> The Dervish speaks not,
> Yet the corridor must be traversed.
> Amidst a thousand flowers, seek,
> The corridor, laden with honey.
> Four doors await passage,
> No need for carriage or company.
> Neither coach nor companion required,
>     The corridor's hand lies empty.

Becoming a Sufi and a Darwīsh is not simply a matter of uttering these words repeatedly. A Darwīsh is not one of words and speech. One who is of the Tariqat and a Darwīsh must have a state of being that allows them to set foot on the stage of the Tariqat. But what are these stages? Shah Ismail refers to four steps. One who wants to become a Darwīsh must go through four stages. First, they must go through the stages and steps of the Tariqat under the guidance of a mentor or a Pir. After this stage, they must associate with those who have passed through these stages and steps and have reached degrees of perfection. Then, when they are of the Tariqat, they must also be of those who help others. Shah Ismail also wants to define and formulate the people of Tariqat. He uses the word Darwīsh. According to Shah Ismail, Darwīsh signifies something, and that something is:

> Darwīsh voice admits guilt's tether,
> Round it shapes, descending hither.
> Symbolized thus, his paths unfold,
> Darwīsh way, a tale untold.

The emblematic essence of a Darwīsh manifests in the dusty descent and humble submission to dust, embodying profound humility. In both the Gnostic Tradition and Irfan, soil serves as a potent symbol of humility. This humility is encapsulated in the metaphorical interpretation of "to be round," signifying a state of profound humility and submission. Imam Ali (a) elucidates this concept in sermon 192 of Nahj al-Balaghah, underscoring the intrinsic connection between humility and the humble nature of soil. Thus, for a Darwīsh, embracing the dusty and descending to dust symbolizes not only humility but also a profound spiritual journey characterized by submission and humility, echoing the timeless wisdom of Imam Ali (a):

> And for what is in that of expressing the liberation of faces with dust in humility and the adherence of the noble organs to the earth in humility.
>
> ALI IBN ABI TALIB, 2005: 192

The tradition of prostrating oneself to the ground symbolizes humility, a theme Shah Ismail employs in his poetry. In one verse, he utilizes the concept of "Torab," meaning soil, which carries multiple layers of meaning. It signifies not only the physical earth but also serves as a reverential nickname for Imam Alī (a). According to Shah Ismail, one should embrace humility by becoming akin to the dust, burying the exoteric self in humility, and submitting to the authority of Imam Ali (a). Thus, in Shah Ismail's view, embodying the qualities of modesty and humility, and recognizing the spiritual authority of Imam Ali (a), defines the essence of a true Darwīsh.

In Shah Ismail Khatai's language, the hallmark of a Darwīsh—according to his verses—is modesty and humility. Shah Ismail equates possessing these traits with the qualifications of a Spiritual Sojourner. He emphasizes this by stating that a Darwīsh must tread a path, implying a journey of spiritual growth. Modesty and humility are integral to Tariqat and the path of spiritual journeying. Throughout Islamic history, various Sufi orders, except the Naqshbandi, have attributed their lineage of spiritual authority (Walayah) to Hazrat Ali (a). This connection is widespread, spanning regions from the Caucasus to India, and from North Africa to the Balkans and Anatolia. The symbolism of dirt and dust suggests a person's readiness to embrace humility. Entry into these spiritual stages often requires guidance from a spiritual teacher (Pir). The journey through the stages of "Sharia," "Tariqat," "Knowledge," and "Truth" is pivotal for those venturing into this valley of spiritual enlightenment.

Shah Ismail's legacy presents a paradox wherein his contributions to theoretical Irfan and Sufism are overshadowed by his portrayal as a warrior king.

Despite his pivotal role in shaping key concepts in these fields, critical discussions on the evolution of Sufism and the Gnostic tradition in Iran often omit mention of Shah Ismail. Instead, he is predominantly remembered as a ruler wielding a sword, with his intellectual endeavors receiving scant attention.

This skewed perception has led to the formation of false ideas about Shah Ismail among Iranians, both within and outside Iran. While he should be recognized as a man of the pen, his scholarly pursuits have been marginalized in historical narratives, while his military exploits have been magnified. This imbalance in representation has perpetuated a one-dimensional view of Shah Ismail, wherein his intellectual legacy remains largely unrecognized, contributing to a distorted understanding of Iranian intellectual and theoretical developments.

Shah Ismail's literary contributions occupy a paradoxical position in the historical and cultural discourse of the Islamic world. While his works are celebrated and revered in regions such as Anatolia, Turkey, and the Balkans—where he is venerated as a saint by Alevis and Bektashis and his writings hold the status of sacred texts—his literary legacy is met with skepticism and even denial within Iran. This contrasts sharply with the recognition accorded to other prolific monarchs of the 15th century, such as Babur, Sultan Selim (Mohebi), and Shibak Khan, whose writings are universally acknowledged without dispute. The dichotomy between Shah Ismail's exalted status abroad and his contested reputation within Iran reflects a nuanced and complex historical narrative, highlighting the interplay between political, cultural, and religious dynamics in shaping the perception of his intellectual and literary contributions.

Shah Ismail's utilization of Irfan to consolidate his political forces is a subject of historical scrutiny. In couplet number 34 of his poetry, Shah Ismail portrays himself as the lone Shah in Karbala, intertwining political authority with spiritual significance. His fusion of politics and religion reflected a worldview where the two were inseparable, with Shah Ismail and his followers, the Qizilbash, not merely viewing him as a political leader but also as a spiritual guide, referred to as "Wali" Tariqat. Accounts from Venetian travelers who visited Iran shed light on the deification of Shah Ismail by the Qizilbash, who believed him to embody divine attributes, even going so far as to regard him as the "Mahdi." However, conflicting reports suggest tensions between Shah Ismail and Qizilbash leaders over such interpretations, hinting at internal discord within the movement.

Shah Ismail's poetic compositions not only served his political agenda but also harbored messianic and Mahdist undertones, contributing to a saviorist narrative. Studies, such as those by Professor Gudmar Aneer, delve into the intertwining of Mahdavit beliefs with Shah Ismail's ideology, particularly among

Qizilbash, Alavi, and Bektashi tribes. Aneer's research posits that a strong strain of promiseism prevailed within these groups, with Shah Ismail embodying messianic expectations and visions of salvation, drawing parallels with figures like Akbar Shah in India. In this context, Shah Ismail's persona and poetry were instrumental in shaping a collective consciousness that fused political ambition with spiritual aspirations, anchoring his movement in a narrative of divine providence and deliverance.

In his analysis of the evolution of the Diwan collection of Shah Ismail, Rasul Ismailzadeh notes that Shah Ismail's political engagement began at the young age of fourteen. This timing suggests that the poems included in the Diwan could not have been composed prior to this age. Given that Shah Ismail passed away at the age of thirty-seven, it is evident that he created this Diwan over approximately twenty-four years. During this period, his understanding of Irfan and his political aspirations evolved simultaneously.

Stating whether Shah Ismail was innovative or not is premature without thorough examination of his texts. Firstly, Shah Ismail's writings need to be meticulously studied and analyzed. Secondly, they should be compared with the works of his contemporaries to contextualize them within the broader tradition of Irfan. Until these critical steps are undertaken, it remains premature to claim innovations attributed to Shah Ismail. Current scholarship has primarily concentrated on the introduction and acknowledgment of the existence of Shah Ismail's Diwan. It is now essential for scholars in the fields of Hekmat, Gnosis, Irfan, and Sufism to engage deeply with this text, conducting thorough analyses to ascertain whether it genuinely presents any innovative elements.

Ismailzadeh has identified certain poems in Diwan Shah Ismail with an asterisk, suggesting they may not be authored by Shah Ismail himself. It is prudent to set these verses aside, acknowledging the possibility that they were added at a later time. Ismailzadeh's research likely represents the inaugural scholarly examination of Diwan Shah Ismail. Many of the concepts found within Diwan Shah Ismail are deeply entrenched in the longstanding tradition of Gnostic teachings and Irfan. Shah Ismail's work undoubtedly aligns with this rich tradition, reflecting his place within it.

The Safavid Tariqat, attributed to Sheikh Safiuddin Ardabili, traces its roots back to Ardabil and shares ties with the Zahidiya Tariqat in Gilan. The familial connection between Sheikh Zahid Gilani, the father-in-law of Sheikh Safiuddin Ardabili, and the Safavid lineage further solidifies this relationship. Over two centuries, the Safavid tradition of Irfan and Tariqat gradually evolved, drawing influence from texts originating in the regions of Azerbaijan, the Caucasus, and Anatolia. This evolution was propelled by the evangelistic journeys undertaken by figures like Sheikh Haider and Sheikh Junaid, Shah Ismail's father and grandfather, spanning from these regions to the Balkans, Kurdish territories of Turkey, Iraq, and Syria, where their teachings gained traction and influence.

Within this rich tradition, Shah Ismail emerged as a significant figure who articulated concepts of Irfan, Gnosticism, and Nazari through poetry, following in the footsteps of many mystics and sages of the Gnostic tradition. The use of poetry as a medium for philosophical expression is not unique to Shah Ismail; throughout history, philosophers and sages across cultures, including Greece, Iran, and ancient Rome, have utilized poetry as a means of conveying their ideas. Figures like Molla Hadi Sabzavari, a Sadra philosopher, composed their most profound philosophical treatises in poetic form. In this context, Shah Ismail can be considered as a poet-philosopher or poet-sage, akin to luminaries such as Jami and Nizami, who employed poetry not only for aesthetic purposes but also as a vehicle for philosophical discourse and profound contemplation.

# CHAPTER 12

# On the Reciprocal Relationship between Shiism and Sufism

## 1   Introduction

This chapter delves into the intertwined intellectual dynamics between Sheikh Safi-ad-Din Ardabili and Sayyed Haydar Amoli, and their profound impact on the emergence of the Safavid dynasty and Shah Ismail in Ardabil, Iran, and across the Islamic world during the 16th and 17th centuries. The Safavid reign, spanning nearly 220 years, holds significant historical importance, yet its influence extends far beyond the temporal confines of its era. The Safavids' imprint on Iranian society remains palpable today, particularly evident in their formulation of societal structures and institutions, notably the fusion of religion and governance. Despite the advent of modernity in Iran, the Safavid legacy endures, shaping contemporary discourses on the relationship between religion and government. This enduring tradition of thought finds expression in the works and teachings of figures like Sayyed Haydar Amoli and Sheikh Safi-ad-Din Ardabili, serving as a foundational framework for understanding the ongoing interplay between religion, governance, and societal development in Iran.

Sheikh Safiuddin Ardabili lived during the years 1356–1381 AH, amidst the Ilkhanate era. Sayyed Haydar Amoli, born in 1341 AD in Amel, resided in the Caspian Sea region. Often overlooked in discussions on Sufism and Sayyed Haydar Amoli is the significance of the "Caspian Sea Basin." This region not only encompasses one of the largest lakes globally but also serves as a focal point for civilization and intercultural studies.

Today, the southern Caspian Sea is bordered by provinces such as Gilan, Mazandaran, and Golestan. To the east and west lie territories belonging to countries like the Republic of Azerbaijan, the Republic of Dagestan (now part of the Russian Federation), and the Republic of Kalmykia, alongside other regions within Russia such as the Astrakhan region, Kazakhstan, and Turkmenistan. This diverse geographical area hosts a tapestry of religions including Islam, Christianity, Judaism, and Buddhism, forming what is termed the "Caspian Sea Region." Over centuries, both Shia and Sunni sects have coexisted in this region, reflecting its religious plurality. Furthermore, the prevalence and spread of Sufism hold particular importance in the Caspian Sea area, shaping its spiritual landscape profoundly.

In the region of Dagestan, two prominent Tariqats, "Qadiriyya" and "Naqshbandi," hold sway, while in Kazakhstan and Astrakhan, diverse branches of Sufism flourish. During the era of Sayyed Haydar Amoli, Sufism exerted a profound influence in the southern Caspian Sea area. A central and pivotal theme in Sayyed Haydar Amoli's discourse is the "interaction between Shiism and Sufism," which he intricately explores within the framework of theoretical Nazari and his intellectual paradigm.

Sheikh Safiuddin Ardabili's spiritual journey reached its zenith under the guidance of Sheikh Zahid Gilani in the Gilan region, where he attained the highest level of Spiritual Sojourn. Following the passing of Sheikh Zahid Gilani, the mantle of leadership in the Zahedieh Tariqat was passed on to Sheikh Safiuddin Ardabili, underscoring his profound significance. The Zahedieh Tariqat, originally belonging to the Safavid lineage, was thus renamed in recognition of Sheikh Safiuddin Ardabili's esteemed position.

As a leading figure in Sufism with Shiite inclinations, Sheikh Safiuddin Ardabili played a pivotal role in shaping the spiritual landscape of the Azerbaijan region, particularly in the city of Ardabil. During the reign of Shah Ismail, whose influence extended beyond present-day political boundaries, Iran was founded under the theoretical framework and Tariqat propagated by Sheikh Safiuddin Ardabili. In examining the shared principles and dialogues between Sayyed Haydar Amoli and Sheikh Safiuddin Ardabili, several commonalities and discussions emerge, reflecting their interconnected roles in advancing spiritual and intellectual discourse in the region.

## 2      Spiritual Crisis: Turning Point in the Life of Mystics

Around the age of thirty, Sayyed Haydar Amoli undergoes a profound spiritual crisis, grappling with fundamental existential questions. Like many mystics and sages, his life narrative features a pivotal turning point where conventional social, political, cultural, and scholarly teachings no longer suffice to satisfy his quest for meaning. Struggling to find solace and fulfillment through external avenues, he embarks on a journey of introspection and inner exploration. Sayyed Haydar Amoli says:

> Engaging in formal and professional sciences not only fails to lead to existential knowledge or Maerefatollāh, but it also exacerbates human doubts and uncertainties.
>
> AMELI, 1368: 42

In the evolution of Irfan, Gnosticism, Sufism, and Hekmat both within the Islamic world and in global spiritual traditions, significant figures often encounter a pivotal turning point in their lives. For instance, Nasir Khusraw led an outwardly engaged life until his thirties, attaining high degrees of worldly success, before undergoing a profound spiritual crisis. Essentially, the journey of anyone immersed in Spiritual Sojourn, Sufism, and Irfan is marked by a crucial spiritual turning point.

In a poignant verse from the Quran, Prophet Ibrahim's inquiry to God resonates deeply: "My Lord, show me how You give life to the dead." God's response probes Ibrahim's belief, to which he asserts, "Yes, but [I ask] only that my heart may be satisfied." (Baqarah: 260) This exchange encapsulates a profound truth: even revered figures like prophets and saints grapple with existential questions, seeking assurance in their faith.

The narrative underscores that even those with divine insight, intuition, and deep contemplation are not exempt from wrestling with the concept of God's existence. Rather, their encounters with the divine continually challenge their understanding and beliefs. The hallmark of these exceptional individuals— be they mystics, prophets, or saints—is not merely their sanctity, but their relentless pursuit of truth and meaning. This pursuit often leads them to confront what is known as a spiritual crisis, as evidenced in the life of Sayyed Haydar Amoli.

A mystic, therefore, is characterized not by passive acceptance of outward appearances, but by a fervent quest to transcend the superficial and delve into the depths of spiritual truth. They seek to traverse the journey from the exoteric to the esoteric, driven by an insatiable thirst for enlightenment and understanding.

The journey from the Exoteric to the Esoteric marks the foundational principle of Sufism, Irfan, and Gnosticism. When we examine figures like Sheikh Safi-ad-Din Ardabili and Sayyed Haydar Amoli, we find a distinction that goes to the heart of Shia thought on Walayah and sets it apart from other religious traditions.

The key disparity lies in their approach to distinguishing between the Exoteric and the Esoteric aspects of faith. It is this focus on delving into the Esoteric that forms the cornerstone of all Sufi and Irfan traditions. The scholars and sages who have delved into the realms of Irfan often trace their lineage back to this fundamental principle, attributing it to Imam Alī (a) and his teachings on the multiplicity of Esoterics.

This notion might initially surprise us, but it holds immense significance, particularly in contemporary interpretations within various schools of thought and philosophical discourses. The concept of interpretation suggests that behind every phenomenon lies a deeper reality, veiled behind a curtain. Every outward manifestation has a hidden dimension, an Esoteric truth waiting to be uncovered.

In this context, both Sayyed Haydar Amoli and Sheikh Safi-ad-Din Ardabili converge, forming a theoretical connection grounded in the notion of the Esoteric. Their teachings and insights reflect a shared commitment to unveiling the deeper truths concealed within the outward appearances of existence. Thus, their philosophical and spiritual legacies intertwine, underscoring the profound importance of embracing the Esoteric in the pursuit of spiritual enlightenment and understanding.

In the mystical realms of Sufism, the notion of the "secret" holds profound significance, highlighting a unique aspect of human consciousness. Among all beings in existence, it is humanity alone that possesses the capacity to contemplate, hold, and comprehend secrets. This ability does not stem from inherent superiority, but rather from a fundamental characteristic of human nature: need. Driven by an innate longing for self-awareness and fulfillment, humans embark on a quest to uncover secrets, a journey that ultimately leads to the genesis of prayer—a profound dialogue between the seeker's yearning and the divine realm. Through this intricate interplay between the secret and human need, individuals come to recognize their own limitations and yearn for a connection with a higher power, known as "God", in religious contexts and "Allah" in Islam and Sufism. This divine entity, often referred to as the "yar," becomes the cherished friend of the seeker, fostering a deep and intimate bond that transcends the mundane.

In the path of Tariqat, seekers reach a profound realization: that the Supreme Being is not merely a distant deity, but a beloved companion. This awareness propels them to cultivate a sincere and intimate friendship with the Divine, characterized by unwavering devotion and commitment. However, this spiritual journey is not without its challenges. Along the path, individuals confront their own shortcomings and failures in fulfilling the obligations of friendship within the context of Tariqat. Yet, rather than discouragement, this recognition serves as a catalyst for growth and transformation. It inspires seekers to redouble their efforts, striving earnestly to honor the sacred bonds of friendship on their spiritual journey. In moments of realization, when individuals acknowledge their faults and shortcomings, they echo the wisdom of Saadi, recognizing the humility in confessing their faults to God, as none can truly fulfill the right of His Lordship.

In the realm of Tariqat and spiritual journeying, the interaction with God stands in stark contrast to Aristotle's notion of engaging with a first mover.

Instead, for the Salek and those affiliated with Tariqat, God assumes the role of a cherished companion, transcending mere cosmic force. Within this profound relationship, the dynamics of need and secrecy transform into the essence of prayer and supplication, navigating the complexities of ontological and existential dialectics.

## 3     The Link between Shiism and Sufism

In his book *Jami al-Asrar wa Manba al-Anwar*, Sayyed Haydar Amoli endeavors to guide seekers towards an understanding that the universe is imbued with both "mystery" and "light" (Amoli, 1368). This illumination is not merely physical but metaphysical, suggesting that existence transcends mere materiality and that matter itself is derived from light. For those traversing the path of Tariqat, comprehending the interplay between secret and need is crucial for navigating towards enlightenment. The concept of "light" in Sayyed Haydar Amoli's perspective serves as a symbol of spiritual enlightenment, representing the inner illumination that unites Shiism and Sufism. By elucidating this connection, Amoli fosters a holistic approach to spiritual growth, guiding individuals towards embracing the inner light that illuminates the path towards divine understanding and union. What role this light plays in bridging Shiism and Sufism remains a pivotal question in Amoli's teachings.

In his book, Sayyed Haydar Amoli delineates three foundational pillars: 1) Tawheed, or the Oneness of God, 2) the Secrets of Tawheed, and 3) the Secrets of Sharia (Amoli, 1368). He critiques the prevailing state of Islamic discourse, asserting that it often reduces Sharia to a mere set of rules, emphasizing blind adherence over genuine understanding. Amoli contends that Sharia holds deeper dimensions, constituting "secrets" that must be unraveled for true comprehension. These secrets, embedded within Sharia, serve as pathways to monotheism and its inherent mysteries. Without grasping and internalizing these secrets, individuals risk reducing Sharia to a mechanical practice devoid of existential significance. For Amoli, Sharia's essence lies in its hidden truths, which beckon individuals to recognize their inherent need and the enigmatic nature of the world. Failure to apprehend these secrets perpetuates a superficial understanding of monotheism, relegating Sharia to a posthumous exercise devoid of spiritual depth. In essence, Amoli urges individuals to delve into the essence of Sharia, for therein lies the key to unlocking the profound self-awareness inherent in understanding this "secret."

In his spiritual journey and intellectual framework, Sayyed Haydar Amoli endeavors to bridge the gap between Shiism and Sufism, drawing inspiration from the work of Sheikh Safi-ad-Din Ardabili's "Qara Al-Mashul" (Ardabili, 1386). Throughout Islamic intellectual history, various challenges have arisen, notably the tensions between jurists, mystics, and philosophers. Each of these factions operated within distinct paradigms, as described by Thomas Kuhn in *Structures of the Scientific Revolution* (Kuhn, 2016). These paradigms, while self-sufficient, often led to conflicts due to differing frameworks and assumptions. Even within shared frameworks such as jurisprudence, mysticism, or philosophy, disparities in insight further fueled discord. Some advocated for the excommunication of philosophers or deemed mysticism as outside the realm of religion, while others dismissed intuition or revelation as lacking in validity.

In the sixth century, figures like Sheikh Ishraq observed this discord within the Islamic world, where some adherents championed Hellenic reason, others emphasized revelation or Semitic rationality, and yet another faction focused on mysticism and illumination, as seen in the works of Suhrawardi. These divergent perspectives, rooted in intuition, revelation, or rational proof, perpetuated ongoing conflicts. Notably, Sayyed Haydar Amoli and Sheikh Safi-ad-Din Ardabili echoed these observations, recognizing the challenge of reconciling disparate paradigms within Islamic thought. Their efforts aimed to foster understanding and unity amidst intellectual diversity, seeking common ground beyond doctrinal differences.

They asked Sheikh Shibli about the meaning of "And before thee also the messengers We sent were but men, to whom We granted inspiration: if ye realise this not, ask of those who possess the Message" (Quran 10:43).

The Ahl al-Dhikr (People of Remembrance) are those who say "la ilaha illallah" (there is no god but Allah), but not merely by uttering the words. They must also understand the profound meaning of this declaration. In this sense, the gnostics who attain knowledge through "la ilaha illallah" are distinct from the general Ahl al-Dhikr. The latter group remains confined to the mere words, repeating "la ilaha illallah" without comprehending its essence. They represent the common folk. The gnostics, on the other hand, have grasped the true meaning of "la ilaha illallah." They possess knowledge of its essence and have access to the divine treasury of secrets. When asked a question about the Remembrance, if they lack an immediate answer, they seek guidance from God and provide a response (Ardabili, 2007).

Sheikh Safi-ad-Din Ardabili delves into the dichotomy of Exoteric and Esoteric, highlighting its significance within Islamic thought.

Suhrawardi's "hekmat-e eshraq" stands as a masterpiece of intellectual thought from the sixth century, blending rational proof, intuition, and revelation-based rationality within its framework. Sayyed Haydar Amoli shares a similar concern of organically linking Sufism with Shiism, viewing both Sufis and Shiites as uniquely significant. In his work *Jami al-Asrar wa Manba al-Anwar*, Amoli draws upon intellectual reasoning, intuitive insights, and revelations from himself and other sheikhs. His central thesis posits that true Shiites are inherently Sufis, and true Sufis are inherently Shiites, emphasizing the concept of "Sir Walayah." At the core of both Amoli's and Sheikh Safi-ad-Din Ardabili's perspectives lies the notion of the "secret," which serves as a catalyst for human need. This need, in turn, becomes the locus for the emergence and cultivation of the secret, ultimately manifesting in prayer—a profound expression of human vulnerability that situates individuals within the realm of servitude in this existence.

## 4      The Influence of Sayyed Haydar Amoli and Sheikh Safi-ad-Din Ardabili on Shah Ismail

The historical intersection of Sufism with political power, exemplified by the contributions of Sayyed Haydar Amoli, Sheikh Safi-ad-Din Ardabili, and the eventual rise of Shah Ismail and the Safavid government, represents a significant paradigm shift in the evolution of Islamic thought and governance. Traditionally, Sufism was perceived as a domain focused on esoteric spirituality, distanced from the practicalities of societal and political structures. However, the Safavid era marked a crucial turning point wherein Sufism transitioned from a secluded mystical practice to an influential force in shaping socio-political systems. This transformation not only redefined the societal role of Sufism but also prompted a critical intellectual reexamination of its theological foundations, fostering a synergy between spiritual authority and political leadership.

At the heart of this intellectual reevaluation lies the critique advanced by Sayyed Haydar Amoli regarding the metaphysical interpretations of Ibn Arabi and his notable commentator, Qaysari. Qaysari upheld a hierarchy of sainthood that positioned Jesus (PBUH) as the seal of absolute saints and Ibn Arabi as the seal of bound saints. In contrast, Amoli offered a profound reinterpretation, asserting that the seal of absolute saints is Imam Ali (a), while the seal of bound saints is Imam Mahdi (a). This theological revision not only aligned sainthood with Shia eschatological beliefs but also reoriented the metaphysical narrative to support a framework wherein spiritual authority could actively engage with temporal governance. By doing so, Amoli effectively bridged the gap between mystical thought and political responsibility, embedding Sufism within the fabric of societal leadership.

The intellectual groundwork laid by figures such as Amoli, coupled with the spiritual legacy of Sheikh Safi-ad-Din Ardabili, facilitated the Safavid synthesis of Sufism and political authority under Shah Ismail. By integrating Sufi principles with statecraft, the Safavids established a model of governance that harmonized spiritual legitimacy with political power, thereby transforming Sufism into a pivotal instrument of state formation. This paradigm not only enhanced the role of Sufism within the socio-political sphere but also signified a broader shift in the Islamic world, where mystical thought and practice became intrinsic to the mechanisms of governance and societal organization. This synthesis marked a departure from the historical detachment of Sufism, positioning it as a central force in shaping the identity and trajectory of the Safavid state.

The integration of Sufism with political power, catalyzed by the intellectual contributions of figures such as Sayyed Haydar Amoli and Sheikh Safi-ad-Din Ardabili, signifies a transformative moment in the perception and practice of Sufism within Islamic societies. This convergence marks a departure from the conventional portrayal of Sufism as a secluded, introspective tradition, redefining it as an influential force deeply embedded in the political and social structures of its time. By bridging the realms of mysticism and governance, this paradigm shift underscores the evolution of Sufism into an active participant in shaping the historical and societal trajectory of the Safavid period.

A critical dimension of this transformation lies in the reinterpretation of Ibn Arabi's teachings through the lens of Shiite Hekmat, or Gnosis, as advanced by thinkers like Amoli. This reinterpretation integrated the theoretical foundations of Sufism with Shiism, resulting in a synthesis of Hekmat and governance. Such intellectual innovation illuminated the emergence of Shah Ismail and the Safavid state under the spiritual framework established by Sheikh Safi-ad-Din Ardabili. Here, Irfan (mystical knowledge) transcended its theoretical origins, becoming an integral element of historical and practical governance. This progression highlights the capacity of metaphysical thought to engage with the political realm, dissolving the perceived boundaries between spiritual insight and statecraft.

At the heart of this discourse lies the profound question of the relationship between Hekmat and governance: Is governance merely the application of rule and enforcement, or does it embody the principles of existential wisdom and Gnosis? Should governance be equated with coercive power, or does it serve as a manifestation of enlightened leadership rooted in philosophical and mystical insight? The contributions of Ardabili and Amoli offer a compelling framework for addressing these inquiries, presenting a dialectic between Hukum (rule) and Hekmat that extends beyond historical confines to resonate with contemporary political challenges. Their intellectual legacy compels us to reevaluate governance not as an exercise of authority alone but as a mode of existential engagement informed by profound wisdom.

In essence, the fusion of Sufism, Irfan, and Hekmat with governance transcends theoretical abstraction, embedding itself in the practical dynamics of human societies. This synthesis challenges reductionist notions of rule enforcement, advocating for governance rooted in insight, ethical wisdom, and existential understanding. By redefining the political sphere as an arena of spiritual and philosophical engagement, this discourse not only reshapes our understanding of historical governance but also provides a timeless lens through which to address modern political and societal complexities. The legacy of thinkers like Amoli and Ardabili continues to inspire a reevaluation of leadership paradigms, emphasizing the enduring relevance of integrating wisdom with power.

# CHAPTER 13

# The Impact of Sayyed Haydar Amoli on Shah Ismail: Fostering Unity between Shiism and Sufism

## 1    Introduction

In the historical context of Iran, the interplay between Irfan, or Sufi mysticism, and Shiism predates the Safavid era. Both traditions shared common spiritual threads, with Sufi practices and beliefs often intertwined with Shia spirituality. However, it was during the Safavid period, particularly under the reign of Shah Ismail, that the relationship between Shiism and Sufism reached a pinnacle. Sayyed Haydar Amoli's teachings played a crucial role in fostering this convergence. His emphasis on the unity of spiritual principles within Shiism and Sufism laid the groundwork for Shah Ismail's vision of a unified Safavid state where both traditions coexisted harmoniously.

Under Shah Ismail's rule, the Safavid Tariqat flourished, with Shiism and Sufism becoming integral components of Safavid governance and society. The blending of these traditions created a unique religious and cultural identity for the Safavid empire. However, as political dynamics shifted over time, the influence of the Safavid Tariqat waned, eventually giving way to new religious and ideological movements. Despite its decline, echoes of the Safavid Tariqat's legacy can still be felt today, with traces of its teachings and practices enduring in various spiritual circles within Iran and beyond.

Mirhaidar Ameli and Sheikh Safi-ad-Din Ardabili lived during overlapping periods, despite a 15-year gap between their lifespans. Mirhaidar Ameli was born in 1319 AD and passed away in 1385 AD, whereas Sheikh Safi-ad-Din Ardabili was born in 1252 AD and died in 1334 AD. This means that Mirhaidar was only 15 years old when Sheikh Safi-ad-Din Ardabili passed away, marking the end of an era that profoundly influenced the spiritual and intellectual landscape of their time.

## 2    The Gnostic Tradition of Sayyed Haydar Amoli

According to Mir Haider Amoli, the Imami religion encompasses two dimensions: the Exoteric, which encompasses the knowledge of the Imams and includes Sharia, Islam, and Faith, and the Esoteric, which delves into their deeper sciences, comprising Tariqat, truth, and certainty. Mir Haider Amoli posits that Shia and Sufi are two terms denoting the same ultimate truth, which is the Muhammadan Sharia.

French philosopher Corbin explored the Gnostic views of Sayyed Haydar Amoli in two articles, later compiled into a book titled *Sayyed Haydar Amoli: Description of His Life, Works, Opinions, and Cosmology* by Nozer Aghakhani, translated into Farsi. What is intriguing about Corbin's approach to Amoli is his deep engagement with continental philosophy, particularly with ontological concerns influenced by thinkers like Martin Heidegger. Corbin sought alternatives in Eastern thought to transcend Western nihilism, and the concept of existence, central to Amoli's philosophy, caught his attention. This concept provided a potential bridge between Western existentialism and Eastern mysticism, offering a fresh perspective on being that resonated with Corbin's philosophical inquiries.

In Sayyed Haydar Amoli's narrative, he delineates two forms of monotheism: Divine Monotheism, categorized as Exoteric Monotheism, and Existential Monotheism, referred to as Esoteric Monotheism. What is significant in Esoteric Monotheism, and how it connects to Corbin, Heidegger, and the German tradition, is the notion of existence. According to Amoli, within Esoteric Monotheism, human existence is perceived as absolute, free from determinations that confer actuality. This epistemological presentation in Amoli's intellectual framework harmoniously synthesizes the paradigms of Shiism and Sufism, paving the way for the emergence of the "Ardebil School" under Shah Ismail.

Amoli asserts that only the Shiite Sufi possesses the capacity to attain truth, underscoring the irreplaceable role of the twelve imams in this pursuit. This linkage between Sayyed Haydar Amoli and Shah Ismail, also known as Shah Khatai, signifies a convergence of spiritual and political authority, wherein the Safavid ruler embodies the synthesis of Shiite and Sufi principles advocated by Sayyed Haydar Amoli, as stated in the book *Jame' al-Asrar*:

> And if it is said that Sufism is based on the way of the Sunnis and their principles and rules, then how can they be considered true Shias? I answer that Sufism, although like Shiism has many sects, its true sect is one, and that is the sect that is described by these attributes: namely, carrying the secrets of the Imams in the way that is fitting, and believing in them, that is, the Imams (a) in both Exoteric and Esoteric.
>
> AMULI, 1989: 41

3      The Influence of Sayyed Haydar Amoli on Shah Ismail

The synthesis of Sufi and Shiite elements, cultivated within the framework of
Haydar Amoli's Gnostic Tradition two centuries prior to Shah Ismail's ascent,
finds eloquent expression in Shah Ismail's Gnostic worldview and his reverence for the Ahl al-Bayt. An illustration of this fusion can be found in *Diwan
Khatai*, where on page 450, we encounter:

> Those who love Hazrat Muhammad and Ali dearly
> God willing, they don't get tired and don't stay on the roads
> Those who have seen the face of Imam Hossein
> God willing, they will not be deprived of Imam Hussain.

Those who love Muhammad and Ali dearly, God willing, they will neither get
tired nor stay on the road. Those who see Imam Hussain's face, God willing,
will not be deprived of meeting Imam Hussain (a).

In Shah Ismail's poetry and perspective, one can discern the embodiment
of Sayyed Haydar Amoli's discourse on the Esoteric viewpoint and the synthesis of Shia-Sufi thought. Sayyed Haydar delineates three realms of knowledge:
philosophical, theological, and divine or existential. He suggests that the former two are acquired through diligent effort, constituting forms of acquisition
and achievement. However, he posits that the knowledge of existence, which
rejuvenates the soul, is not merely attained but rather discovered within one's
own being, manifesting as a profound taste and revelation. Shah Ismail says
about receiving existence on page 458 couplet number 13:

> In a city weary of its own existence, I roamed,
> How delightful is the encounter with Mohabat, sweetly combed.
> My eyes fixated on one thing alone,
> How delightful is the encounter with Mohabat's gentle tone.

Once more, Shah Ismail elucidates, "I journeyed through the city of my being
and embarked on a Spiritual Sojourn within its confines." Here, the essence
of existence emerges as a pivotal notion in Shah Ismail's philosophy, echoing
the sentiments expounded by Seyyed Haider Amoli. Shah Ismail contends that
to attain such profound existential knowledge, love and affection are indis-
pensable, coupled with an intuitive perspective—a form of cognition rooted
in existential understanding. Thus, the Spiritual Sojourn within the realm of
existence culminates in the union, for it is through love that unity is achieved.
This narrative carries forth the legacy of Sayyed Haydar Amoli's teachings

within the Ardabil school, particularly in Shah Ismail's discourse. However, the neglect of this semantic and conceptual continuum within the Gnostic tradition in Iran and the Turkish-speaking world poses a significant question. What steps must be taken to rectify this oversight now?

As it has been discussed earlier, Seyyed Haider differentiates between two perspectives within Imamiyyah concerning the Exoteric and Esoteric views. The Exoteric dimension concerns itself with the exegesis of the imam's knowledge, while the Esoteric delves into the profound role of the imams in this context. In Shah Ismail's perspective, the view of the imams transcends mere superficiality; he embraces an Esoteric understanding. For Shah Ismail, the imams are not relegated solely to historical figures of the past; rather, he perceives them as integral to an existential relationship. Their significance lies not only in their past deeds but also in their ongoing influence on spiritual consciousness.

Regarding the neglect of Shah Ismail's reflections on the tradition of Irfan and Gnosis in the Turkish language-speaking world, it is crucial to highlight the broader context of linguistic and cultural dynamics. The marginalization of the Turkish language within Iran's public sphere represents more than the suppression of a linguistic medium; it symbolizes the dismissal of an entire tradition, worldview, and cultural heritage that has enriched Iranian society. This expulsion has stifled the nourishing flow of Turkish language's contributions to Iranian culture's growth and excellence.

Furthermore, the Safavid Tariqat tradition did not emerge solely with Shah Ismail; rather, it represents a continuation of deeper spiritual currents. While Shah Ismail played a pivotal role in its development, the tradition did not abruptly vanish after his era. Instead, it likely continued, evolving and adapting over time, albeit with varying degrees of visibility and influence.

Even scholars well-versed in the realms of Irfan, Hekmat, or Gnosis, along with the theoretical and Sufi traditions, have, through their theoretical frameworks and assumptions, somewhat detached Shah Ismail from both the Shiite tradition and the Turkish Irfan tradition, whether intentionally or inadvertently. In the book *Thaqalain: 'Irfan (Mysticism): Theoretical and Practical Principles of 'Irfan and the Safavid Spiritual Path*, Seyed Salman Safavi provides a foreword and introduction written by Seyyed Hossein Nasr. Seyyed Hossein Nasr says:

> Over centuries, Iran has nurtured numerous luminaries in the realms of Hekmat (Gnosis) and Irfan. From Ibn Sina and Suhravardi to Mirdamad, Mulla Sadra, Haj Molahadi Sabzevari, Agha Ali Modares, Mirza Mahdi Ashtiani, and Allameh Tabatabai in the domain of Hekmat, to Bayezid, Sheikh Safiuddin Ardabili, Sheikh Bahauddin Amoli, Agha Mohammad

Reza Qomshaei, and countless others in Sufism, Iran boasts a rich tapestry of spiritual heritage. This land has given rise to the richest and most
diverse literature of Irfan globally. Persian Irfan literature stands unparalleled, adorned with masterpieces from luminaries such as Sanai, Attar,
Rumi, Hafez, Shabestri, Jami, and numerous other titans in the field.

SAFAVI, 2013: 29

In discussing figures like Sheikh Safi-ad-Din Ardabili, Seyyed Hossein Nasr
highlights a historical oversight rather than deliberate exclusion. However,
many scholars, in their historiography of Irfan, Hekmat (Gnosis), and Sufism,
have indeed included Sheikh Safiuddin Ardabili while overlooking Shah Ismail.
Nasr's emphasis on "Iran" as the focal point of his study is understandable,
as it has been a hub of spiritual and intellectual activity. Yet, his assertion
that Persian Irfan literature is unrivaled may inadvertently limit the scope of
inquiry to texts in Persian alone.

This perspective on Iran's cultural and linguistic diversity is not eternal but
rather a product of historical circumstances and academic trends. The confla-
tion of Iran with the Persian language is a relatively recent phenomenon. Shah
Ismail and Hakim Hidji, among others, did not perceive Iran solely through the
lens of Persian language and culture; they embraced its multifaceted nature.
Their choice to write in Turkish reflects this diversity and challenges the notion
of Iran as synonymous only with Persian.

Indeed, Iran's historical legacy extends far beyond Persian, encompassing
languages like Arabic, Turkish, and others. Figures like Molla Hadi Sabzavari
and Ibn Sina wrote extensively in Arabic, showcasing the linguistic richness of Iran's intellectual heritage. However, this theoretical framework that
prioritizes Persian texts may inadvertently neglect valuable insights from
non-Persian traditions. Recognizing Iran's linguistic and cultural diversity is
crucial for a more inclusive and comprehensive understanding of its intellectual legacy. Another important point is that Seyyed Hossein Nasr formulates the "Hadith of the thaqalayn" mentioned in the book *Erfan-e Thaqalayn*
(Safavi, 2017) as follows:

The Hadith of the Thaqalayn holds a significant place within the narrative of this book. In this renowned Hadith, highly regarded among Shia
adherents, the Prophet Muhammad articulates his intention to leave
behind two invaluable legacies for his followers upon his departure from
this world: the Holy Quran and his progeny (Ahl al-Bayt). This Hadith
possesses both an outward appearance and an esoteric dimension. Its

outward appearance is clear and requires no further elucidation. However, its esoteric aspect warrants exploration. Beyond its literal and external meanings, the Holy Quran harbors internal and esoteric dimensions that have been expounded upon by various interpreters of Irfan over numerous centuries. From the interpretations of Imam Jafar al-Sadiq to those of luminaries such as Ibn Arabi, Meibdi, Ibn Aghabeh, and scholars from the Gonabadi tradition, these interpretations delve into the profound spiritual truths embedded within the Quranic text.

The Hadith of the Thaqalayn, intricately linked to the essence of this book's message, holds profound significance among Shia adherents. In this renowned tradition, the Holy Prophet Muhammad declares his intent to bequeath two invaluable legacies to his followers upon his departure: the Holy Quran and his Ahl al-Bayt. This Hadith is both outwardly evident and imbued with esoteric depths. While its outward appearance requires no elucidation, its esoteric dimension warrants acknowledgment.

Beyond its literal and external meanings, the Holy Quran possesses internal and esoteric layers that have been expounded upon by scholars of Irfan across centuries. From the interpretations of Imam Jafar al-Sadiq to the insights of luminaries like Ibn Arabi, Ahmad ibn Ajiba, and scholars from the Gonabadi tradition, these interpretations delve into the profound spiritual truths enshrined within the Quranic text.

An intriguing aspect to note is the absence of Shah Ismail's interpretation of the Hadith of the Thaqalayn within Seyyed Hossein Nasr's perspective. For instance, in verse number 7, Shah Ismail offers a unique formulation of interpretation for the Hadith of the Thaqalayn:

Those who love Muhammad and Ali with all their hearts,
God willing, they will never grow weary or falter on their paths.
Those who have beheld the face of Imam Hussain (a),
God willing, will never be deprived of meeting Imam Hussain (a).
Those who have partaken of the blessings of Imam Zain al-Abidin, (a)
Who have imbibed the knowledge of Imam Muhammad al-Baqir, (a)
Who have reached Imam Jafar al-Sadiq (1) with sincerity,
God willing, they will never stray from this path.
Those who have come from the presence of Imam Musa al-Kadhim (a),
Who have sacrificed their heads and souls and found their congregation,
Those who have poisoned Imam Reza (a),
God willing, they will not find refuge in the Court of Intercession.

A day will come when the Book of Deeds will be read,
In the hands of the Prince of Intercession, it will be held.
If Imam Taqi (a) and Naqi (a) awaken,
God willing, our blossoming bud will not wither.
Khatai says that this work will come to an end one day,
The longing for the Mahdi will one day seize this world.
God willing, the prince will not be wronged.

Returning to the words of Seyyed Hossein Nasr, he notes that Shah Ismail offers an interpretation of the Hadith of the Thaqalayn that is not only rare but also potentially unique.

"Itrat" also holds a deeper significance. It encompasses not only the Shia Imams, as commonly understood, but also denotes the occult and esoteric teachings of religion that they imparted and transmitted to their chosen disciples. Hazrat Ali (a), recognized as the vanguard of Sufism, served as the foremost inheritor of the inner teachings and Walayah derived from the Prophet. The reverence accorded to Hazrat Zahra (PBUH) serves as a universal reminder of the spiritual legacy of Umm Abiyh for Muslims. Hazrat Imam Hassan (a) disseminated these teachings through tranquility and silence. The Dua Arafah of Imam Hussain (a) is regarded as a repository of Irfan. Furthermore, the Al-Sahifa al-Sajjadiyya of the fourth Imam, Imam Sajjad (a), and the narrations of the fifth and sixth Imams abound with teachings of Irfan. The mystics of the eighth Imam, Hazrat Reza (a), acclaim him as the Imam of inner teachings and guidance, the progenitor of a significant Irfan legacy. These revered figures are acknowledged as the spiritual beacons of their era, even within the mystic circles of the Sunni world. Finally, Hazrat Hojjat bin Al-Hassan al-Askari, revered as a paragon of Shiite Irfan, is esteemed as a living embodiment and contemporary source of the inner realm of Islamic revelation (Safavi, 2017: 30).

In a parallel interpretation, Shah Ismail, nearly 500 years prior to Seyyed Hossein Nasr, echoes a similar sentiment in couplet number 7 within the chapter of the twelve Imams and their role as spiritual beacons. He emphasizes that individuals whose connection with Muhammad and Ali transcends mere outward association, but rather stems from the depths of their souls, will never falter on their path nor lose their way. Seyyed Hossein Nasr also delves into this spiritual and esoteric dimension within the chapter on the Hadith of the Thaqalayn, similarly referencing figures like Imam Sajjad, Imam Baqir, and Imam Sadiq. According to Shah Ismail, those whose bond with Imam Sadiq (a) is rooted in sincerity, truth, and righteousness will remain steadfast until the fulfillment of Shah Ismail's vision, reaching the reign of Hazrat Mahdi (a) as his words permeate throughout the world.

Had Seyyed Hossein Nasr's theoretical framework embraced a more inclusive and pluralistic understanding of Iran, one that transcended Persian-centric interpretations and recognized Iran as a spiritual hub encompassing diverse traditions, including Persian, Turkish, Arabic, and Kurdish, then surely texts like this would have found resonance in his perspective. Figures like Shah Ismail, who played pivotal roles in shaping the evolution of Hekmat, Gnosis, and Sufism in Iran, would not have been overlooked within such a framework.

Today, the status of the Safavid tradition or Tariqat is nuanced. While it may not hold the same prominence as it did in the past, elements of its legacy endure through various channels. Some individuals still identify with and uphold aspects of the Safavid tradition, albeit in diverse ways. Those who align with this tradition may interpret its foundations differently, drawing from both historical perspectives and contemporary insights. Seyed Salman Safavi outlines the main pillars of the Safavid Tariqat, emphasizing its spiritual and theoretical underpinnings.

As it has been discussed earlier, the essence of love and affection permeates throughout Diwan Shah Ismail. In his verses, Shah Ismail underscores that the journey towards truth and spiritual enlightenment, as well as the attainment of divine communion, are unattainable without the presence of love (Mohabat) and intuition. Similarly, Shah Khatai echoes these sentiments in his Diwan, encapsulating the essence articulated by Seyed Salman Safavi.

> In a city weary of its own existence, I roamed,
> How delightful is the encounter with Mohabat, sweetly combed.
> My eyes fixated on one thing alone,
> How delightful is the encounter with Mohabat's gentle tone.

Shah Ismail asserts that "love" stands as the primary catalyst for movement, transformation, and flourishing. He emphasizes that encountering and embracing truth necessitates the presence of affection and love. Similarly, Shah Khatai affirms this notion through his Spiritual Sojourn at the boundaries of existence, elucidating that Tariqat cannot be pursued without Mohabat.

Seyed Salman Safavi says about Sheikh Safi-ad-Din Ardabili and the foundations of Tariqat Safavid:

> According to Safi-ad-Din Ardabili, the optimal path of Spiritual Sojourn, or Tariqat, is rooted in love, mirroring the way of Prophet Ibrahim. The teachings of the Safavid Tariqat Irfan draw from multiple sources, including the Quran, the guidance of the Fourteen Infallibles, spiritual experiences, and the exemplary lives of the saints. Spiritual progression

necessitates strict adherence to Sharia's directives, with adherents continuing to uphold these principles throughout their lives. Key principles of the Safavid Tariqat include knowledge, devotion to God, love, trust, striving in the greater Jihad, promoting and honoring the practices and teachings of the Fourteen Infallibles, awaiting the arrival of Hazrat Hojjat, exhibiting good character, offering fatwas, engaging in social cooperation, demonstrating courage, aiding the oppressed, and serving the people. The Safavid Tariqat stands as a primary spiritual tradition.

SAFAVI, 2017: 40

If we refrain from exaggeration, the concepts of generosity, bravery, aiding the oppressed, and administering justice, which Seyed Salman Safavi describes as "social cooperation," are pervasive throughout Diwan Shah Ismail. Following Sheikh Safi-ad-Din Ardabili, who epitomized the Safavid Tariqat? Seyed Salman Safavi elaborates:

Tariqat Sheikh Safiuddin from the perspective of the dynasty to Imam Ali b. Musa al-Rida (a) and Imam al-Muhaddin, Imam Alī (a) arrive. After his death, his son Sheikh Sadr al-Din Musa and after him Khvajeh Ali Safavi, Sheikh Ibrahim, Sheikh Junayd and Sheikh Haider guided and trained the disciples and after Sheikh Haider, Shah Ismail.

SAFAVID, 2016: 37

But what was the fate of this Tariqat after Shah Ismail, and what is the state of the Tariqat today? Seyed Salman Safavi says the following in this regard:

In the contemporary era, the Safavid Tariqat has been upheld by figures such as Ayatollah Seyyed Shahabuddin Safavid Hammami, Ayatollah Shushtri, Ayatollah Mollah Hossein-Qoli, Ayatollah Seyyed Ali Ghazi, and Seyyed Salman Ibn Hajj Seyyed Abbas Ibn Haj Aghamirza Safavid Hammami. These individuals, who have been students of esteemed scholars like Ayatollah Sheikh Abbas Yazidi Allameh Seyed Mohammad Hossein Tabatabai and Ayatollah Seyed Ali Qazi, serve as custodians of the tradition. Seyyed Salman, the 14th successor of Sheikh Safi, has also established connections with the Shadhili Tariqat through Seyyed Hussain Ibn Waliullah Kashani Shazli. With their extended authority, they have played a pivotal role in the revitalization of the Alevi Safavid Tariqat in contemporary times, both in Iran and in various parts of Europe. Thus, the Safavid Tariqat remains vibrant and active today.

While the Safavid Tariqat persists in its movement and continuity in both Iran and Europe today, the absence of Shah Ismail and his contributions within the dynasty and formulation presented by Seyyed Hossein Nasr and Seyed Salman Safavi raises questions. Notably, there exists a fundamental disparity between Nasr's perspective and that of Seyed Salman Safavi regarding Shah Ismail. Unlike Nasr, Seyed Salman frequently references Shah Ismail in his works, yet Nasr neglects to acknowledge the significance of Shah Ismail's Tariqat.

The question we have raised necessitates a rigorous response from both the academic and scholarly communities, as well as from those engaged with Irfan and the Gnostic Legacy, both in Iran and globally. It is essential to provide an objective analysis devoid of emotional biases or confrontational attitudes. Unfortunately, many Iranians, including researchers, perceive Shah Ismail solely as a warrior without acknowledging his noteworthy contributions. This perspective is flawed and warrants correction; biased and hostile viewpoints cannot erase this question. Some unbiased scholars assert that Shah Ismail's message found expression through his pen rather than his sword. Today, Shah Ismail's Divan and his teachings hold significant value in regions such as the Balkans, Anatolia, Turkey, Bulgaria, parts of Iraq and Syria, and within Iran. However, to engage with this material analytically and academically, we must recognize the Turkish language as an integral part of Iran's cultural fabric in the public sphere. This acknowledgment would facilitate the reevaluation and revitalization of these texts.

As we conclude this book, we are contemplating ambitious projects for the future. One such project involves translating *Diwan Khatai* into Persian and providing a comprehensive interpretation of Khatai's philosophical views for Iranian audiences. Additionally, we plan to compile interpretations from the traditions of Irfan in the Balkans, Anatolia, and the Caucasus, presenting them in the form of stories attributed to Shah Ismail. Through these endeavors, we aim to critically reassess and reconstruct Shah Ismail's position within the global tradition of Irfan. While these projects may be extensive, our profound and enduring love and devotion to Shah Ismail Khatai propel us forward. As a fitting conclusion to our research, we offer a poignant poem by Shah Khatai about Imam Ali (a):

> I possess a body, yet my essence is Ali,
> In my veins flows blood that's pure Ali.
> I require neither office nor courtly sway,
> My true realm and station is Ali's way.
> Like a drop submerged in the vast sea's scope,

I'm immersed in Ali's ocean, my only hope.
In this realm of Jacob, where worlds may whirl,
Ali's the Canaan, my guiding pearl.
These words I speak, they are not mine alone,
In matters of truth, Ali's wisdom has shown.
My guide, my mentor, in all that I claim,
In this journey of life, Ali's is the name.

# CHAPTER 14

# Conclusion

Shah Ismail Safavi should not be examined solely as a military leader or the founder of the Safavid dynasty; rather, it is essential to deconstruct the conventional and stereotypical representations of his character and critically reconstruct his intellectual dimensions. Such an approach allows us to perceive Shah Ismail not merely as a political figure but as a transformative agent in the epistemological and cultural shifts of his era. This re-evaluation situates Shah Ismail within a broader intellectual framework, enabling a nuanced understanding of his role in shaping the sociocultural and philosophical currents of his time. Moreover, the Khatai tradition, as a central manifestation of aesthetic and mystical knowledge, warrants close analysis to uncover its profound connections to the intellectual and social contexts of his period.

This critical perspective offers new avenues for engaging with contemporary intellectual challenges. Overcoming the limitations of nihilism and subjectivism necessitates drawing upon epistemological approaches such as aesthetic thinking and knowledge by presence, which provide opportunities for generating alternative perspectives and enriching critical methodologies. By foregrounding these approaches, we can move beyond reductive interpretations and uncover the potential of Shah Ismail's thought to inspire novel frameworks for understanding both historical and modern socio-intellectual dynamics. The interplay between his philosophical vision and the broader Khatai tradition further emphasizes his significance as a thinker whose legacy transcends his immediate political accomplishments.

In this light, Shah Ismail Safavi and the Khatai tradition represent pivotal concepts for rethinking sociological and epistemological questions. They serve as tools for reconstructing intellectual history and addressing fundamental issues in knowledge formation. By critically reinterpreting his contributions, we can unlock theoretical insights that extend beyond his historical context, offering conceptual resources for engaging with present-day concerns. This process not only deepens our comprehension of Shah Ismail as a figure of intellectual significance but also broadens the scope of sociological inquiry into alternative forms of knowledge production and critical engagement.

The fundamental question here is: What position do Shah Ismail Safavi and the Khatai tradition occupy within the broader realm of global thought and intellectual discourse? This question is not merely a historical or academic concern but serves as a starting point for philosophical reflection on the interaction between diverse cultures and their impact on the formation of intellectual frameworks. Shah Ismail Safavi, as the founder of the Safavid dynasty, represents more than a historical figure. His intellectual and cultural legacy, particularly in the form of the Khatai tradition, provides fertile ground for a deeper analysis of mystical and philosophical currents in the Global South. The Khatai tradition, as a prominent manifestation of mystical knowledge, raises essential questions about how such legacies can be evaluated within the context of global intellectual discourses.

Understanding Shah Ismail's intellectual stature and analyzing the Khatai tradition are not only vital for interpreting Iranian history and culture but also necessary for exploring the mutual influences of Global South and Western philosophy and their relevance to contemporary epistemological and philosophical challenges. This issue opens up an opportunity to re-examine intellectual traditions and reassess legacies like the Khatai tradition to propose new frameworks for ontological and epistemological analysis. By doing so, we gain the ability to uncover the potential of these traditions to contribute to global intellectual dialogues and to address pressing philosophical and sociological questions.

Such an approach enables a richer comprehension of the interaction between Global South and Western intellectual systems and offers innovative frameworks for tackling global issues in philosophy and the sociology of knowledge. By reflecting on Shah Ismail's contributions and the Khatai tradition within a broader intellectual context, we can transcend conventional historical narratives. This perspective invites a rethinking of the role of these traditions in shaping not only the historical trajectory of thought but also their ongoing relevance in confronting modern intellectual challenges and fostering cross-cultural understanding.

A central issue that has arisen in Western philosophy since the Enlightenment, particularly under the influence of Kantian and neo-Kantian paradigms, is the question of the possibility of non-conceptual thinking. This form of thinking, which seeks to transcend the dominant conceptual structures of modern philosophy, challenges the boundaries of modern rationality and its ability to grapple with the intricacies of a complex and interconnected world. The dominance of conceptual frameworks in modern thought has often constrained the scope of philosophical inquiry, leaving unresolved fundamental questions about the potential for modes of understanding that lie beyond these limitations. This challenge has become increasingly urgent as contemporary global issues demand intellectual frameworks capable of addressing problems that defy reduction to purely conceptual analysis.

Max Weber's sociology provides a striking example of this conceptual constraint. His emphasis on subjectivism and instrumental rationality offered a systematic analysis of modernity's dynamics but ultimately remained confined within the boundaries of conceptual rationality. While his work sheds light on the mechanics of modern social structures, it fails to present a path for overcoming the epistemological and ontological limitations imposed by these frameworks. This inadequacy leads to a pressing question: Can alternative intellectual traditions provide resources for rethinking these limitations? Addressing this question requires venturing beyond the intellectual boundaries of Western modernity and engaging with non-Western or pre-modern traditions that propose different epistemological and ontological paradigms.

One significant approach to this inquiry lies in the exploration of traditions that prioritize knowledge by presence. This mode of knowledge emphasizes direct, experiential awareness rather than abstract, conceptual reasoning, offering a fundamentally different perspective on understanding. By engaging with such traditions, it becomes possible to envision new intellectual pathways that challenge the dominance of conceptual thought and allow for a redefinition of humanity's place within the modern world. These alternative frameworks not only enrich the discourse on the nature of knowledge and existence but also hold the potential to address contemporary philosophical and sociological challenges. In doing so, they pave the way for a more holistic, inclusive, and dynamic engagement with the complexities of modern life.

In Global South traditions, particularly within the framework of knowledge by presence, the concepts of direct and acquired knowledge hold a central and profound significance, offering a distinctive approach to understanding reality. Knowledge by presence refers to an immediate and intuitive awareness of truth, contrasting sharply with acquired knowledge, which relies on conceptual structures and linguistic articulation. This form of knowledge opens a new horizon for understanding, free from the constraints of abstract reasoning. Mehdi Haeri Yazdi, a prominent contemporary philosopher, has extensively analyzed and articulated this concept, demonstrating its philosophical depth and applicability. In particular, this type of knowledge finds a vivid reflection in the wisdom and mysticism of Shah Ismail Safavi, whose intellectual legacy bridges traditional epistemology and contemporary intellectual needs.

The concept of knowledge by presence provides a pathway to transcend the conceptual frameworks that often appear restrictive in modern thought. It represents a mode of understanding rooted in direct experiential truth rather than mediated, abstract constructs. Within the philosophical and mystical traditions of Shah Ismail, this knowledge emerges as a tool for navigating between the limits of traditional epistemological paradigms and the pressing demands of modern intellectual discourse. By incorporating such insights, knowledge by presence offers not only a profound rethinking of the nature of reality and human understanding but also serves as a resource for addressing the challenges of reconciling traditional wisdom with contemporary perspectives. This synthesis has the potential to redefine intellectual engagement in both Global South and global philosophical contexts.

Non-conceptual thinking, or the ability to think beyond the confines of conventional concepts, is one of the defining features of Contemplative philosophy and the intellectual heritage of Shah Ismail Safavi. This approach to thought seeks to transcend the limitations of linguistic and conceptual structures, offering a fresh and profound avenue for engaging with truth. Contemplative philosophy, rooted in the principles of light and intuition, presents a form of knowledge by presence that emphasizes direct, experiential awareness rather than reliance on abstract, acquired knowledge. Shah Ismail's intellectual contributions vividly embody this perspective, blending mystical insights with philosophical inquiry to create a robust framework for exploring the deeper dimensions of reality. His work reflects a unique synthesis where the boundaries of conventional reasoning dissolve, allowing a more intuitive grasp of existential truths.

The legacy of Contemplative thought, deeply grounded in the epistemological tradition of knowledge by presence, provides a transformative lens for reexamining foundational concepts such as existence, truth, and consciousness. This tradition's emphasis on light and intuitive understanding offers a pathway to surpass the constraints of acquired knowledge, which often depends heavily on linguistic and conceptual mediators. In Shah Ismail's intellectual endeavors, this Contemplative framework manifests not only through his mystical reflections but also in his philosophical engagements with ontological and epistemological questions. By merging these realms, Shah Ismail developed a model of non-conceptual thinking that challenges conventional epistemologies and provides a means for navigating complex intellectual and existential challenges. His legacy invites a redefinition of the human relationship with reality, rooted in an experiential and intuitive connection to truth.

Shah Ismail's integration of mystical principles and Contemplative philosophy established a paradigm of thought that remains profoundly relevant across time and cultural contexts. His approach demonstrates how the synthesis of mystical intuition and philosophical rigor can inspire solutions to both timeless and contemporary intellectual challenges. This mode of thinking extends its relevance beyond abstract philosophical inquiries, offering insights into social, cultural, and existential issues. Shah Ismail's intellectual heritage serves as a reminder that transcending the boundaries of conventional thought requires a deliberate embrace of intuition and direct experience as complementary to reason. By fostering such a synthesis, he has provided a framework that continues to influence and inspire discussions about the nature of truth, existence, and the human condition. By the human condition I refer to key events of human life. In other words, the human condition can be conceptualized as the characteristics and key events of human life, including birth, learning, emotion, aspiration, reason, morality, conflict, separation and death. By looking at these key events through the Khataian perspective then we realize that the human condition could be interpreted beyond the gamut's of nihilism-cum-subjectivism; i.e., within the parameters of knowledge by presence.

# References

## In Persian

Alaei, M. (2000). The Discourse of Consensus [Persian title: Goftman-e Vefagh]. Tehran, Iran: Naqd-e Farhang.

Al-e Ahmad, J. (2012). Journey to the Land of Azrael [Persian title: Safar be velayat-e Azrael]. Tehran, Iran: Ferdows.

Al-e Ahmad, J. (2016). On the Service and Betrayal of Intellectuals [Persian title: Dar khedmat va khianat roshanfekran]. Tehran, Iran: Nashr-e Pir-e Omid.

Al-e Ahmad, J. (2023). The Tat People of Blok-e Zahra [Persian title: Tatneshinha-ye Bloke Zahra]. Tehran, Iran: Ars.

Ali ibn Abi Talib. (2005). Nahj al-Balagha, (M. Dashti, Trans.). Tehran, Iran: Islamic History and Culture Research Office.

Amuli, S. H. (1989). The Comprehensive Secrets and the Source of Lights [Persian title: Jame' al-asrar va manba' al-anvar] (H. Corbin & O. Yahya, Eds.). Tehran, Iran.

Ardabili, S. S. (2007). The Black Collection [Persian title: Qara Majmuah] (H. M. Sidiq, Ed.). Tabriz, Iran: Nashr-e Akhtar.

Asadabadi, S. J. (1929). Naturalism: A Refutation of Materialism [Persian title: Nichrieh, ya, Naturalism dar rade madi gari va tabii gari]. Tabriz, Iran: Entesharat-e Din va Danesh.

Batani, M. (2000). Language and Thought [Persian title: Zaban va Tafakkor]. Tehran, Iran: Agah.

Bidel, 'Abd al-Qādir. (2001). Dīvān-e Bīdal Dehlavī (Ed. Akbar Behdārvand). Tehran: Enteshārāt-e Negāh. Ghazal 1187.

Chomsky, N. (2010). Cartesian Linguistics (A. Taherian, Trans.). Tehran, Iran: Hermes.

Eqbal Ashtiani, A. (1945). The politics of language [Persian title: Siasat-e Zaban]. Yaghma, Issue Number. Tehran, Iran.

Esmaeilzadeh, R. (2011). Shah Ismail Safavi Khatai: Collected Works [Persian title: Shah Esmail Safavi Khatai: Koliyat Divan, Nashatnameh, Dahnameh, Qoshmalar Farsija Sherler]. Tehran, Iran: Entesharat-e Beynolmelali Al-Hoda.

Farabi, A. (2010). The Enumeration of the Sciences [Persian title: Ehsā al-Olūm] (H. Khodiyojam, Trans.). Tehran, Iran: Entesharat-e Elmi va Farhangi.

Foroughi, M. (2000). The Course of Philosophy in Europe [Persian title: Seyr-e Hekmat dar Orupa]. Tehran, Iran: Niloufar.

Ghanirad, M. A. (1999). The Sociology of the Rise and Fall of Science in Iran (Islamic Period) [Persian title: Jame' shenasi-ye Roshd va Oful-e Elm dar Iran (Doreh-ye Eslami)]. Tehran, Iran: Madinah.

Hasanzadeh Amoli, H. (1986). Texts of Wisdom on the Bezels of Wisdom [Persian title: Nusūs al-Hikam bar Fusūs al-Hikam]. Tehran, Iran: Nashr-e Farhangi-ye Raja.

Husseini Tehrani, S. M. (1987). The Essence of the Essence on the Path and Conduct of the Elite [Persian title: Resaleh-ye Lab al-Labab dar Seyr va Soluk-e Oliyal albab]. Tehran, Iran: Entesharat-e Allamah Tabatabai.

Husseini Tehrani, S. M. (2008). Theology [Persian title: Allahshenasi]. Tehran, Iran: Entesharat-e Allamah Tabatabai.

Ibn Khaldun, A. (2004). The Muqaddimah: An Introduction to History [Persian title: al-Ibar : Tarikh Ibn Khaldun] (A. Ayati, Trans.). Tehran, Iran: Institute for Humanities and Cultural Studies.

Ibn Munawwar, M. (2000). The Secrets of Oneness in the Stations of Sheikh Abu Said [Persian title: Asrar al-Tawhid fi Maqamat Shaykh Abu Said] (Z. Safa, Trans.). Tehran, Iran: Ferdows.

Ibn Turkah Isfahani, S. (2000). Introduction to the Principles [Persian title: Tamhid al-qavaid] (S. J. Ashtiani, Ed.). Tehran, Iran: Bustan-e Ketab.

Jorjani, M. S. (2023). Persian Treatises of Mir Sayyed Sharif Jorjani [Persian title: Rasael-e Farsi-ye Mir Sayyed Sharif Jorjani] (Z. S. Abtahi, Ed.). Tehran, Iran: Mahmoud Afshar.

Kasravi, A. (1999). Sheikh Safi and His Lineage [Persian title: Sheikh Safi va Tabarash]. Tehran, Iran: Ferdows.

Kokab, M. & Corbin, H. (2009). Seyyed Haydar Amuli: Biography, Works, Thoughts, and Cosmology [Persian title: Seyyed Haydar Amuli; Sharh-e Ahval, Asar, Ara va Jahanshenasi] (N. Aghakhani, Trans.). Tehran, Iran: Haqiqat.

Kuhn, T. (2017). The Structure of Scientific Revolutions (A. Javadzadeh, Trans.). Tehran, Iran: Farhang-e Nashr-e No. (Original work published 1962).

Mansour, J. (2023). The Constitution of the Islamic Republic of Iran [Persian title: Qanun-e Asasi-ye Nezam-e Jomhuri-ye Eslami-ye Iran]. Tehran, Iran: Doran.

Marx, K. (2007). Capital (I. Eskandari, Trans.). Tehran, Iran: Ferdows. (Original work published 1867).

Miri, S. J. (2013). Developments in the North Caucasus and Their Impact on the National Security of the Islamic Republic of Iran. Tehran, Iran: Institute for Humanities and Cultural Studies.

Miri, S. J. (2019). Re-Reading the Idea of a National Unity Language: Re-Reading the Discourse of Archeological Nationalism [Persian title: Bazkhani-ye Ideh-ye Zaban-e Vahdat-e Melli: Bazkhani-ye Goftman-e Nasyonalism-e Bastan Gera]. Tehran, Iran: Naqd-e Farhang.

Miri, S. J. (2020). Iran in Five Narratives [Persian title: Iran dar Panj Ravayat]. Tehran, Iran: Naqd-e Farhang.

Miri, S. J. (2021). The General Theory of Religious Reform [Persian title: Nazariyeh-ye Amm-e Eslah-e Dini]. Tehran, Iran: Naqd-e Farhang.

Miri, S. J. (2023). Beyond Secular and Religious Knowledge: Allamah Mohammad Taqi Jafari, Architect of Open Horizons [Persian title: Farasuyi Marefat-e Sekular va

Marefat-e Dini: Allamah Mohammad Taqi Jafari Memar-e Ofoqha-ye Baz]. Tehran, Iran: Naqd-e Farhang.

Mosleh, A. (2021). Allamah Tabatabai's Conventional Perceptions and the Philosophy of Culture [Persian title: Edrakat-e Etebari-ye Allamah Tabatabai va Falsafeh-ye Farhang]. Tehran, Iran: Entesharat-e Pegah-e Ruzgar-e No.

Motahhari, M. (2020). Mutual Services of Islam and Iran [Persian title: Khadamat-e Motaqabel-e Eslam va Iran]. Tehran, Iran: Sadra.

Mousavi, S. J. (2017). Safavid Mysticism and Literature of That Era [Persian title: Tasavof-e Asr-e Safavi va Adabiyat-e An Doreh]. Tehran, Iran: Amir Kabir.

Nasr, S. H. (2003). Sufi Essays [Persian title: Amuzehha-ye Sufiyan az Dirooz ta Emrooz] (M. H. Amini & H. Heydari, Trans.). Tehran, Iran: Entesharat-e Qasideh Sara.

Nasr, S. H. (2021). Three Muslim Sages (A. Aram, Trans.). Tehran, Iran: Amir Kabir. (Original work published 1964).

Olucay, O. (1993). Shah Khatai and Alevism: Beliefs and Tradition, Elements and Ethics [Persian title: Shah Khatai va Alavi-gari; Bavarha va Sonnat, Anasor va Akhlaq]. Adana, Turkey: Hakan Ofset.

Pourhasan, Q. (2020). Al-Farabi and al-Huruf: An Inquiry into Al-Farabi's Linguistic-Philosophical Reflections [Persian title: Farabi va al-Horuf: Jostari dar Tamalat-e Zabani-Falsafi-ye Farabi]. Tehran, Iran: Sadra Islamic Philosophy Foundation.

Sadi, M. (2022). Gulistan of Sadi (G. Yusufi, Ed.). Tehran, Iran: Khavarazmi.

Sadr, S. M. (2004). Nay and Ney (A. Hejazi Kermani, Ed. & Trans.). Tehran, Iran: Imam Musa Sadr Cultural and Research Institute.

Safavi, S. S. (2013). Thaqalain: 'Irfan (Mysticism): Theoretical and Practical Principles of Irfan and the Safavid Spiritual Path. London: LAIS Press.

Safavi, S. S. (2017). The Mysticism of the Two Weights: Theoretical and Practical Foundations of Safavid Mysticism and Tariqa [Persian title: Erfan-e Thaqalayn; Mabani-ye Nazari va Amali-ye Erfan va Tariqat-e Safaviyeh]. Tehran, Iran: Salman Azadeh.

Shahbazi, A. (2004). Jewish and Parsi Plutocrats: British Colonialism and Iran [Persian title: Zarsalarane Yahudi va Parsi, Estemar-e Britania va Iran]. Tehran, Iran: Institute for Political Studies and Research.

Shariati, A. (2019). Rediscovering Iranian Islamic Identity [Persian title: Bazshenasi-ye Howiyat-e Irani-ye Eslami]. Mashhad, Iran: Sepideh Bavaran.

Tabatabai, S. M. & Motahhari, M. (2000). The Principles of Philosophy and the Method of Realism [Persian title: Usul-e falsafeh va ravash-e realism]. Tehran, Iran: Sadra.

Tamimi Amadi, A. (2016). Pearls of Wisdom in the Treasures of Speech [Persian title: Ghurar al-Hikam fi Durar al-Kalim]. Qom, Iran: Dar al-Hadith.

Zia-ebrahimi, R. (2019). The Emergence of Iranian Nationalism (H. Afshar, Trans.). Tehran, Iran: Markaz.

## In English

Chularatana, J. (2008). The Shiite Muslims in Thailand from Ayutthaya Period to the Present. MANUSYA: Journal of Humanities, Special Issue No. 16.

Gallagher, A. (2004). The fallible master of perfection: Shah Ismail in the Alevi-Bektashi tradition (Doctoral dissertation). McGill University, Montreal, Quebec.

Markoff, I. (1993). Music, saints and ritual: Sama' and the Alevis of Turkey. In G. M. Smith & C. W. Ernst (Eds.), Manifestations of Sainthood in Islam (pp. 95–110). Isis.

Nasr, S. H. (2013). The history of Sufism and theoretical mysticism in Iran from the beginning until now. Transcendent Philosophy Journal, London Academy of Iranian Studies, 14(1), 1–36.

Olsson, T. (1998). Epilogue: The Scripturalization of Ali-Oriented Religions. In T. Olsson, E. Ozdalga, & C. Raudvere (Eds.), Alevi Identity: Cultural, Religious and Social Perspectives (pp. 199–208). Curzon.

Savoy, R. (1980). Iran under the Safavids. Cambridge University Press.

Shankland, D. (1998). Anthropology and ethnicity: the place of ethnography in the new Alevi movement. In T. Olsson, E. Ozdalga, & C. Raudvere (Eds.), Alevi Identity: Cultural, Religious and Social Perspectives (pp. 15–22).

# Index